HARDWIRING FLOW

Systems and Processes for Seamless Patient Care

"I coined a term a few years ago, rather awkward but to the point: 'gaspworthy'—as in, obviously, the audacity and power of the proposed program make you no less than gasp. Well, this is clearly a 'gaspworthy' effort. The healthcare debate is complex, but I have long believed that the true breakthroughs in healthcare will come, not primarily from external policy overhauls, but from the likes of superior application of programs such as 'flow' described herein. The big point: The approach laid out here is within the grasp of any hospital; it requires no alteration of outside forces. Hence, in my view, not to follow a path like this is a breach of duty to our patients as much as an inappropriate treatment protocol. Read it. Absorb it. Act. No excuses. Yes, 'gaspworthy.'"

—**Tom Peters, One of the most influential business thinkers of all time,**
Author of *Reimagine: Business Excellence in a Disruptive Age*
and *In Search of Excellence*

"A highly original and unexpected application inspired by the flow theory of optimal experience to the problem of managing patient flow in treatment centers. This book will be very helpful to anyone who is concerned to make sure that waiting for services will be minimal, and as enjoyable as possible—a huge boon in these days when wasting time is worse than wasting money."

—**Mihaly Csikszentmihalyi,**
Professor of Psychology and Management,
Claremont Graduate University, Claremont, CA

"Hardwiring Flow *was an unexpected page-turner, full of instructional insights to the world of emergency physicians and their patients. Visionary in scope and innovative in application, Mayer and Jensen have produced a work that will change medicine as we know it.*"

—Angela F. Gardner, MD, FACEP,
President, American College of Emergency Physicians

"*To the extent timing is important, Thom Mayer and Kirk Jensen have hit on the right topic at the right time in their recent book,* Hardwiring Flow. *The entire healthcare industry is focused on cost, and their work on flow and systems does a terrific job of introducing the science, math, and art of flow management. As we are all grappling for new tools, this book is a welcome tool kit.*"

—Bruce Crowther, FACHE,
CEO, Northwest Community Hospital, Arlington Heights, IL

"Hardwiring Flow *is a tactical and comprehensive how-to approach to solving the most challenging of healthcare problems. This book not only provides detailed solutions to flow issues, but provides an easy-to-understand and readable review of critical physician and staff issues that make or break a system's ability to provide effective and efficient care. I found this book extraordinarily helpful and relevant to the black hole of patient flow.*"

—Stephen Beeson, MD
Author of *Engaging Physicians* and *Practicing Excellence*

"*Waits and delays do not have to be a routine part of patient care. In* Hardwiring Flow, *Dr. Mayer and Dr. Jensen expertly present proven theories and strategies to guide improvements in hospital-wide patient flow. The authors' practical approach makes the theories and strategies readily implementable. I highly recommend the study of this book to anyone who has the good fortune to work in a hospital. The potential impact on patient and staff satisfaction, safety, and the bottom line is enormous.*"

—Kevin Nolan, MA,
Statistician, Associates in Process Improvement

HARDWIRING
FLOW

Systems and Processes for Seamless Patient Care

Thom Mayer, MD, FACEP, FAAP
and Kirk Jensen, MD, MBA, FACEP

Published by:
Fire Starter Publishing
913 Gulf Breeze Parkway, Suite 6
Gulf Breeze, FL 32561
Phone: 850-934-1099
Fax: 850-934-1384
www.firestarterpublishing.com

ISBN: 978-0-9840794-6-9

Library of Congress Control Number: 2009935124

Printed in the United States of America

To my wonderful wife and best friend, Karen; to my sons, Christopher and Michael, for their inquisitiveness and zest for life; and to my parents, Earl and Naomi, for "hardwiring" my values.

—Kirk Jensen, MD, MBA

To my beautiful, brilliant, and always inspiring wife, Maureen.
To our three sons, Greg Mayer,
2nd Lt. Kevin Mayer, United States Marine Corps,
and Josh Mayer.
To Josh's wife, Valerie, and their daughter, Eve.
To the memory of my parents, affectionately known as
Grandpa Jim and Grandma Bette.
And to the memory of my father-in-law, John Bernard Henry, MD,
who was a scientist, author, and man of epic measure.

—Thom Mayer, MD

TABLE OF CONTENTS

Table of Contents

FOREWORD

In our work with hundreds of organizations, we've found that even if you get the people component right in healthcare—the right person at the right place—it still doesn't ensure success. We're in an industry where everything has to be working well—from the equipment to the technology to the facilities to the systems. Nothing is more frustrating than working so hard to get the people component right but still not achieving the desired outcomes. This leads to losing the people component due to the staff's own frustration with how the systems work and discouragement that they are working so hard and not accomplishing what their calling is, to take great care of patients.

Dr. Thom Mayer and Dr. Kirk Jensen have always been impact players in healthcare. Dr. Thom Mayer is the chairman of the board of BestPractices, Inc., and a medical director for Studer Group.® He has been widely recognized as one of the nation's foremost experts in leadership, management, customer service, and flow in healthcare. He is also recognized as an expert in emergency medicine, pediatric emergency medicine, trauma, and sports medicine. Dr. Kirk B. Jensen has spent over 20 years in emergency medicine management and clinical care. Board-certified in emergency medicine, he has been medical director for several Emergency Departments and is chief medical officer for BestPractices and a medical director for Studer Group.

Both Dr. Mayer and Dr. Jensen have practical experience; they have done it and are still on the field. They take the thinking to the doing, which leads to becoming. In healthcare, we spend *a lot* of time thinking, but Dr. Mayer and Dr. Jensen help us move to doing. It is by doing that we get the outcomes and by doing consistently that we accomplish our goal—we become great places for patients to get care, employees to work, and physicians to practice medicine.

Dr. Mayer's and Dr. Jensen's commitment to excellence in achievement and unwillingness to accept the status quo makes healthcare better for all. As a reader of this book, you will have the processes, tactics, and techniques to achieve and maintain excellence.

Sincerely,
Quint Studer

ACKNOWLEDGMENTS

This book is the product of our combined efforts on this subject accumulated over a total of 25 years of clinical practice and working with, learning from, and mentoring hospital teams across the country, while also applying these principles in the hospitals and healthcare systems with which we work on a daily basis. Therefore, it is very much born from the combined efforts of a large number of health professionals whose hard work and insights have contributed to our current understanding of flow and its dramatic impact on the lives of our patients and those who care so courageously for those patients.

At BestPractices, Inc., we wish to thank the members of the Physician Leadership Team, including Doctors Robert Cates, Glenn Druckenbrod, Luis Eljaiek, Jr., Rick Place, John Howell, Dan Hanfling, Raul Armengol, Damian Banaszak, Scott Weir, John Maguire, Hannah Grausz, Maybelle Kou, Mary Ann McLaurin, David Postelnek, Michael Born, Vince Sevier, Anthony Kitchen, Wayne Cayton, Gary Senula, and Gary Fraley. We also want to thank our entire Senior Leadership Team, including Eric Minkove, Andrea Bondi, Dan Kirkpatrick, and the incomparable Kaye Wear, whose tireless work over 30 years has improved the lives of both patients and physicians. Joy Sparks-Gavira was, as usual, a joy to work with and was critical to the timely submission of the manuscript. Ashley Jones and Alice Lingerfelt also made major contributions to the work. Robert Milks was of great help in producing and editing the manuscript.

At our client hospitals we have been fortunate in the extreme to work with a consummate group of healthcare leaders: Reuven Pasternak, MD, Knox Singleton, William Flannagan, Jr., Mark Stauder, Wayne Diewald, Toni Ardabell, Charles Barnett, Bruce Crowther, Leighton Smith, MD, Dale Beatty, Mike King, Bob Kane, and George Manchester, MD.

At Duke University Medical Center, many thanks for the many insights over many years to Doctors Victor Dzau, Sandy Williams, Bill Fulkerson, and Michael Morsberger and Molly O'Neill.

At Studer Group, Quint Studer has been a mentor and source of unparalleled inspiration, and we are deeply grateful for his friendship and the faith he has put in our work. BG Porter has also had a major impact on our work and the book reflects his impact as well. About Jay Kaplan, MD, there are not enough words to express our deep respect and gratitude for the countless insights we have gained in listening to his lectures over the years. Our colleague Stephen Beeson, MD, has greatly expanded our view of leading physicians and we are grateful for his insight. Finally, after publishing over 15 books between us, no editor has ever been as efficient, pleasant, insightful, and wise as Bekki Kennedy. The book would not have seen the light of day without her Herculean efforts.

We'd also like to thank the entire team at DeHart & Company Public Relations for their proofreading and design services—as well as handling many of the million-and-one unforeseen details that crop up when bringing a project like this to fruition.

Many individuals and organizations have contributed to our evolving knowledge of how to improve patient flow. Studer Group, with its vast body of work in the arena of Evidence Based Leadership, is one of them. The firm's insights on aligning employee behaviors and processes as well as getting physicians engaged have been invaluable. In addition, we would like to recognize the central role played by the Institute for Healthcare Improvement (IHI) in advancing this science. Much of the material in this book was developed as part of work in IHI programs and with IHI staff and faculty members. We gratefully acknowledge the leadership of both of these organizations in this area.

Many people with diverse backgrounds and viewpoints have helped guide our thoughts on flow, management, and leadership over the years, including Tom Peters, Peter Block, Peter Senge, Rob Strauss, MD, Mel Gottlieb, Will Galtney, Mihaly Csikszentmihalyi, Len Berry, Don Berwick, MD, Kevin Nolan, Roger Resar, MD, Deb Kaczynski, Marilyn Rudolph, Jody Crane, MD, MBA, Chuck Noon, PhD, and Eugene Litvak.

Acknowledgments

Many thanks to our families for their patience and understanding with our long dedication to this book, the underlying intellectual content underpinning it, and the many long hours we were away from home speaking at meetings and working with hospitals and healthcare systems to make flow a reality. In particular, our wives, Karen Jensen and Maureen Mayer, were, in every sense of the word, full collaborators in the genesis of the work, and if there is any wisdom herein, it comes in no small measure from them. Any failures or errors of omission or commission are entirely ours.

We encourage the readers of this book to contact us if we can be of assistance in any way.

Thom Mayer, MD, FACEP, FAAP thom@best-practices.com

Kirk Jensen, MD, MBA, FACEP kjensen@best-practices.com

CHAPTER 1

DEFINING FLOW:
THE FOUNDATIONS OF FLOW

"When I use a word," Humpty Dumpty said, in rather a scornful tone,
"It means just what I choose it to mean—neither more nor less."

*"The question is," said Alice, "Whether you **can** make words mean so*
many different things."

"The question is," said Humpty Dumpty, "which is to be master—that's all."

—*Lewis Carroll,* **Through the Looking Glass**

After a combined half-century study of the concept of flow, we have come to at least one ironclad conclusion: *Words matter!* By this we mean that, properly used, words communicate some combination of data, knowledge, or wisdom, which, taken together, help guide our efforts and those for whom we are responsible as healthcare leaders. Specifically, it is essential that we use our words with precision, so that there will be clarity with regard to what is meant, what needs to be done, when it needs to be done, and, whenever appropriate, how it needs to be done.

Into this mindset comes the increasingly important concept of the flow of patients through our hospitals and healthcare systems. (Throughout this book we use the term *flow* to refer to "patient flow" unless otherwise specifically noted.) With the importance of the precision of words and the weight they carry in mind, we enter into somewhat perilous waters when it comes to defining flow. On the one hand, it is a widely used and commonly understood term. Yet on the other hand, it is a term that has been poorly and inconsistently defined. We ourselves have defined flow in previous works, though, as we will see, we believe that previous definitions of flow are not as helpful as our current thinking is on this subject. Or, as former United States Supreme Court Judge Potter Stewart noted about another subject:

I may not be able to define it, but I know what it is when I see it.

Many people say the same about flow, with perhaps the important modification that, "I may not be able to define flow, but I know both when it is there—and when it isn't!" More to the point, our patients know when flow is there—and when it isn't. The term *flow* is used almost with an inherent assumption that we understand its meaning, even if it hasn't been precisely defined.

With this caveat in mind, we begin this chapter with a brief review of the origins of flow, including the seminal work of Mihaly Csikszentmihalyi (1990, 1993, 1996, 1997) as well as the thoughts others (including ourselves) have had with regard to defining flow in healthcare. We then present what we see as the most valuable and pragmatic definition of flow, including examples of its application in practical settings. Finally, we briefly introduce the Flow Toolkit™, the elements of which are discussed in greater detail in the following chapter.

FLOW'S ORIGINS: MIHALY CSIKSZENTMIHALYI AND THE EXPERIENCE SAMPLING METHOD (ESM)

Mihaly Csikszentmihalyi, a brilliant psychologist then working at the University of Chicago, began studies in the mid-1970s designed to identify the root sources of happiness in individuals from varying educational, financial, and societal backgrounds. By utilizing pagers programmed to signal the subjects at different times of the day, Csikszentmihalyi then had his subjects record their mental status, their state of happiness, their state of frustration, and other pertinent information in what he described (1990) as the experience sampling method (ESM). In distilling and analyzing these data, Csikszentmihalyi noted that he identified a phenomenon he referred to as "flow," describing a new "psychology of optimal experience."

Csikszentmihalyi identified eight factors comprising the flow experience (1990):

1. Goals have clarity.
2. Feedback is immediate and clear.
3. Challenges are evenly matched with skills required.
4. A feeling of intense focus develops.
5. You escape "inward and forward"—the periphery recedes.
6. You are in control—but "on the edge."
7. Self-consciousness disappears—but returns even stronger.
8. The sense of time seems transformed.

These fundamental elements constitute the basis of flow as described in his original research. Csikszentmihalyi acknowledged his study of Maslow's concept of self-actualization and creativity in his work, but clearly expanded its horizons through the ESM method and the conclusions to which it led. Of some interest, Csikszentmihalyi listed several examples from healthcare in his original 1990 description of flow, including the feeling that highly trained surgeons have in the course of performing challenging, yet achievable, surgical procedures requiring great skill.

The eight characteristics describe the elements noted during the experience of flow. Because flow is a positive phenomenon, it is therefore one those who have experienced it seek to repeat. This observation led to the insight that those who are able to replicate flow experiences have what Csikszentmihalyi (1996) called complex personalities, which he describes as comprising five fundamental characteristics known as "The 5 Cs."

1. **Clarity.** Those with complex personalities have a deep ability to retain a clear and intense realization, both as a whole and moment to moment, of their goals, real-time feedback concerning those goals, and the ability to read that feedback immediately as to their progress—or lack thereof—toward attainment of the aim.

2. **Center.** The ability to center, focus, distinguish feedback from distraction, and fuel feedback while extinguishing distraction is a key feature of complexity in pursuit of flow.

3. **Choice.** Of all the possible choices of action to be taken, which among them proceeds to flow? Complexity involves a continuous (if tacit) dialogue asking, "Why?" and "Why not?" The choice to accentuate flow experiences arises out of this dynamic tension.

4. **Commit.** Attaining flow consistently occurs for those who can not only follow clear, centered actions that have been chosen but also have the ability to care for and commit to the course of action. They never "go through the motions," but are instead deeply invested in the outcome.

5. **Challenge.** The final characteristic of complexity is a seemingly innate ability to constantly "up the ante" in seeking further challenges and levels of attainment of more advanced goals over time. Having gotten to one level by meeting or exceeding difficult challenges, those with complex personalities then "reset the thermostat" to the next level and the next set of challenges. Or, as the saying goes: "There is no finish line—the victory is in the running!"

These five elements comprise the bedrock aspects of the experiences of those who have attained flow and seek to continuously repeat the experience by expanding the horizons of flow. Flow and complexity are thus intimately related in that flow is described by the eight characteristics *that occur in the flow experience itself,* while the "5 Cs" describe the elements observed in those with complex personalities *who seek to replicate flow experiences on an ongoing basis.* As we reflect on our experiences with flow in healthcare, Csikszentmihalyi's taxonomy of flow and complexity describes what we have seen accurately and precisely. However, we have felt that more work needed to be done to answer the question "How can we apply this to the phenomenon of flow in healthcare?" And even more importantly, "How can we best define flow in healthcare systems and processes?"

While the book *Flow: The Psychology of Optimal Experience* (1990) has been justifiably honored and popular, there was very little initial application of the flow concept to healthcare. Of particular interest is the following insight (1990):

Flow cannot be pursued. It must ensue.

Csikszentmihalyi meant that to apply to the experience of flow for the individual experiencing flow. For healthcare leaders, the challenge is clearly to prove that insight wrong with regard to creating flow in the healthcare system. In other words, we must find ways to assure that we can develop a practical and pragmatic definition of flow that allows us to illuminate the pathway toward flow for other healthcare leaders, who must be trained to create the optimal conditions in which flow can ensue.

THE ORIGINS OF FLOW IN HEALTHCARE

As the precepts and principles of industrial models of improving quality (including continuous quality improvement, total quality management, and other models) began to be applied to healthcare in the 1970s and 1980s, one area of particular emphasis was the concept of *variation* and its effect on the ability to consistently deliver quality care. An emerging sense developed that reducing this variation, particularly through the redesign of processes, could have a substantial impact on the fundamental way in which healthcare was delivered. The 2003 white paper published by the Institute for Healthcare Improvement (IHI) "Optimizing Patient Flow: Moving Patients Smoothly Through Acute Care Settings" stated the problem succinctly:

Patients and providers alike regard waits, delays, and cancellations
as a normal part of getting and giving care. Particularly in hospitals,
waiting seems intrinsic and, to many, intractable.

In many ways, the fundamental problem is helping leaders understand that poor flow may be intrinsic to many of our systems, but our challenge is to prove not only that it is not intractable but that specific tools exist to dramatically improve flow. Without ever specifically defining "flow," the white paper did begin to discuss the intersection of three vectors as possible components in understanding flow:
1. variation;
2. waits and delays; and
3. a fundamental mismatch between demand and capacity.

5

To our knowledge, this was the first publication specifically addressing flow in the patient care setting, and its primary emphasis was on reducing process variation. It also reiterated an insight (Covey 2004) originally made by Arthur W. Jones, a knowledge-management specialist at Xerox's famous Palo Alto Research Center (PARC), and later popularized by Dr. Donald Berwick (1996) as the first law of improvement:

Every system is perfectly designed to achieve the results it achieves.

Partially as a result of working closely with IHI in its development of the concept of patient flow and partially through independent interest and research, we developed an alternate, somewhat more nuanced definition of flow, which we published previously (Jensen et al. 2007). Our view then was that flow comprised five essential features, which we delineated there.

1. flow as efficiency and cycle times;
2. flow as reduced variation, increased predictability, and improved forecasting;
3. flow as systems thinking;
4. flow as empowered providers exceeding expectations; and
5. flow as demand-capacity management.

Flow as Efficiency and Cycle Times

While flow could simply be defined as turnaround time (TAT), our view has been that turnaround time *alone* is insufficient to define flow. In general, people tend to believe that "faster is better," but in healthcare we have seen cycle times alone as insufficient for effective flow. In healthcare, we need to learn and live by the adage:

We must be fast at fast things and slow at slow things.

For example, in the Emergency Department, in general, the faster we can evaluate a sprained ankle and treat it, the better. If we can speed the process of obtaining a radiograph of the ankle and put the patient and provider together faster, the better it is for the patient and the provider. (Indeed, using evidence-based approaches such as the Ottawa Ankle Rules [Bachmann et al. 2003], radiographs in certain cases can be safely eliminated altogether.)

However, for patients with moderate to severe but nonspecific abdominal pain, a certain amount of time is necessary to take a history, examine the patient, establish intravenous access, perform appropriate laboratory and imaging studies, and determine the patient's course and response to treatment over time. For the abdominal pain patient, how fast is too fast and how long is too long? By way of extreme example, 20 minutes is probably too fast (unless a critical abdominal crisis requiring immediate surgery is present), and 12 hours is undoubtedly too slow. However, if the patient has clear-cut appendicitis, confirmed by history and physical examination, is it really necessary to confirm the diagnosis with imaging studies when it is apparent from history and physical examination? There are countless other examples to help demonstrate that, while turnaround times and efficiency and effectiveness are an important component of flow, they are insufficient and inadequate to solely define flow.

Flow as Reduced Variation, Increased Predictability, and Improved Forecasting

While we believe that IHI's original insight about reducing variation as one of the keys to improving flow is valid, we do not think reducing variation alone will attain flow. To be sure, the tools of statistical process control, statistical analysis, and focusing deeply on variation are all important to improving flow. However, as we will see, reducing variation is less important than *reducing variation that does not add value*. More on this concept later, but we also believe the reduction of variation must be supplemented by an ability to increase predictability so we can forecast the demands that will be placed on healthcare.

By way of an extremely simple example, there is an old saying that, "You can't predict what's coming to the Emergency Department!" While on its surface this saying makes some sense, in fact if statistical analysis is applied to the ED, we not only know how many people are coming but also what types of illness and injuries they will have by time of day, day of the week, and season of the year. For example, we often tell our ED patients:

"I knew you were coming—I just didn't know your name!"

Thus, while there are some surprises in the ED, there is also a high level of predictability regarding the healthcare we provide. To the extent that we are able to forecast patient demand, we increase our ability to improve flow.

Flow as Systems Thinking

In many respects, flow is a complex interaction between multiple systems, all of which are designed to improve the health and safety of the patient. Healthcare involves a series of service transitions in a complex fabric of various providers weaving their efforts into a systematic effort on even the simplest initiatives. Doctors, nurses, laboratory workers, radiologists, radiology technicians, and a vast array of other healthcare workers interact to varying degrees in the care of a given patient in the healthcare system. If these processes—and the people who provide those processes—are not positively and proactively cooperating to develop a seamless system, in fact, the provision of our healthcare begins to appear to the patient and the family as having been "functionally siloed," in that service handoffs and transitions are not effectively handled. To most effectively assure that this coordination occurs, we must align strategic incentives across the various aspects of healthcare in a systems approach. For more on the importance of a systems approach to healthcare, see Peter Senge (2006), Tom Peters (2003), John Kotter (1996), Quint Studer (2008), and Peter Block (Block 2002).

Flow as Empowered Providers Exceeding Expectations

While we want to reduce variation to help improve patient flow, we also want to make sure that our healthcare providers are well educated and well trained, and that they are *empowered* to exceed expectations whenever possible. Empowerment simply means that those providing the service have the ability to adapt the service to meet or exceed the needs of the patient or family during the course of the provision of that service. A simple way of illustrating this is by asking this question:

Do you have a thick-rulebook company—or do you have a
thin-rulebook company?

In other words, if the rulebook is so thick that the provider has to "look up" the right way to deliver the service, it is highly unlikely that that service will be pleasing to either the patient or to the person providing care to the patient. However, if your company has a commitment to well-thought-out values, principles, and strategies—including the core value of reducing variation—and then empowers the employee or groups of employees to provide the service according to those values, principles, and strategies, that is a "thin-rulebook company" and a very pleasing one to both those providing the service and the patients who receive superior service from those employees. In addition, understanding a patient's expectations and meeting—or exceeding—them is critically important to improving flow. As we'll discuss later, the simplest way to understand patients' expectations is two simple words: *Ask them!* The clearer we can be with regard to what the expectations are, the more likely we are to be able to meet or exceed them. To a certain degree, flow exists to the extent that we are able to not only understand expectations but exceed them.

Flow as Demand-Capacity Management

As we will discuss in more detail, service capacity simply cannot be stored and is in that respect a perishable commodity. The more a system has bottlenecks or rate-limiting steps built into it, the less it has flow as an essential characteristic. Matching service demand with service capacity is a critical component of flow and requires a number of tools, strategies, and interventions, which, thankfully, are becoming increasingly well honed and understood.

Evolving a More Practical Definition

While the preceding definition of flow is perhaps more comprehensive than previous iterations, we have come to view it as more cumbersome and less possessed of utility. The principles making up flow in this definition all have proven their validity since the definition was proposed; still, we believe it is necessary to evolve it to a much more succinct and practical definition. Part of that definition is an understanding of flow as "the movement of patients through the network of queues and service transitions that characterize modern healthcare" (Jensen and Crane 2008). But what is it *about* that movement that speaks to flow existing or not existing, being improved or declining? These questions led to our current focus on defining flow as the process of adding value and eliminating waste during the course of our patients' journey through the healthcare system.

DEFINING FLOW AS VALUE ADDED AND WASTE ELIMINATED: THE BENEFIT-TO-BURDEN RATIO

With the above thoughts in mind, we took a deeper dive into a definition of flow that affords a more practical means of identifying, training for, and accentuating flow. Fundamentally, it is an attempt to find ways in which flow *can* be pursued and not just ensue.

In some respects, the genesis of the concept of flow grew out of an increasing focus on applying leadership and management principles to healthcare. To be sure, applying these leadership and management principles was an extremely important trend. Out of that movement and the literature supporting it has come a truism with origins in the well recognized and widely respected works of Joseph Juran (1989), W. Edwards Deming (1986), and William Shewhart (1939), among others, which is:

Quality exists to the extent that value is added to a product or service.

This concept is precise, concise, and widely accepted. In our experience, though, it is not of particular utility in guiding which of many clinical options we should pursue, much less how we might measure value and therefore quality. Further, how is the nurse or doctor at the bedside able to put this definition to use for the good of the patient? Thus, while the statement on its face seems true and has what the statisticians would call "face validity," it has little practical applicability unless we can define the term *value*.

With these thoughts in mind, we recalled the insights learned from one of America's preeminent researchers on service excellence, Dr. Leonard Berry from Texas A&M University, who has described the importance of analyzing the benefits and burdens inherent in the delivery of a product or service (Berry 1995, 1999; Berry and Seltman 2008). Berry notes that value comprises a simple ratio of benefits received versus burdens endured to receive those benefits. In considering the complexity of flow through the healthcare system—and in particular the importance of system appreciation—we have come to appreciate the validity and utility of the following definition:

Flow exists to the extent that value is added to a product or
service during a patient's journey through the queues and service
transitions in healthcare.

In other words, at each step of the patient's journey through the
healthcare system, those providing the care should ask the following
questions:

Does this add value?

How does this add value?

To the extent that the process or service adds value, flow has increased. If
it has not added value, flow is, at best, neutral. And if it has subtracted value,
flow has decreased.

The next question becomes how we define the terms *value* or *value added*.
Here is where the brilliance of Leonard Berry's formulation appears (1999).

Value is defined as a ratio of the benefits received versus the burdens
endured as the service is delivered.

Graphically, this formulation looks like this:

Flow = Value Added Services = $\dfrac{\text{Benefits Received}}{\text{Burdens Endured}}$

Thus, if you want to increase flow in the system, you need to increase
value by addressing the benefit-to-burden ratio. By this definition, anything
that increases benefit increases value and therefore flow, so long as the burdens
involved in increasing the benefit do not increase more than the benefit itself
(but more on this later). A very simple example is the routine use of standing
physician orders to proactively manage pain in certain groups of patients by
the use of oral pain medication. This effort increases benefit by alleviating
pain in a more timely fashion. But what if the pain medication has to be given
intramuscularly (IM) or intravenously (IV)? In this case, both the numerator
(the benefit of relieving pain) and the denominator (the burden endured from

a shot or an IV) change as well. Presumably, the discomfort of the shot or establishing an IV is a burden exceeded by the benefit of the pain relief provided by the more rapid and, in some cases, more powerful agent being given by the IM or IV route. To the extent that the benefit (pain relief) exceeds the burden (the discomfort of the shot or IV), value has been added and therefore flow has improved. This example also shows that, just as there is a flow equation of a value-added-benefit-to-burden ratio for the patient, there is also one for the nurse who provides the care. Specifically, the presence of the standing order for pain medication in certain groups of patients precludes the nurse having to call the doctor, wait for the return call, get a medication order, prepare the medication, and finally give the patient the medication—all of which are burdens for a busy nurse who is often overtaxed in the first place. By eliminating or decreasing these burdens, a hospital adds value and improves flow for the nurse as well as for the patient.

The benefit-to-burden ratio as a definition of flow through adding value can be applied to virtually any process or activity in healthcare by asking three fundamental flow questions:

1. What are the benefits received?
2. What are the burdens endured?
3. Would you tolerate this ratio?

The last question is perhaps the most important, at least for any organization that professes to put the patient first. If it isn't good enough for you or, more importantly, a member of your family, why is it good enough for your patients?

We can add a further subset of questions to each question. For the benefits, are they obvious? If so, you should reaffirm them, to assure that the patient and family realize them. If they are not obvious, you should inform patients about them by using scripts or Key Words at Key Times™. (See Chapter 3.) Here's a simple example involving privacy, an important aspect of the patient's perception not only of the courtesy of the healthcare experience but of flow as well. Closing the curtain or door to the room is a way of assuring the patient's privacy. But this can be a non-obvious benefit, and we can use these key words to make it more obvious:

"Mr. Rodriguez, shall I close this curtain *for your privacy?*"

By using these words, we can not only make the benefit more obvious but also give the patient a choice in the matter. Sometimes the results can surprise you, as we learned one night from an ED patient with whom we had used the above script. His response was classic:

"No, thanks. I'd rather enjoy the show!"

We learned from him that we are always "onstage" in healthcare and are providing "The Show" to the patient. (We discuss the "onstage" concept further in Chapter 3.)

With regard to the burdens endured, are they necessary or unnecessary? If they are necessary, explain why they are necessary at each step of the way, and the patients' flow experiences will improve. If they are unnecessary, eliminate them! Figure 1.1 illustrates the concept of flow as value added and the questions we need to ask as we improve flow in healthcare.

Figure 1.1: The Benefit-to-Burden Ratio Defining Flow in Healthcare and Steps to Accentuate Benefits and Eliminate Unnecessary Burdens

- **What are the BENEFITS RECEIVED?**

    Obvious? - Re-affirm them
    Non-obvious? - Inform them

- **What are the BURDENS ENDURED?**

    Necessary? - Explain them
    Unnecessary? - Eliminate them

WOULD YOU TOLERATE THIS RATIO?

The calculus of the benefit-to-burden ratio results in a sometimes dizzying number of combinations in which value can be increased and flow can be improved through working on both the numerator (benefits) and the denominator (burdens). As Figure 1.2 illustrates, there are almost infinite possible pathways to increase value; we just need to explore them.

Figure 1.2: Mechanisms to Increase, Decrease, or Keep Static Variables of Benefits and Burdens and Increase or Decrease Value

---

The Calculus of Flow

Changing the Benefit to Burden Ratio

Increased Value	Decreased Value
↑ Benefit, → Burden	→ Benefit, ↑ Burden
↑↑ Benefit, ↑ Burden	↑ Benefit, ↑↑ Burden
→ Benefit, ↓ Burden	↓ Benefit, → Burden
↑ Benefit, ↓↓ Burden	

↑ Increase, ↓ Decrease, → Same

A helpful tool in this task is value-stream mapping (Nash and Poling 2008; Lee and Snyder) or VSM; it offers a highly visual method of describing processes, services, and systems in a way that accentuates the specific actions and places that increase value. We describe it in more detail in Chapter 3. Understanding queues (and the elimination of non-value added queues) and service transitions is also critical to finding ways in which to increase flow through increasing benefits and decreasing burdens. Finally, both evidence-based medicine and Evidence-Based Leadership[SM] are of great importance because they help leaders standardize the approach to the healthcare we provide. As we noted and will discuss further, reducing variation that does not add value is a key part of improving flow.

A Word About Evidence-Based Leadership

To understand flow, it helps to first understand Evidence-Based Leadership. Indeed, the principle of flow is a powerful example of EBL in practice.

What *is* EBL? Basically, it's a strategy centered on using behaviors and tactics collected from around the country that have been proven to yield the best possible outcomes. Organizations that embrace EBL standardize these "best practices" and hardwire them into their systems and processes so that they remain in place as leaders come and go.

Just as the American healthcare industry uses evidence-based medicine (EBM) to guide clinical decisions, its leaders should be committed to Evidence-Based Leadership (EBL) in order to create sustainable results.

There are three fundamental components to EBL:
1. aligned goals;
2. aligned behavior; and
3. aligned processes.

It's the very presence of this alignment that allows the principles we discuss in this book to take root and flourish inside an organization. At least from the patient's perspective, every staff member who provides care is exercising leadership. When everyone is working together, using standardized practices, flow can ensue.

To learn more about Evidence-Based Leadership and its connection to hardwiring flow, please visit www.studergroup.com/hardwiringflow. There, you'll find a downloadable PDF that explains how healthcare organizations use EBL to create consistently great outcomes for employees, physicians, and, of course, patients.

FLOW AND THE CONCEPTS OF VALUE ADDED AND NON-VALUE ADDED (WASTE)

A corollary of the definition of flow as the connection of activities adding value to the patient's healthcare experience is that we can classify our processes, using the benefit-to-burden ratio, as value added or non-value added. As our previous discussion implies, if the benefit-to-burden ratio increases, we have added value. If it decreases, value has decreased, and the change should properly be considered non-value added. But a much better term for non-value added is the more precise description of what such activity provides the healthcare system—*waste!* Anything that doesn't add value is not just the *absence* of value, it is the *diversion* of resources from the value stream. Further, because our resources—and the time and energy of those who lead and manage those resources—are severely capacity-constrained, waste is also the *destruction of possibility*, since it consumes time, effort, and energy that could otherwise create value and improve flow elsewhere. As Taiichi Ohno noted, "Waste is any expenditure of time, money, or other resources that doesn't add value" (Black and Miller 2008).

A simple question arises about waste, which is: Is waste the presence of something negative or the absence of something positive? In fact, waste encompasses elements of both, to varying degrees. Figure 1.3 lists the seven types of waste as defined by Ohno in his original work.

Figure 1.3: The Seven Types of Waste That Must Be Eliminated

1. Waiting
2. Transportation
3. Processing
4. Inventory
5. Movement
6. Defective products or services
7. Overproduction

We should thus learn to distinguish burdens from waste. Burdens are the necessary parts of the current processes constituting the flow experience. They may not be pleasant, but they add value to the process or service. For example, anyone who has ever had to drink oral contrast prior to an abdominal CT scan will tell you that it is a burden—it doesn't taste great and it takes time to circulate through the GI tract before imaging can begin. But it is, at least in the correct circumstances, a burden that adds value in that it allows the radiologist to better delineate the intra-abdominal organs. Another example of a necessary burden is the need to obtain access to the femoral vessels in a cardiac catheterization. It is uncomfortable, carries the risk of bleeding, and requires various means of hemostasis following the procedure, but it is a burden that must be endured to permit the procedure. (To be sure, considering the benefit-to-burden ratio has led us to introduce certain ways of lowering the pain or discomfort burden, including topical anesthesia or the use of amnestic agents such as Versed®.)

To return to the example of oral contrast in abdominal CT scans, many hospitals have progressive radiologists who have studied the issue and the medical literature and have determined that oral contrast is not necessary in routine abdominal CT scans, except in certain circumstances. Based on collaborative efforts between radiology and the clinicians ordering the studies, they have *eliminated waste by eliminating the burden* of the oral contrast. This action adds value and improves flow, in this case for the patient, the nurse, and the ordering physician. As we'll see in the next chapter, the use of oral contrast is a rate-limiting step or bottleneck, so the elimination of waste creates further value and flow by eliminating the time required to drink the contrast and allow it to circulate. *This creates capacity in a severely capacity-constrained system.*

For example, an Emergency Department that had an annual volume of 95,000 patient visits found through retrospective review that it completed 20,500 abdominal CTs per year, each of which, by policy, required the administration of oral contrast. Again, retrospective chart review indicated that the use of oral contrast added, on average, 155 minutes to a patient's length of stay in the ED. (Note that the very process of studying the rate of utilization is an example of increasing the predictability of the study, a key step in improving flow.) A collaborative effort of the departments of Radiology, Emergency Medicine, and Surgery resulted in the development of evidence-based guidelines to restrict the use of oral contrast, except in certain defined cases. Following adoption of these guidelines, the use of oral contrast in abdominal CTs dropped from 20,500 to 2,700. This tactic had two extremely positive flow outcomes. First, for the 17,800 patients who *didn't* have to have oral contrast, their burden was decreased not only by the 2.5 hours shaved off their ED length of stay but also by eliminating the burden of drinking the oral contrast. Second, by eliminating the waste caused by the unnecessary burden of oral contrast (since it did not add value but did add to the burden), this Emergency Department created nearly 46,000 *hours* of additional capacity (17,800 CTs times 155 minutes of delay per CT). Since the overall length of stay for this ED was 4 hours and 15 minutes, this action created potential capacity for over 10,000 additional patients.

While reducing variation is a common tactic used to improve flow, this example shows how we can sometimes dramatically improve flow by actually *increasing variation*. In this instance, the hospital increased variation by creating two pathways (oral contrast versus no oral contrast) where there previously had been one pathway (oral contrast for all patients). Increasing variation created the potential to treat an additional 10,000 patients per year while shaving over 2 hours off the length of stay for over 15,000 patients.

This somewhat counterintuitive phenomenon of selectively increasing variation to improve flow has been noted by others as well. In their landmark work defining high reliability organizations (HROs), Weick and Sutcliffe (2007) noted:

Much to our surprise, reliability does not mean a complete lack of variation. It's just the opposite. It takes *mindful variety* to assure stable high performance.

Successfully leading flow initiatives requires a deep understanding of this concept: *How much and what type of variation is the right variation, meaning of course the variation that improves value?* In developing this skill, two points deserve particular emphasis. First, as we have mentioned previously and will develop further in Chapter 4, leading flow requires creatively assessing which of the alternate ways of providing processes and services leads to value creation and waste reduction. Skill in experimentation is necessary to guide these efforts. If variation is blindly eliminated, experimentation is stifled and potential improvements in flow are lost. Second, if elimination of variation is the primary criterion for improvements in flow, there is very little room for diversity, which is a key ingredient of successful healthcare organizations. This concept includes not only diversity of culture, race, and ethnicity but also of learning styles and viewpoint about what success might look like. Thus, creativity, experimentation, and mindful diversity are necessary in determining how much and what type of variation best creates value.

These examples show that some burdens are necessary and can create value, while others do not and should therefore be eliminated. (It also shows that all of our processes need to be continuously revisited, since their value changes as the science changes, as the example of oral contrast for CT scans shows.) All this discussion leads us to an important insight about value added, burdens, waste, and flow:

All waste is burden, but not all burden is waste.

Armed with the new vision that the benefit-to-burden definition of flow allows and with the Flow Toolkit outlined next and in detail in the next chapter, leaders and managers need to become "flow detectives," who prowl their units in search of the culprits (usually systems and processes, more rarely people) who provide no benefit and increase burdens to patients and providers alike. By sleuthing through their domain, they can help their staff identify those things that work effectively through the use of tools like value-stream mapping. Those areas should be accentuated. Similarly, we can identify areas that need to be eliminated, because they're waste. It's a combination of two forms of "hunt," as Figure 1.4 shows.

Figure 1.4: The Two Kinds of Hunts

Flow is...

- **A continuous Treasure Hunt to add value**

- **A continuous Bounty Hunt to eliminate anything that doesn't add value**

The bounty hunt and treasure hunt approach requires us to lead our units with a new spirit (described in more detail in Chapter 3), which encourages innovation in value identification and creation and a healthy disrespect for tradition in the merciless elimination of waste or non-value added processes or services. As we apply the calculus of the benefit-to-burden ratio, leaders must be aware of the constant dynamic tension between these two questions:

_____

Why are we doing it this way if it doesn't add value?

Why not do it another way that adds more value?

_____

These two questions are put to pragmatic use in our efforts to use flow as a way of assuring we design healthcare systems that get it right. We believe there are six clinical elements that we need to get right:

1. the right resources;
2. to the right patient;
3. in the right environment (bed);
4. for the right reasons;
5. with the right team;
6. at the right time—*every time!*

At each of these "right" inflection points, we need to consider how to use the benefit-to-burden ratio to increase value, maximize flow, and eliminate waste in a team-based environment and in a fashion that predictably delivers consistent results.

One additional concept is important in our definition of flow: expectations and their role in determining value. A deep understanding of patient expectations is central to improving flow, because we can't manage value unless we understand what benefits and burdens the patient expects. Broadly stated, expectations occur when we believe, usually for good reason born out of careful reflection upon our experiences, that certain things are reasonably certain to come about. To expect something is not to prejudge it or to fail to be open to the richness of new experience, but rather is the way to get mentally ready for the challenges of the day. With all deliberate actions, we (and our patients) make assumptions regarding the most likely of the many reactions that might occur and proceed accordingly. These implicit and explicit assumptions guide our choices. But equally importantly, they serve as the *infrastructure* for how we experience the world. Without infrastructure, it is impossible to assess our experiences, much less progress to better flow through improved value. Expectations are much like careful planning, which allows for excellence in execution. The dynamic tension between planning and execution is an old one and is illustrated by the healthy debate between two great generals in World War II. General Dwight D. Eisenhower, Supreme Commander of the Allied Expeditionary Force in Europe, believed that plans were the fundamental aspect of successful warfare, while his colorful and controversial Commanding General George S. Patton of the U.S. Third Army thought that "Execution, not plans, is the key to successfully defeating the German Army" (Axelrod 2006). Who was proven correct? Most students of military history would say that both of them were, depending upon the circumstances of the particular battle. Operation Overlord, the Allied assault on Fortress Europe on the Normandy beaches on D-Day, June 6, 1944, relied heavily on detailed planning. However, the Battle of the Bulge in December 1944 did not allow time for extensive planning and instead relied on Patton's brilliant execution.

Discovering patient and family expectations in healthcare is fundamentally essential to creating value. As we mentioned previously, the best way to discover patients' expectations is encompassed in two words: *Ask them!* Studies done by Studer Group (Meade, Kennedy, and Kaplan 2008) concerning hourly rounding found this question the most helpful in discovering expectations:

What's the *one thing* we can do to make this an excellent experience and exceed your expectations?

Once we have discovered their expectations, we can then use our flow detective skills to develop a road map for how to improve flow by creating value and eliminating waste through the benefit-to-burden ration as our patients move through the service transitions and queues of healthcare.

To summarize briefly, flow is defined as adding value to processes or services by increasing benefits, decreasing burdens, or some combination of both when applied to the movement of patients through the network of service transitions and queues that characterize modern healthcare. Leaders must be trained in and become expert at identifying opportunities to increase value (the treasure hunt) and eliminate waste (the bounty hunt) by using tools such as value-stream mapping, queuing theory, service transitions, EBM, and EBL to guide their detective work. That detective work will assure we have the right resources for the right patients in the right environment for the right reasons with the right team at the right time—every time!

THE FLOW TOOLKIT™

With the definition of flow as value added through the benefit-to-burden ratio in mind, the question becomes:

If that's what flow is, what tools are the ideal
ones to use to optimize flow?

The Flow Toolkit was developed over years of research in leading and coaching teams attempting to improve flow in their environments. It comprises seven key components, which we describe in detail in the next chapter. All of the aspects of the Flow Toolkit are helpful, but, as with any toolbox, there are different tools for different jobs. Effective flow leadership requires not just knowledge of the tools but the wisdom to know which tools to use in each circumstance. That is the focus of Chapter 2.

CHAPTER 2

HARDWIRING FOR FLOW: KEY STRATEGIES FOR IMPROVING FLOW

"Genius is 1 percent inspiration and 99 percent perspiration."

—*Thomas A. Edison*

If you've ever worked in an Emergency Department, you've probably experienced something like this: You're relaxing in the ED one morning with nothing to do when all at once five patients show up in triage. The five patients are each processed one by one through triage and registration. The five patients each get a room, and five different nurses do their nursing assessments while the physician waits—and then the ED physician faces five patients at the same time. Delays begin to build. More patients arrive and suddenly patients are waiting and your team is harried and frustrated.

As an ED physician or director or manager, our initial responses might include the following: Why weren't the patients brought back immediately? Why the sequential processes and the sequential assessments? Why not a heads-up notification to everyone on the team that we were going from zero to sixty miles per hour in a short period of time? As an ED physician or director or manager, our initial responses might be to find someone to blame. Those were certainly among the initial thoughts and responses of one of the authors when in training years ago as an emergency physician, and later in the role of leading and managing a busy Emergency Department; for example, when lab results weren't coming back in a reliable and timely manner, we'd go find the lab director and manage the situation (some might construe this as complaining...). If radiology turnaround times were prolonged, that too might be a situation that needed "active managing."

Then an article by Don Berwick changed our way of looking at things—and our lives. In that article (1996), Berwick discussed the first law of improvement we mentioned in Chapter 1: "Every system is perfectly designed to produce the results it produces." In the ED example, you could blame someone or something, but in truth, no one is to blame. If five patients show up at the same time and your triage system puts them through sequentially, the effect is not difficult to predict. If five patients are assessed at the same time by five nurses and then those five charts are placed in the physician's "To Be Seen" queue, the effect is not difficult to predict. If five radiology studies are ordered on five patients at the same time, the effect is not difficult to predict. The system was designed to produce the results it produced. If you want a different outcome, you have to change the system.

Our system of healthcare is a system of patient flows and hand-offs. It is critical to realize several things about this system. First, it is a network connecting the various parts of the hospital and the journey that the patient takes through the hospital: We're all part of this together, and what we do affects other parts of the system. The ED is connected to the ICU. The ICU is connected to the OR. The discharge processes in one affect the admission processes of the others. The patient care network comprises multiple queues and multiple service transitions, and, as we'll see, the queues and waits can often migrate within the system. For patients arriving in the ED, waiting to register is a queue. Waiting for triage is a queue. Waiting for a room is a queue. Waiting to see a doctor is a queue. Service transitions occur when a patient is handed from nurse to doctor to lab technician to X-ray technician and then back to a nurse. The better you manage the queues and optimize or even in some cases eliminate the transitions, the smoother the patient flow. Second, the rate at which patients arrive varies over time, as does the type and complexity of patients. Third, those arriving patients with different medical conditions require different procedures, respond to treatment differently, and stay varying amounts of time. Fourth, physicians and nurses vary in how they work—work styles, risk tolerance, and capacity. In other words, variation—variations in flow, clinical conditions, and workforce patterns and capabilities—impacts patient flow significantly. If not managed effectively, it can and will overload the system.

The delays we often see in healthcare systems today are not inevitable. By improving patient flow, you can manage your healthcare system effectively. To do so, the first step is to see that system as being a set of processes and transitions. If you want to produce different results, you must change and improve your processes and smooth your transitions. "Changing processes" may sound abstract, but in fact it relates directly to the reason many of us got into this field in the first place: Quality patient care and excellent patient satisfaction are largely outcomes of good systems and processes, as well as the aptitudes and attitudes of those performing the processes. The surest way to deliver quality outcomes and great patient satisfaction is to deliver great operational service. And the critical factor often missing in delivering great operational service is managing effectively patient flow.

Consider the following comment from a participant in a seminar on improving flow led by one of the authors:

At my hospital we did implement this model. And we went
from a left-without-being-seen rate [in the ED] of 9 percent
down to 1 percent. So it does work. It's actually very miraculous.

You may not be able to work miracles, but you can improve patient flow by understanding and implementing some key strategies. In fact, when you understand the key strategies of flow, improvements in flow are not miraculous—they are *expected*. The seven key strategies for improving flow are:

1. Demand-capacity management;
2. Real-time monitoring of patient flow;
3. Forecasting service demand;
4. Queuing theory;
5. The Theory of Constraints;

6. Managing variation; and
7. System appreciation.

We will discuss each of these in this chapter and in later chapters when the strategies are relevant. Taken together, they'll give you the intellectual tools and the mental models you need to improve patient flow in your system, and thereby improve your system of healthcare delivery. Doing so is also good for your business. But the number one reason for getting your patient care processes right is that it's good for your patients and it's good for the people who take care of your patients.

SEVEN STRATEGIES TO IMPROVE FLOW

Demand-Capacity Management

Healthcare is a service, not a physical item that can be stored on a shelf and retrieved whenever it is needed. If an hour goes by when a doctor or nurse can't deliver care, that service time and opportunity are gone forever. When those five patients suddenly arrived in the ED and the queues began to form, the clinical service time available before they arrived can't be recovered or used. If you keep track of the number of patients arriving in your hospital over a certain amount of time and plot that number and that time on a graph, you will see fluctuation. Demand during a period of time varies. This is true for any unscheduled system—an ED, emergency surgery, unscheduled transfers, and so on. When demand is lower than the capacity of the healthcare system, resources will be underutilized. At times of peak demand, when it exceeds capacity, they can be overwhelmed.

Years ago, the notion of "capacity" meant we decided how much service capacity we needed—not only space but doctors and nurses as well—and we built facilities and staffed them accordingly. Then budgets (and DRGs) became a primary concern, money became a scarce resource, and the emphasis changed to staffing for averages. In some ways, this approach makes sense, but in other important ways it doesn't make sense at all, because it means that half the time, demand exceeds capacity. In other words, half the time, you are probably having a bad day. What is worse is that if you are having a bad day, your patients are having an even worse day.

Matching Capacity to Demand
Managing demand and capacity together can be done in two ways:
1. Smoothing patient demand; or
2. Matching service capacity to meet it.

Both involve tracking data and responding accordingly. Because they confront the same kinds of peaks and valleys, service businesses have developed strategies to help match capacity to demand—strategies equally useful in healthcare settings. Figure 2.1 shows a number of these, both for managing demand and managing "supply," or capacity. Some of these are discussed in more detail in Jensen, Mayer, Welch, et al. (2007).

Figure 2.1: Demand-Capacity Management Strategies

Managing Demand	Managing Supply
• Scheduling	• Customer participation
• Partitioning/ segmenting demand	• Cross-training
• Developing complementary services	• Shared capacity
• Offering price incentives	• Innovative scheduling and shift work
• Developing reservation systems	• Flexible capacity
• Promoting off-peak demand	• Using part-time employees

Four Key Questions for Demand-Capacity Management
The most important aim in demand-capacity management is to *establish a measure of patient demand by hour (or relevant period of time), and design a system to handle it.* In achieving that aim, there are four key questions to ask:
1. How many patients are coming?
2. When are they coming (month, day, and time)?

3.   What resources are they going to need?
4.   Is our service capacity going to match patient demand?

The answers to these questions are predictable. You can study and analyze your visits for the last week, month, or year, and then use this data to plan. You can figure out what resources you will need by day, by shift, and even by hour. You can evaluate whether your department is prepared to deliver those resources. You can study the demand for anything and everything—space, ancillary services, human resources—and then see if, on average, you can meet that demand. Track your data to answer the four questions for each of these areas, and then match staffing and capacity to patient arrivals and demand. For example, match ED lab and radiology service capacity to the demand for these services. Remember, we are all part of the system: ED directors and hospital administrators should understand when their EDs are busy and when they are slow. In the process of tracking the data, break down arrivals by chief complaint, triage, emergency medical-services arrivals, emergency severity index (ESI) level, and ancillary utilization. Last but not least, develop a response plan for times when demand unexpectedly spikes. (If demand "unexpectedly" spikes predictably over time, reset the demand-capacity equation to meet the "new reality.")

Key Principles for Demand-Capacity Management

Once you've tracked the data, you need to predict the demand based on the results and then act on what you've learned. This is one of the basic principles of matching capacity in your system to the demand it has historically experienced—and will continue to experience. These principles are:

1.   Predict demand based on historical data.
2.   Match service capacity to patient demand.
3.   Make daily predictions and plans.
4.   Implement a real-time dashboard for key cycles and monitor it.
5.   Respect the desires, concerns, and goals of the people on your team.

Part of implementing the plans that are formed is setting in advance triggers for various actions and, as we mentioned, forming effective backup plans. Take steps in advance, as well, to handle peak loads, for example by establishing "flow huddles" or "board rounds" (which we will discuss later), appointing a patient-flow coordinator, setting up an advanced triage team in the ED and placing ED admissions into inpatient beds, and, once again, creating a backup plan. In the ED, for example, if we know every Friday night is going to be difficult, why not build in some backup strategies for Friday night, such as extra staffing? If every Friday night is overwhelming, then your system is designed to be overwhelmed on Friday nights. You are planning on being overwhelmed on Friday night. (You already have a plan, but you need a better one.) You can improve the system with backup plans and surge capacity.

Real-Time Monitoring of Patient Flow

Would you drive down a busy interstate highway at night at 70 miles per hour without your headlights or dashboard lights on? Of course not. Yet many of our healthcare systems do the equivalent every day. We work without being able to see what lies immediately ahead, and we seldom have a dashboard with real-time performance metrics to see how our patient care processes are currently doing, let alone tell when we are going to run out of gas.

Service businesses have used dashboard technology for years. McDonald's uses "Hyperactive Bob," infrared cameras mounted on its stores' roofs to monitor incoming traffic and linked to computers with software allowing the stores to predict what the "soccer mom" in the SUV with four kids is going to order. This prediction gives the store a five-to-ten minute jump on what demand is likely going to be. The result? The company has cut waste in half and reduced the waiting time for customers. The restaurant chain T.G.I. Friday's uses a computer system to track "table turns," the average length of time from seating customers to putting the table back in service for another customer. When table turns increase—even by a few minutes—managers are alerted to speed up processes and divert resources to put the capacity of the system back into compliance with demand. After all, for the T.G.I. Friday's manager, table turns mean revenue and revenue means profitability. Healthcare desperately needs to learn this lesson and put such technology to work so that we have a real-time dashboard for patient flow.

Dashboards in Healthcare

Hospitals can and do make use of the same idea. Here's an example of one that did:

Luther Midelfort Hospital introduced a hospital-wide intranet dashboard along with a system for capping patient flow to units that were overwhelmed. Under the new system, all hospital units could self-grade how busy they were and put a halt temporarily to new admissions while they handled what patients they had. Hospital units and administrators could monitor hospital-wide patient flow unit by unit and disseminate this information to key departments and personnel. By enabling better use of hospital capacity, load-leveling, and the judicious deployment of reinforcements, the dashboard led to increased revenue of about $200,000 per month, increased the percentage of patients who were put into a bed within one hour from 23 percent to 40 percent, and reduced ED diversions from 12 percent to between 1 and 2 percent. Impressively, the overall number of open nursing positions decreased from about 10 percent to 1 percent.

You may think establishing a dashboard like this will involve a substantial expenditure to set up. Think again. Overlook Hospital, with its PATRACK system, for example, was doing this 15 years ago with a DOS-based program. It's a basic tracking tool recording the patient's name, chief complaint, position, nurse, and treatment or lab done or not done. You may very well have this information tracked in your system already—it is simply not being used as well as it should be. What you need and deserve in addition is simple software to pull it out and track in real time your key (or critical to quality-CTQ) process indicators or metrics. It may not be simple—but it's not very complicated, either. Ten years ago one of us mentioned this to the IT gurus at a company we were working with, and they built their own real-time dashboard in a month. *The data are in your system already.* As so often happens in healthcare, much of the data we need to lead flow are there but are not being extracted and put to pragmatic use.

The Overlook dashboard has various screens monitoring different ED functions. For the Emergency Department as a whole, you can visualize and monitor where you are in trouble and why you are in trouble. Matching capacity to demand becomes more scientific than simply calling for "More doctors! More nurses!" It may be, "More x-ray techs!" or "More beds!" It may be, "We need to get the admitted patients admitted." We are all part of the healthcare system; we are all in this together. Monitoring key processes, identifying when, where, and why our service processes are overloaded and then strategically applying needed resources benefits us all—patients and caregivers alike.

Key Questions for Real-Time Monitoring

Here are key questions for real-time monitoring:

1. How many patients are we currently caring for?
2. When do they need what services?
3. How does our service capacity match patient demand?
4. What are our contingency plans?
5. What does this patient need *next?*
6. What are the rate-limiting steps?

A final piece of advice: If you're considering buying a tracking system for use as a dashboard, make sure it can automate tracking information, monitor real-time demand and capacity, forecast, and mine data. If it can't, ask why not and see if it can be customized to do so—or don't buy it.

Forecasting Service Demand

If you check the weather report in the morning before you go out, you are taking advantage of forecasting. You may simply want to know whether to take an umbrella or a sweater. There are, however, more significant reasons for forecasting. In your own life, you may want to know whether your flight is likely to be on time. Is it going to snow on your way to work tomorrow—or, perhaps of greater concern, on your way home? If you are headed to the beach, what are the prospects for rain, or even a hurricane? The point is that forecasting plays a significant role in our daily lives, and it should play an equally significant role within your hospital system. For, in fact, you can predict patient flow. That is, you can project unscheduled arrivals with an accuracy rate of 80 to 85 percent. You don't know the patients' names, but you know how many are likely to come, why they are coming, and what resources they will likely need.

Consider this common scenario:

Most years, during the middle of flu season, people will say, "This is the worst flu season ever. We had no idea it was going to be this bad." When the year ends and the CDC statistics are released, it turns out this flu season was average—a typical one. It adds credence to the adage, "The worst crisis is always the current one!"

You can predict what your ICU demand will be, what your ventilator demand will be, and what the number and severity of flu season patient admissions in the ED are going to be. When you predict demand, then you can match resources to that predicted demand.

How Can You Know What Patient Flow Will Be?

Figure 2.2 shows patient flow for an ED, based on arrivals, patient volume, and arrival by hour of the day. This is the graph of the patient arrival activity in your ED. How can we be sure it applies to you? It's the graph of activity in any ED in the United States. The actual number of patients per hour may vary, but the curve is the same. You can begin to forecast patient flow from such data, but once you have the data, you can take it a step further. You can similarly track hourly census in the ED, not only the number of arrivals but the number of patients actually in your department at particular times. A further step is plotting the demand for lab and radiology services. Compile these types of data and you can forecast patient flow with a high degree of accuracy.

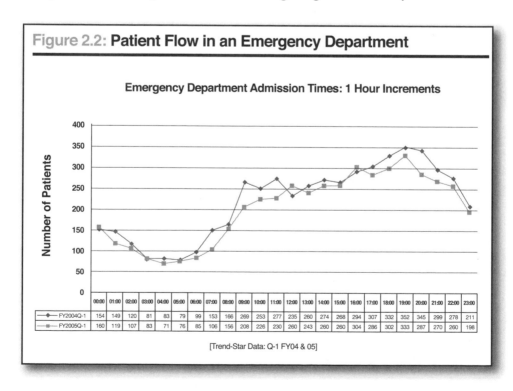

Figure 2.2: Patient Flow in an Emergency Department

Emergency Department Admission Times: 1 Hour Increments

	00:00	01:00	02:00	03:00	04:00	05:00	06:00	07:00	08:00	09:00	10:00	11:00	12:00	13:00	14:00	15:00	16:00	17:00	18:00	19:00	20:00	21:00	22:00	23:00
FY2004Q-1	154	149	120	81	83	79	99	153	166	269	253	277	235	260	274	268	294	307	332	352	345	299	278	211
FY2005Q-1	160	119	107	83	71	76	85	106	156	208	226	230	260	243	260	260	304	286	302	333	287	270	260	198

[Trend-Star Data: Q-1 FY04 & 05]

Here's how you go about forecasting admissions from the ED, for example:

1. Gather at least 30 days' data on admissions by day of the week.
2. Stratify admissions data by type and number per shift by day of the week.
3. Stratify further by diagnosis and type of bed needed.
4. Use the data to predict admissions for the next day by type and number per shift.
5. Communicate admissions predictions in real time to the patient placement staff.

For minimal delays and high throughput, your healthcare team and leaders need to predict admissions for individual units and the capacity to accept admissions for those units. The team then needs to assess, using a designed decision-making structure or process, the predicted demand and capacity of each unit and determine whether the unit or the hospital requires a plan to meet the predicted or expected demand if it will be greater than predicted capacity. If so, a plan should be developed and implemented to deal with the mismatch, and the hospital should (at the end of the day or by the morning of the following day) evaluate the success or failure of the defined plan to match capacity to demand. The next step is to redefine the effectiveness of the plans over time in response to what the evaluation of the plans reveals. In other words, are there recurrent troublesome scenarios, recurrent demand-capacity mismatches, that require a more permanent solution or set of solutions. Remember that trouble is often easier (safer, less expensive, and more gratifying) to prevent than to fix.

Forecasting Methods

Many forecasting methods are available. If the inputs (e.g., patient arrivals, lab draws, OR cases) are relatively stable over time, then time-series models (moving averages, exponential smoothing) or causal models (regression, econometric) should suffice. Significant service or operational changes, however, such as opening a new ED, a new patient care tower, or an outpatient surgical center, require both expert opinions and analysis of historical patterns. Sensitivity analysis or modeling "what if" scenarios can also help. For most of the forecasting purposes you're likely to need, using moving averages, establishing a trendline with adjustments made by expert opinion, or exponential smoothing will usually prove enlightening and rewarding.

In healthcare, three often-used forecasting methods are a percentage adjustment of previous historical activity, following a 12-month moving average, or modeling a trendline. These three common forecasting models in healthcare are quantitative in nature—they use historical data as statistical inputs. Each method, though, can benefit from adding expert knowledge based on review of the data by experienced consultants who can suggest adjustments based on their knowledge—a form of qualitative forecasting. Here are brief descriptions of the three methods:

1. Percentage adjustment is your best estimate of what will happen in the future based on percentage increase or decrease in performance over the previous 12 months.

2. Moving average calculates the average number of patient visits for the previous 12 months; it recalculates each month based on the previous 12.

3. A trendline statistically derives a best-fit line using regression analysis based on historical data to determine how accurate earlier planning was compared with the actual number of admissions in the previous 12 months.

For more detailed discussion of these forecasting methods, see Jensen, Mayer, Welch, et al. (2007).

A Factor of Change to Be Aware Of

Here's something we know intuitively about healthcare: Our patients are getting sicker. In their forecasting efforts, hospitals and healthcare systems will need to take into account a factor that indeed all parts of society will face: the aging of baby boomers. That demographic bulge will especially affect hospitals: Americans are living longer, healthier in many respects but also living longer with chronic illnesses. Peter Sprivulis has found that caring for older patients requires more time, more bed space, more laboratory tests, and more imaging. This trend is going to continue, and healthcare systems need to be prepared. Sprivulis discovered that a linear relationship exists between age and complexity in healthcare (the amount of workup and care a patient needs). Hospital work is increasing in complexity as the hospitalized population ages, and the increasing complexity carries a burden: About 60 percent of patients result in more than 90 percent of the work. High-complexity patients require more resources and a greater intensity of healthcare services. (Fatovich, Nagree, and Sprivulis 2005).

As your work to improve patient flow goes forward, you will need to keep these points in mind as you track data and make plans. The baby boom generation will need healthcare, and they have high expectations of service. Ensuring effective patient flow is going to become even more important in matching capacity to demand under these conditions.

Key Questions for Forecasting

The key questions for forecasting are similar to those for earlier strategies:

1. How many patients are coming?
2. When are they coming?
3. What services are they going to need?
4. Is our service capacity going to match patient demand?

As we noted, if service capacity is not going to match demand, then you need to formulate a plan to handle the forecasted mismatch.

Queuing Theory

If you've ever waited in a line at Starbucks, you've experienced a queue. If you've waited in a line to register for a motel room, you've been in a queue. (Often we seem to choose the wrong line at the supermarket or bank.) If you're serving patients in the ED, you're working in a queuing model or system. More formally, we can define a queuing system as any system with unscheduled or uncontrolled arrivals. (It is important to note, however, that "unscheduled or uncontrolled arrivals" does not mean they are completely unpredictable, particularly if we have the right data.) In healthcare, emergency surgeries follow a queuing model, and so do unscheduled patient transfers. Queuing theory is the art and science of matching fixed resources to unscheduled demand. Engineers have worked on queuing theory for 50 years. They've discovered that even though systems that are queuing models involve unscheduled demand, and such demand—in the case of healthcare systems patient inflow and service times—is random, we can predict how those systems will behave. The Poisson distribution, developed by the nineteenth-century French mathematician Siméon Poisson, describes unscheduled arrivals into an unscheduled system or process. One of the key relevant consequences of queuing theory is that when demand on the system increases, the response is nonlinear. This property has profound implications.

One of those significant implications is illustrated in Figure 2.3. This graph of MICU utilization and patient rejection shows that at 0 percent use of capacity (utilization = 0), the MICU is, as we might expect, empty, and the odds of a rejection of a request for an ICU bed ("rejection rate") are zero. If the MICU is full, the odds of being rejected are close to 100 percent. Notice that as the curve reaches and surpasses 60 percent utilization, it starts to take off. This is not a linear curve; it is a geometric one, a logarithmic curve, meaning that the observed data (in this case, the need for an ICU bed) reflect a sharp increase in rejections as patient utilization increases. For the patient and the provider, this means that the rejection rates—which to the user-patient and provider alike are a system failure—rise dramatically as utilization increases above 60 percent. A utilization rate of 80 to 85 percent is often the optimal point for a queuing system to operate. Above that rate, it is not only possible but highly likely that there will be "no room at the inn" for patients in need of services.

What does this mean from a practical standpoint? If an ED typically sees 150 patients per day and admits 25 percent (37) of them, 10 of whom will need MICU beds, MICU utilization rates over 80 percent at the beginning of the day bode poorly for obtaining MICU beds in a timely fashion, barring a concerted effort to obtain a substantial number of MICU transfers to other units or to obtain discharges. Under these circumstances, we can *forecast* not only our projected MICU needs for the ED but also the need to use flow tools to address this demand-capacity mismatch.

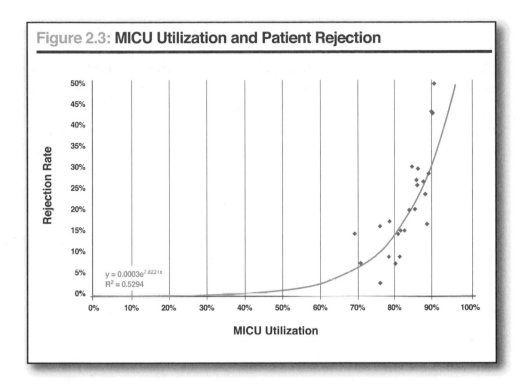

Figure 2.3: **MICU Utilization and Patient Rejection**

$$y = 0.0003e^{7.8221x}$$
$$R^2 = 0.5294$$

Implications of Queuing Theory for Patient Flow

What does this mean in the context of patient flow? *You don't need to understand the math to understand the principles and their implications.* **Many** organizations try to reach 100 percent utilization—following an assembly-line model or mentality: If everyone is busy and every bed is occupied at all times, then we must be maximizing productivity. But this is a flawed model. Running at 100 percent capacity in a system with unscheduled arrivals and variable service times is not the most effective way to operate. In fact, it's describing a system that will not work optimally much of the time. Since 80 to 85 percent utilization is often the optimal spot on the curve (in systems with unscheduled arrivals and high degrees of variability), this is where you probably want your systems to operate. The good news is that if you are at 95 percent utilization of your capacity, small changes can lead to a significant improvement and reduction in waiting times and rejections. Healthcare systems that have been able to drop to 80 to 85 percent usage of capacity, even 90 percent, have found they can better handle inflows and variation, and as a result, throughput has gone up, and so have profits and worker satisfaction. (Another caveat: The more you can predict demand, reduce variation, and streamline service delivery, the higher up the utilization curve you can operate.)

As you might guess, dropping that utilization percentage involves using the strategies we've been discussing. In the ED, for example, use historical data to estimate the number of beds and staff needed at different times throughout the day. For the hospital as a whole, again using historical data, estimate the number and types of daily admissions from the ED, the OR, and outpatient sources. Examine both average and peak daily inpatient census and ED admissions. Consider the following questions:

1. When do admissions arrive?
2. What type of admissions are they?
3. When do admissions move into inpatient beds?

Use the data that you gather to predict what will happen tomorrow and form a plan to deal with it today. Managing queues involves several possibilities: Alter the arrival process; alter the service process; and manage queues that do form more efficiently. Service businesses deal with queues by implementing efficiencies in their processes or by expanding capacities. If your resources as a healthcare system are limited, focus on operational efficiency, quality, and reliability and prioritize the available resources.

Here is an example of a business that manages queues in its work:

A company that handles billing for emergency medicine services has a number of operators handling telephone calls in its office. It mounted a large television monitor in the office, which functions as a real-time dashboard. The dashboard works on a color-coded system, by color of bars across the operators' data bars. Green across an operator's bar means that person is available to take a call. A red bar means the worker is on a customer call. The dashboard monitor shows the number of calls waiting, the average length of a call, the number of operators available at a given point in time, and the number of calls diverted because of busy operators. When most of the bars are red, everyone in the office who is not on a call knows they are likely to be needed soon. And when all bars are red? The next call rings in the boss's office.

Not only does the dashboard show what's going on now, in real time, it allows the company to mine historical data to predict volume and length of calls and plan service accordingly. When were there a high proportion of red bars? When did the office get busy? How long did calls take? All of the answers are in the data from the dashboard.

Figure 2.4 shows this dashboard. Healthcare systems can similarly take a significant step to improve the accuracy of their predictions by tracking their data. Another step for managing queues is to understand and implement lessons from the psychology of waiting.

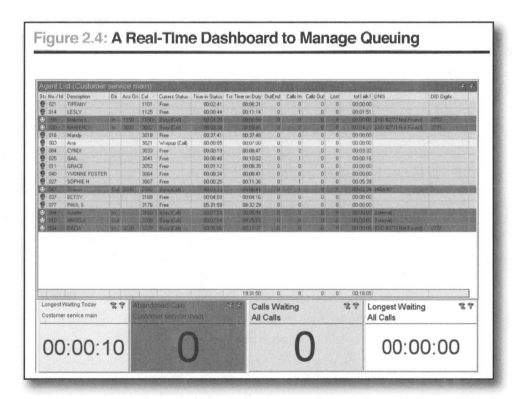

Figure 2.4: A Real-Time Dashboard to Manage Queuing

The Psychology of Waiting

When you have to wait for a table at a restaurant or in a checkout line at a grocery store, you're likely to become frustrated if the delay stretches on, while you stand there with nothing to do but wait. Businesses have become adept at managing waiting by their customers so as to minimize that frustration, indeed to deflect it. Disney is the master of this process, but many successful businesses take advantage of the psychology of waiting. Maister (1985) has identified eight principles of that psychology:

1. Occupied time beats unoccupied time.
2. Being in-process beats being preprocess.
3. Anxiety is bad.
4. Limited certainty beats uncertainty.
5. Explained situations beat unexplained ones.
6. Equitable treatment beats unfair treatment.
7. The more valuable the service is, the more tolerable the wait is.
8. Group waits beat solo waits.

Here's an example from healthcare of how awareness of those principles can change patient satisfaction:

A cardiologist friend read about the principles and then applied them in his office practice. He changed nothing else about the practice except how his staff managed the various waits. His patient-satisfaction benchmarking scores improved from worst in his area to first—solely because he managed the waits for his patients.

Maister provides an excellent description of the principles that matter. Here, in connection with healthcare, we'll point out several things:

1. Occupied time beats unoccupied time. In a well run doctor's office, patients move sequentially through various tasks and steps. Patients have material to read or video to watch until the doctor can see them. Moving patients along is more effective than keeping them waiting in one place in the process.
2. Our patients may be anxious. They may by definition be having a bad day already. Simply letting them know what the waits are, why, and what to expect can alleviate family and patient anxiety. If you survey patients as to how often they would like to be contacted while they wait in the ED, for example, they'll say 20 to 30 minutes. If you survey ED staff, they'll say at most once every hour

or two. Establish a deliberate policy of regular contact, and your patients will be more satisfied.

3. If a patient asks how long a CT scan will take, an answer giving a finite amount of time—and an amount a bit longer than the scan will likely take—will lead to a more satisfied patient. (This is a more effective approach than saying, "Soon," "You're next," "When they call for you," or "It's a busy day....")

4. If a Fast Track waiting room in the ED is in the same area as the main waiting room, patients in the latter area, who are not likely to move through as fast as the Fast Track patients, will feel dissatisfaction—they'll notice they aren't moving through as rapidly as the other patients.

5. The more valuable the perception of service, the longer patients will wait. If your facility is considered to be a top-notch ED, surgical center, or hospital, patients will tolerate longer periods of waiting.

 A Word About the Psychology of Waiting:

More information on this important subject is available at www.davidmaister.com and at www.studergroup.com/hardwiringflow, the latter of which has further examples of applying these principles in healthcare.

The Theory of Constraints

If you want the essence of the theory of constraints, you don't need to get an MBA; simply read one book, in fact a novel, *The Goal*, by Eliyahu M. Goldratt (Goldratt and Cox 1992). It concerns a man trying to save his job, his marriage, and his relationship with his son. Read the book and you'll be familiar enough with the concepts of the model (Theory of Constraints—TOC) to start implementing them in your life. The key points to remember are just two:

1. Constraints limit performance; and
2. To improve performance, you have to focus on improving constraints.

Of course, there's more to the theory than those two points. A simple definition is that a constraint is anything that significantly limits the performance of an organization or process in moving toward its goal. A constraint can thus fall into two different categories: a weakness in the system or a scarce resource. A physician or lab technician who performs a certain service may be the only one available to do so, for example, and so can easily become a constraint on the system. When demand for this resource exceeds its capacity, what is known in the TOC as a bottleneck results. In Goldratt's definition, a bottleneck has a precise meaning: It is a part of your process that holds up the flow of the entire system or relevant process, not merely a constraint that is irritating. Constraints can be internal or external resources, people, equipment, inefficient processes, policies, non-bottlenecks, and market forces.

Here are succinct definitions to distinguish between bottlenecks and non-bottlenecks:

1. A bottleneck is any resource whose capacity is equal to or less than the demand placed upon it.
2. A non-bottleneck is any resource whose capacity (ability to serve) is greater than the demand placed upon it.

The capacity of the system equals the capacity of the bottleneck: The slowest process or resource ("rate-limiting") in the service chain governs throughput. Remember that patient care comprises a network of queues and service transitions. The implication from TOC is that a delay at a critical bottleneck delays the entire system. A related implication is that you can reduce time spent at a non-bottleneck but not reduce time spent within the overall system. For healthcare clinicians, this concept will seem extraordinarily familiar, because of its similarity to the concept of the "rate-limiting step," which they all studied in organic chemistry and biochemistry.

Dealing with Bottlenecks

In your efforts to improve flow, you need to assess actions with these principles (TOC) in mind. Here's an example of one such effort and the lesson learned:

A hospital considered how to improve patient flow from the ED by reducing the cycle time for admitting patients from the ED to

inpatient beds. A plan was developed, modeled after a process in
a neighboring hospital: Use an admission nurse. So the hospital
hired five admission nurses and implemented its plan to reduce
cycle time. After trying the new process for a time,
administrators assessed how it had worked. In several ways it
worked well: Patient satisfaction increased, emergency physicians'
satisfaction increased, and nurses' satisfaction increased greatly.
Throughput cycle time in the system, however, did not change.

Does that result mean hiring admission nurses is a bad idea? Certainly
not. What it meant, for that hospital, is that the functions performed by the
admission nurses were not a bottleneck to the overall admission process.
Improving the non-bottleneck had no effect on the system throughput. As a
practical step to improve flow, the hospital should have mapped its process
flow and then tested a small step—hiring one nurse for a designated period,
for example—and then examined whether that step reduced admission
process times. At the outset, perform a bottleneck test:

If we increase the capacity or efficiency of the resource we think
is a bottleneck, would throughput of the whole system increase? Would
we be closer to our goal? If the answer to both these questions is yes,
then we can consider the resource a bottleneck.

TOC is particularly helpful in dealing with complex systems, such as a
healthcare system. In linear, nonbranching systems, identifying bottlenecks is
relatively easy. In complex, branching, highly variable systems, however,
where processes vary from job to job and there are branches and loops,
bottlenecks can shift around and they can be situation dependent. The
bottlenecks can move, from the OR to the PACU to the ICU to the ED. The
critical bottleneck may involve a bed for a time, then a lab test for another
amount of time, then the discharge process. They involve dependent events,
which require certain steps to be performed in a prescribed sequence. In the
ED, for example, patients go from triage to registration to an ED bed to
provider evaluation. An ED chart is required before orders can be placed.
Bottlenecks are also subject to statistical fluctuation. In other words, events
occur that cannot be precisely predicted. To continue with our ED example,

a surgeon is paged; that surgeon normally arrives in the ED within 30 minutes. This time the surgeon is held up in the OR for an hour. Now the response time is 90 minutes rather than the average (usual) 30-minute arrival time. Combining dependent events and statistical fluctuation gives bottlenecks their power and impact.

Consider another example. Partially in an effort to speed the admissions process, a hospital hired a group of hospitalists, who were dedicated to an evidence-based approach to various issues, including CMS measures, length of stay, and clinical pathways. Unfortunately, several of the hospitalists insisted on evaluating all admissions from the ED *in the ED prior to allowing them to be admitted*. Not only did this create a bottleneck for the first patient admitted, but the bottleneck was compounded greatly when several patients waited for admission while the hospitalist sequentially examined, documented, and wrote an order for each patient. This "bottleneck upon bottleneck" phenomenon is unfortunately common.

Managing Bottlenecks

To manage bottlenecks, you need to determine what your constraints are, and which are the most significant for the system: What processes are causing the longest delays? Look at your staff coverage—physicians, PAs, nurses—and how adequately it matches the required coverage hours revealed by your tracking of data and use of your real-time dashboard. Specifically, match the volume and capacity of provider hours to peak demand by day of the week. Examine your processing time: For patients entering the ED, how long does it take once they enter to register, to be evaluated by a doctor, to be admitted to a room? How long does it take to gather data? Once you have the data, how long does a decision on treatment require? And finally, how long after treatment begins is the patient discharged? Is there a fail-safe backup set up to ensure timely discharge? Identifying constraints is not only a matter of mining your past data. Use board rounds and bed huddles to identify them on a daily, ongoing basis. These (board rounds and bed huddles) involve key members of a department who meet at predetermined times, for about 10 minutes, to assess current conditions in the department, anticipate admissions, and analyze patient flow, as well as make disposition decisions.

Design processes to work most effectively in light of the bottlenecks. Decide what you are trying to accomplish and what interventions are possible in your system, forming both short-term and long-term plans to improve the constraints. Make sure you are carrying out critical steps when you consider what you will do when bottlenecks shift. Then plan your interventions and test them. For long-term interventions, concentrate on identifying chronic causes of demand-capacity mismatches and identify wasted inpatient capacity. Table 2.1 offers some suggestions on how to analyze and manage bottlenecks that can occur within a hospital.

Table 2.1: Analyzing and Managing Bottlenecks in a Hospital

Function	Identifying Bottleneck	Potential Intervention	Intermediate Measure
Discharge	Wasted capacity exists for "bed has a patient waiting to go" Predicted discharges often do not take place on time	Discharge team/discharge rounds "Discharge if" orders Discharge appointments	Average time of day of discharge Inpatient wasted capacity due to "bed has a patient waiting to go"
Transitions	Delays exist to transition patients within the hospital Delays exist to transition patients to extended care facilities	Joint team between two units Admission team/nurse Flow coordinator Prediction and synchronization Visibility of beds needing cleaning and matching EVS to demand Efficient care of short stay patients Specialized units (e.g., EAU, CDU) Hospitalists Cooperative agreements with extended care facilities	ED wasted capacity Time from decision to transition to arrival on a unit Bed turnover time Number of off-service patients LOS for patients transitioning to nursing home, SNF, rehab, etc.

Table 2.1: Analyzing and Managing Bottlenecks in a Hospital - con't

Function	Identifying Bottleneck	Potential Intervention	Intermediate Measure
Telemetry or ICU	Patients can't be transitioned to Telemetry/ICU while capacity is available on medical/surgical units	Board rounds Admission/discharge criteria Synchronization MDR Decentralized telemetry beds	Time from ED arrival to ICU or telemetry ICU or telemetry LOS
Certain times	Delays usually occur on certain days or at certain times	Plan for flexing capacity Cap elective admissions Smooth elective admissions	Time from ED or PACU to a unit by time of day or day of week Ratio of variation in ED admissions to elective admissions
Certain clinical conditions	Large delays exist from the ED or PACU for certain types of patients LOS for patients with a certain condition is an outlier compared to other hospitals	Bottleneck analysis on the patient stream to identify interventions Care pathways	ED arrival to floor time for the patient stream LOS for a patient stream

Here's an example of how a hospital identified and managed a bottleneck in its orthopedic unit:

Analyzing data from the real-time demand-capacity tracking system, administrators determined that moving patients out of the PACU was the source of delays. Patients were delayed leaving, which backed up the OR. Investigating further, the analysts discovered that every orthopedic patient left on an anticoagulation regimen. The bottleneck appeared to be getting medication delivered on the day of a patient's discharge. The rationale the system had been operating on was "our patients need this medicine when they're discharged. We are going to get the medicine to them on the day of discharge." This process prolonged discharges, sometimes by a whole day. The hospital had a just-in-time delivery system that wasn't just in time. It was a key constraint. The solution? Keep the same process but set it up to deliver the medication on the day after the operation. The delivery process remained the same; only the timing of it changed. The outcome after trying the test of change? Of 43 patients receiving medication, 43 of them received it on the day after the operation.

Managing Variation

Consider a telephone helpline service. In this example, one person handles all the calls. Each call lasts an average of two minutes. Can the system handle 30 calls an hour without putting anyone on hold? Could it handle 20 calls an hour without having anyone on hold? Figure 2.5 helps answer these questions.

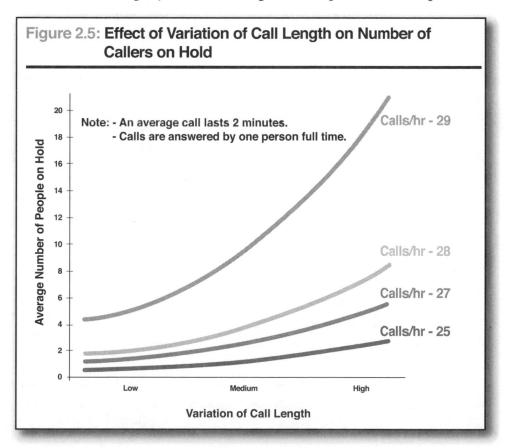

Figure 2.5: **Effect of Variation of Call Length on Number of Callers on Hold**

Note: - An average call lasts 2 minutes.
- Calls are answered by one person full time.

The calls average two minutes, but in fact, some calls take ten seconds, and others last ten minutes.

If there are 25 calls an hour with low variability, most lasting close to the average, almost no one is on hold. With higher variability, a few people are on hold. If the number of callers increases to 29 and the variation (the variation in call length) is low, the number on hold is still fairly low. But look what happens with 29 calls per hour and high variability—the curve takes off in Figure 2.5, and now 18 people are on hold. The average length of the calls is the same, and there aren't that many more callers—but you can see the results. The power and impact of variation begins to emerge in this example.

In healthcare, variation shows up in the difference in diseases and severity in patients and different responses to therapies, as well as in different levels of abilities of providers and different levels of training. There are two kinds of variation, "natural" and "artificial." Natural variation is clinical variability in diseases and professional variability in skills, patient arrival times in the ED, and the duration of surgery. It is random. It is part of flow, and it needs to be managed. Artificial variation is nonrandom. It is elective surgery and time of discharge and the schedule of the nuclear-medicine lab for reporting stress-test results. It is nonrandom. The elements of artificial variation need to be smoothed so that they are predictable and steady and in fact the high variability often associated with it eliminated. Artificial variation often contributes significantly to problems with flow.

Managing Variation

Addressing variation means using the tools we've been discussing to manage queues, match capacity to demand, and manage constraints. Some key points are:

1. Focus on operational efficiency;
2. Prioritize available resources;
3. Flex scheduling;
4. Predict demand;
5. Smooth demand; and
6. Improve the accuracy of predictions.

The example of Luther Midelfort Hospital cited earlier, in which the hospital units capped admissions when capacity reached a certain point, letting administration and other hospital units know that admitting another patient would not be safe or desirable at the moment, points the way toward smoothing patient flow (load-leveling). Doing so optimized system and individual performance and took variation into account. The service outcome wasn't fewer patients, less money, or unhappier employees. The service outcome was more patients, faster throughput time, more money, and happier healthcare workers.

In the ED, standardize the care process by developing protocols for triage and protocols for high-risk and high-volume populations and by using telephone orders, protocols, and pathways to facilitate the admission process. For inpatients, use multidisciplinary rounds and bed huddles to optimize communication and the coordination of care. In these rounds and huddles, the key representatives of departments meet to review the current patient status, schedule tests and procedures, clarify patient goals, identify safety risks, and create a plan for the day. Hospitals can focus on conditions with long length of stay, such as stroke patients, through the use of multidisciplinary rounds to predict and plan for admissions to extended-care facilities, and they can use rounds for preadmission planning for elective surgery admissions. Case managers are another useful asset—they can coordinate admissions, discharges, and transfers; address delays in testing and treatment; and consult directly with physicians to review cases.

Separating and optimizing the flow of outpatients and inpatients helps manage variation. Study the impact of outpatients on flow: the types of patients and the volumes, the beds used where and when, bottlenecks. Optimize inpatient and outpatient flow:

1. Review schedules, and don't group large numbers of similar patients who would compete for beds on the same day.
2. Dedicate beds for same-day patients or outpatients.
3. Create separate, homogeneous units only where they will leverage resources and processes and improve flow.

Appreciation of a System

W. Edwards Deming was the master of business strategy, statistics, and operations whose work led to the practices that made companies such as Toyota so successful. He developed a system of profound knowledge with four components, the first being "appreciation of a system" (the others were knowledge of variation, theory of knowledge, and knowledge of psychology). "Appreciation of a system" means that we have to realize we are part of a system. As we said earlier, we are all in this together, and our actions have an impact on other parts of the system. One of Deming's principles is that a system must have an aim. And the aim of the system must be clear to everyone in the system. If you want to improve patient flow, you need to decide what the aim of your work is. Is that aim clear to everyone in the system? If not, the system will include good people with differing priorities. For some, the primary aim will be patient safety, for others patient satisfaction or workforce satisfaction, and for still others controlling costs. All of those perspectives are relevant and important.

But in order to optimize the system, everyone working in it needs to clearly understand the overall aim of the system. You cannot optimize the entire system by separately optimizing each part of the system. Some people may have to give up something. Every part of the system can't operate at 100 percent of its potential if the system as a whole is going to operate at its maximal or optimized capacity. Some units have to have sufficient slack to take up some of the work of other parts of the system when variation or flow requires it. Often the way current systems operate, people within subsystems focus (particularly with subsystem goals and budgets) on optimizing their own (subsystem or microsystem) performance, often at the expense of other subsystems. Optimizing flow through an entire system is more difficult than optimizing flow through one department. It requires leaders. It also requires a recognized aim for the system and agreed-upon performance metrics. Chris Argyris of the Harvard Business School has focused attention on the fact that many organizations believe they have a clear aim for the system, known to all within the system. He notes, however, the dichotomy between what he refers to as the "espoused theory" (what leadership teams believe is the commonly understood aim) and the "theory in action" (what actually occurs in the day-to-day operations of the organization). (Argyris, 1992, 1993) Deming's focus on a clear aim and Argyris's observation that there is often a discrepancy between what we say and what we do must always be kept in mind. Disciplined leader rounding can help identify these discrepancies between plans and reality.

TEAMWORK AND IMPROVING FLOW

Can you think of a physician or nurse or technician you have known who was clinically proficient but could not perform well as a teammate? Can you think of a good physician or nurse who was skilled in delivering individual clinical care but poor at situational awareness—that is, who was good at taking care of a limited set of patients, but unaware or unresponsive to the overall ebb and flow of patients and patient care in the department? Not just unaware, but unresponsive to the demands of clinical care and service.

Good teamwork matters: Dynamics Research Corporation (DRC) performed a 10-year retrospective study of more than 50 cases in eight Emergency Departments that led to malpractice lawsuits. The DRC study found that an average of 8.8 errors due to poor teamwork occurred per case and that 50 percent of the harm caused could have been avoided with good teamwork. The study projected, in fact, that 80 percent of observed errors could have been prevented with better teamwork. The Joint Commission on Accreditation of Healthcare Organizations studied critical mishaps ("sentinel events") from 1995 to 2002. They discovered the leading cause wasn't professional competence—it was communication, followed by orientation and training.

The implication of these findings is that teamwork is a critical factor of success in healthcare. It is no less important in improving patient flow than in any other aspect of healthcare. Hiring the right people to begin with is one of the most effective things leaders of healthcare systems can do to establish an environment that is both safe and effective—in fact, it is critical to the success of your system. You want an "A-Team." Implementing the measures you've planned to improve flow in your system will be difficult if you field less than your best team. If you're managing or coaching a sports team, you want your best team on the floor at all times. To do so, your entire team needs to be comprised of A-Team members. (This is discussed in more detail in chapter 3.) A-Team members should be good at teamwork; they should trust other members of the team; and they should be good teachers and be willing to do whatever the job requires to achieve excellent results. A sense of humor doesn't hurt, either.

What, on the other hand, should you avoid? B-Team members, in short, are constant complainers who can't or won't do necessary tasks and who are always surprised by events. Our colleague Dr. Jay Kaplan describes them as "CAVE people—constantly against virtually everything. (Kaplan, 2009) The A-Team/B-Team analogy is another way of describing the "highmiddlelow"® or HML concept of Studer Group's evidence-based leadership approach.

This emphasis on team members is not to overlook the important role that the physical and operational environment plays in influencing ability to work in teams as well as individual team member behavior. A noisy, crowded, cluttered, and inefficient physical environment can easily reduce the average A-Team member to B-Team status. Deming's observation that 80 percent of an organization's problems are systems or process problems versus only 20 percent people problems is certainly correct. If we have B-Team processes and systems, however, the importance of A-Team behaviors from the staff increases exponentially. Both systems and people are critical to success. One insight is repeatedly confirmed in our work with hospitals and healthcare systems:

A-Team members can make up for B-Team processes and systems.

B-Team members can destroy A-Team processes and systems.

At times the challenge for administrators is knowing what came first in order to focus on fixing the most critical aspect.

Of course, life isn't easy. Are we all always A-Team members? Periodically looking in the mirror and asking yourself, *Am I an A-Team member (high performer)?* is useful. We assume you're going to say yes. Follow that up with, *Well, okay, I'm an A-Team member at the start of my day; am I an A-Team member at the end of my day? Taking it even further, Am I an A-Team member at 3 a.m.?* The answer to these questions doesn't have to always be "yes"—and likely won't be, if you're honest. But if we understand what we're trying to accomplish, we're more likely to consistently be an A-Team member.

Building Teamwork

Once you have hired the right people, how do you mold them into an effective team? Good teamwork requires the proper mix of skill sets and roles, the right capacity to match the demand, situational awareness, communication, aligned goals and incentives, and transparent metrics so that everyone on the team understands what the aims are and how the accomplishments will be measured. Optimize the mix of physicians, MLPs, RNs, and technical staff. Using the key strategies for improving flow, tailor the hours and staffing to the facility and patient flow. One lesson from TOC is that scarce resources should not be squandered; in other words, skilled practitioners should not be engaged in work that doesn't fit their critical skill sets and team roles. Clinical staff should be seen as roving intellects taking care of patients, and they should be involved in activities that add value to the system at all times.

"After-action reviews" are a concept borrowed from the military that can work for healthcare systems as well. An after-action review involves reviewing a case in a structured way. Study both successful and unsuccessful cases. The goal is to learn from the review and improve in the practices involved in the cases studied. The structure of the review involves asking:

1. What were our intended results?
2. What are the measures we use for assessing?
3. What challenges can we anticipate in similar cases in the future?
4. What have we learned?
5. What will make us successful?

Crew Resource Management

Pretend for a moment you're the pilot of an F/A 18 jet from an aircraft carrier, say the USS *George Washington*. If you've ever seen it from close range, it's a big ship. But pretend you're flying over the Pacific and you have to find something that appears (from your perspective) to be the size of a postage stamp bobbing up and down on the ocean surface in a stiff breeze. You actually have to land on that postage stamp. Now suppose you have just learned the deck crew is brand new, that crew members have gone through basic training on carrier landings but have never worked together before? Your response might well be, "I am not landing on that carrier." Landing on the bobbing carrier deck with the new crew, however, is akin to what we have often done and continue to do in our healthcare systems.

Several branches of the military have carried out research on aviation mishaps, which determined that the pilots and crews involved in the accidents were for the most part experienced fliers, not newly trained crews with little flight time. What also emerged was that common errors in the crashes were often communication problems between crew members, workload management, and task prioritization.

Responding to the lessons from these studies, the military developed a program called crew resource management training—essentially, teaching team members how to work as a team and function as a highly coordinated unit. Follow-up studies showed dramatic improvements in military aviation. Figure 2.6 shows the Navy results; the Army cut the number of deaths per year by 17 and the losses to aircraft by $30 million per year.

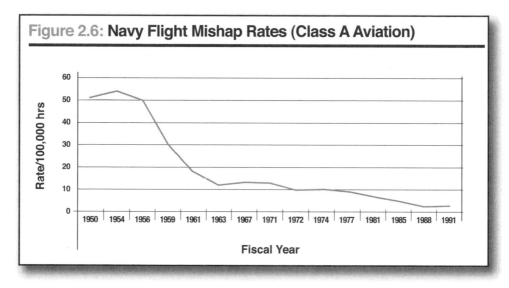

Figure 2.6: **Navy Flight Mishap Rates (Class A Aviation)**

Some professionals in healthcare realized that crew resource management (CRM) training could be applied to emergency medicine, and the MedTeams Project (as have others) has been implementing such training. The Kaiser system under the leadership of Mike Leonard has been training its OR staff in CRM, as has the OSF Staff Healthcare System, led by John Whittington. The core ideas are that teamwork skills are teachable, teamwork does not replace clinical skills, and excellent individual clinical skills do not guarantee an effective team performance in providing care. CRM training, as in the military, teaches healthcare personnel how to work effectively as teams. The training focuses on maintaining team structure and atmosphere, planning and problem solving, communication, managing workloads, and improving other team skills.

The military isn't the only place to review what a crew resource management approach can accomplish. Look at what happens in a Starbucks when a queue begins to form. The cashier concentrates on the customer at the front of the queue, but another employee goes up the line taking orders—queue management. It's also an example of situational awareness. Something else happens in Starbucks: The cashier calls back the order to the customer, following a process of call-outs and check backs. CRM training similarly involves call-outs and check backs, as well as maintaining effective flow and high-quality care through handoffs and maintaining situational awareness through cross-monitoring.

Here's an example from our experience:

Potomac Hospital implemented teamwork training and structuring, in which ED patient care modules were organized by zones and by teams. After introducing these innovations, the hospital examined how they'd worked. One of the effects was a 60 percent decrease in the time for a patient to receive a doctor's evaluation after entering the ED. Other general effects were increased patient satisfaction, workforce satisfaction, and patient safety.

Tools for Teamwork

A useful tool for thinking about teamwork is the S-BAR:

S: Situation
B: Background
A: Assessment
R: Recommendations

For effective teamwork, describe the situation, provide the background to it, assess the situation, and make recommendations for resolving it.

Changing Behavior on the Team: Change Management—Getting Things Done...

Meaningful, lasting changes in behavior come when people motivate themselves. So motivating healthcare providers to change requires convincing them of the benefits of doing so. Conveying a sense of enlightened self-interest is an effective method: *What's in it for me?* Obviously, making the hospital a better place to work because of improved patient flow and jobs within the system becoming less frustrating should be effective in showing benefits.

Getting the Physicians on Board

Chapter 6 addresses engaging physicians in flow in more detail, but here are some of the important concepts. Physicians are key people to involve in making improvements, and motivating physicians requires an understanding of two psychological "contracts," the old physician contract and the new one applicable in the kind of system you're trying to build. Both involve an implied set of "give" and "get" considerations built on three fundamental and long-standing assumptions about what being a physician brings: autonomy, protection, and entitlement. Under the old psychological contract, physicians give in these ways: They sacrifice earnings early in their career and they study hard, they see patients face to face, and they provide good care (as they define it). In return, they get reasonable compensation, a reasonable balance of work and personal life later, autonomy, job security, and deference and respect.

Persuading physicians to sign on to the new psychological contract is a leader's task in building the new system of improved patient flow. Under that new agreement, physicians give in these ways: They are patient-focused; they foster interdependence on their team and throughout the system; they delegate authority; and they are held accountable. In return, they get to be part of an organization sensitive to its market and set to compete successfully in it; they get to influence governance of that organization; they have a voice in making local decisions; and they get compensation linked to organizational success as well as individual performance. (The notion of psychological contracts and related concepts comes from the work of Edwards, Kornacki, and Silversin 2002 and Silversin and Kornacki 2000.)

WILL—IDEAS—EXECUTION

Several critical factors ensure successful execution of your goals and plans, particularly in the context of improving patient flow. We have examined a number of tools, strategies, and mental models necessary for achieving that success in this chapter. These strategies are necessary but not sufficient. Will: the sustained commitment to make a difference. Ideas: the lifeblood of our work. Execution: the ability to actually carry out our plans and to hardwire the gains. This work requires an engaged and informed leadership and a passionate and aroused healthcare team. Thomas Edison did point out that, "Discontent is the first necessity of progress." Gene Kranz, however, during the Apollo 13 mission, inspired us with, "Failure is not an option." Failure is not an option—not for our patients and not for our teammates.

CHAPTER 3

FLOW'S TEAMMATES: CUSTOMER SERVICE, PATIENT SAFETY, LEAN MANAGEMENT, SIX SIGMA, AND HIGH RELIABILITY ORGANIZATIONS

---

*"Think where man's glory most begins and ends
And say my glory was I had such friends."*

—W.B. Yeats, *"The Municipal Gallery Revisited"*

"Folks will judge you by the company you keep."

—*Grandpa Jim Mayer (and your mom & dad)*

"When we won that last-second game over Kentucky, many people said we were lucky. But I think luck favors teams who trust one another."

—*Duke Coach Mike Krzyzewski,* **Leading with the Heart**

These three quotes express similar thoughts in different metaphors. Yeats ties our glory to the friends with whom we choose to associate. Grandpa Jim's metaphor (as a marker for the advice all of our parents have given us) is not just a comment about how our reputations might be lost but also on how they can be won by those on our team. And Coach K reminds us that we are only ever as strong as the trust we have in our teammates. Great insights, all.

In the first two chapters, we have defined flow in a pragmatic fashion (what flow *is*), and defined the elements of the Flow Toolkit (*how* to achieve flow). We extend these thoughts in this chapter by delineating those aspects of current healthcare leadership we see as most likely to increase your leverage in accelerating the pace of change in attaining flow initiatives. These include customer service-patient satisfaction issues, patient safety, lean management, Six Sigma, and high reliability organizations (HROs). These are among the friends, the company we keep, and the teammates we use in service of our goal of attaining flow. Every great coach needs to know whom to "pull off the bench" when the team needs a boost, an additional way of creating excellence. No matter whom you "pull off the bench," utilize Evidence-Based Leadership[SM] (EBL) with these teammates to drive sustainability of results. Without EBL, organizations are jumping directly to aligning processes. This skips the critical components of aligning goals and then behaviors. These teammates are the "sixth man" coming off the bench to invigorate the team at the most critical of times.

In fact, the lessons of the genesis of the sixth man concept are instructive. As it turns out, the initial use of the sixth man idea came from a coach who was hired by Duke University to lead its basketball team at a time of transition for this since-storied program. The coach was hired and began the relocation process to Durham, North Carolina. As fate would have it, he never coached a single game for Duke, as health problems with his daughter precluded completing the move. The coach honorably withdrew and another was quickly found. While he missed the chance to lead what became a great program, he went on to have success in his subsequent job, leading another team. The team? The Boston Celtics. The coach? Red Auerbach, the winner of nine National Basketball Association championships, and the originator of the concept of the sixth man. The sixth man is a highly talented player perfectly capable of starting for the Celtics or for any number of other NBA teams but who instead comes off the bench to rally the team at critical moments. Red found that the sixth man is often the difference between winning and losing (Russell and Steinberg 2009).

All of the flow teammates we discuss here are very much like the sixth man—ready and available to be put to work in the right circumstances to complete the team's mission, in this case the accomplishment of our flow imperatives. We discuss each of these teammates and answer these questions with regard to their contribution to flow:

What are their fundamental precepts and principles?

How do they relate to flow and healthcare?

The role of the flow leader is to act as the coach of the team, knowing how and when to deploy these team members, when to pull these sixth men and women off the bench and into the game.

PATIENT/CUSTOMER SATISFACTION

What Is Patient Satisfaction?

Of flow's teammates, the one perhaps most closely and easily related to flow is patient satisfaction. (For reasons that will be made clearer as we progress, we use the term "patient satisfaction" to refer to "customer satisfaction" as well.) Since we have defined flow as increasing value by increasing benefits while decreasing burdens (waste), it is only logical that patient satisfaction would play a key role in flow (Jensen et al. 2007).

Our approach to patient satisfaction and customer service is perhaps nonintuitive—maybe even counterintuitive. It is based on our work with over 200 hospitals and healthcare systems and has been presented in more detail in a previous book (Mayer and Cates 2004). We begin our discussions with our team on patient satisfaction with a focus not on the "how" but the "why." The question we always lead with is:

"What's the number one reason to focus on patient satisfaction?"

When we ask it, the audience routinely gives us the same answers—it's good for the patient, good for the family, good for market share, and so on— which are all certainly excellent reasons to focus on patient satisfaction. But the number one reason to focus on customer service is: *It makes your job easier!*

In other words, if it doesn't make your job easier, it isn't really customer service. To communicate this insight to your staff, simply pose this question: *Do you offer good customer service on your unit?* Some enthusiastically say, "Yes!" while others shake their heads, "No." But in our experience the majority don't answer yes or no, but instead say, "Sometimes." Or, "It depends!" If that's the case, what does it depend upon?

Are there days you go to work and you see the people with whom you'll be working that day and say to yourself, "All right! Bring it on, because this team of people can make it happen!" Of course "it" does happen, and the question becomes, *What do you call these people?* The answer we always hear is: *The A-Team!* When you question your staff as to the attributes they consider essential to be an A-Team member, what we hear from every healthcare group to whom we speak is the list of characteristics in Figure 3-1.

Figure 3.1: A-Team Members

• Positive	• Teamwork
• Proactive	• Trust
• Confident	• Teacher
• Competent	• Does whatever it takes
• Compassionate	• Sense of humor
• Communication	• Moves the meat

A-Team members (high performers) make the hard work of healthcare easier because of their behaviors. We all want to be A-Team members and we all want to work with A-Team members. Part of this desire is because the alternative is grim: Are there days when you come to work and see the people you are working with and say to yourself, *Shoot me, shoot me, shoot me! I can't work with you—I worked with you yesterday!* That team of people is always referred to as "The B-Team." Figure 3.2 shows the attributes for B-Team members that we hear from staff across the country.

Figure 3.2: B-Team Members

- Negative
- Reactive
- Confused
- Poor communication
- Lazy
- Late

- Constant complainer
- BMW Club
- Can't do
- Always surprised
- Nurse Ratched
- Dr. Torquemada

While physicians often laugh at the insight that every unit has its Nurse Ratched, they may not realize that the nurses know that every unit has its Dr. Runfrom! (All the nurses see this doctor and run!) The B-Team is decidedly a group of people with whom we do *not* want to work, since they make the job harder, not easier. In fact, we always get precisely the same answer when we ask people the following question:

How many B-Team members does it take to destroy an entire shift?
One!

The "A-Team/B-Team" concept is fundamentally a restatement, using different terms, of the fundamental "highmiddlelow" or HML concept of Studer Group. (Studer, 2008) Regardless of whether we describe the performance gap in HML or A-Team/B-Team language, the fundamental issue is the same:

If it doesn't make your job easier, it isn't really patient satisfaction or customer service—it's something else masquerading or pretending to be patient satisfaction.

Dealing with the Performance Gap

I'm hearing leaders say that step one is to get everyone on board. I disagree. You'll never get everyone on board.

—Quint Studer, Results That Last

The experience of Studer Group with hundreds of organizations and hundreds of thousands of employees is that 34 percent of employees will consistently exceed expectations over time—these are the organization's *high performers*. The *middle performers* comprise the steady 58 percent of the organization who will develop and sustain mid to high levels of performance—their results are solid. The remaining 8 percent are the *low performers*, who refuse to budge, who can't, don't, or won't change and produce predictably disappointing results. The low performers view any leadership initiative as temporary, transitory, and, as the biblical verse says, "Even this shall pass away."

One of the most fundamental insights of Studer Group's EBL is this:

Leaders should spend 92 percent of their time on the 92 percent of high and middle performers and no more than 8 percent on the low performers.

As leaders, we have the ability to improve organizational performance through the high, middle, and low conversations. (Detailed examples of the conversations can be found at www.studergroup.com/hardwiringflow.) These conversations create a performance gap by using three skills:

1. Re-recruit high performers by letting them know how much their work is appreciated and having them mentor middle and low performers.
2. Retain and develop the specific skills of the middle performers, so they can legitimately aspire to and have a discrete path toward becoming high performers.

3. Hold low performers accountable to an "up or out!"
philosophy. It is almost always better to work short-
handed than to continue to tolerate low performers.

The outcome: Your high and middle performers will
increase their performance. The low performers will remain at the
same level. This creates a "performance gap" that is noticeable to
the entire team. When the low performers are dealt with by moving
them up or out of the organization, the entire performance curve
shifts to the right.

For more information on the performance gap and HML
conversations, go to www.studergroup.com/hardwiringflow.

As we describe in more detail in Chapter 4, many great thinkers, but
most notably Abraham Maslow, have noted that all meaningful and lasting
change is intrinsically motivated, not extrinsically motivated. Asking people
to change because "the Boss says so!" is far less likely to be successful than
tapping into intrinsic motivation by helping them understand that it makes
their job easier.

A second insight critical to understanding the relationship of flow to
patient satisfaction comes as we consider this question:

Are they patients or are they customers?

To answer this question, we use a thought exercise we call "The Patient-
CustoMeter™" (Figure 3.3).

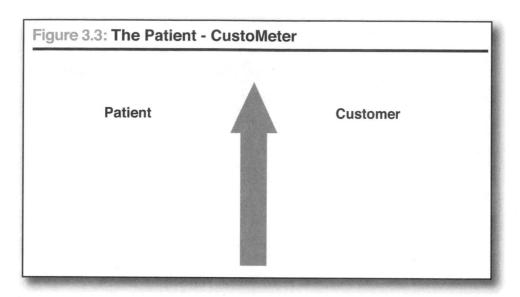

Figure 3.3: **The Patient - CustoMeter**

Patient   Customer

We simply ask the members of our team to respond to three clinical scenarios and state candidly whether they consider the examples as more like patients or customers. There are examples for each type of team to which we are presenting, but we use Emergency Department examples here.

Scenario 1. A 67-year-old woman is brought to the ED by paramedics with a chief complaint of "crushing" substernal chest pain. As soon as the paramedics arrived on the scene, the woman went into ventricular fibrillation. They gave her an immediate countershock and she returned to normal sinus rhythm, but certain segments on her EKG are extremely elevated, so she clearly has a massive anterior myocardial infarction. Is she more a patient or more a customer?

Scenario 2. A 3-year-old child is brought to the ED by the parents at 3 a.m., having been seen by the pediatrician at 3 p.m. The pediatrician diagnosed left otitis media, gave them fever-control instructions, and started the child on antibiotics. The parents nervously bring the child to the ED with a temperature of 99.2°F, saying they "can't get the fever down." (*Not that this would ever happen, of course.*) Is the child more a patient or more a customer?

Scenario 3. Scenario 3 is precisely the same as Scenario 2 with
this difference—this is *your child!*

Without exception, we are told that Scenario 1 is a patient, while Scenario 2 is a customer. (On Scenario 3, the needle wavers a bit…) Because the woman with the heart attack is so desperately in need of technical assistance and lifesaving care, members of healthcare teams say she is a patient. Because the child's illness is not life-threatening (to us—it seems as if it is to the parents), the child—and the parents—seem much more like customers. Not surprisingly, we will use more science skills with the woman and more patient satisfaction skills with the parents. But in fact, they are always both patients and customers, to varying degrees, as illustrated in Figure 3.4. As the figure shows, if someone is 80 percent patient, that person is still 20 percent customer.

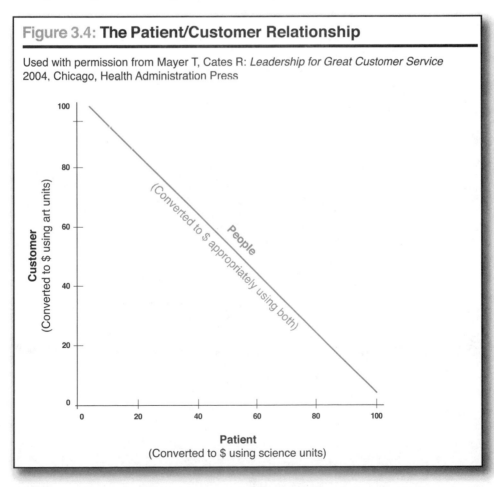

Figure 3.4: **The Patient/Customer Relationship**

Used with permission from Mayer T, Cates R: *Leadership for Great Customer Service* 2004, Chicago, Health Administration Press

Thus, in every clinical scenario, we need to make a customer service diagnosis as well as the clinical diagnosis. We do this by using a simple diagnostic rule:

The more horizontal they are, the more they are a patient.

The more vertical they are, the more they are a customer.

In fact, in the care of inpatients, we are in the business of taking patients from horizontal to vertical. We need to assess what percentage patient they are and apply science-technical skills to their illness or injury. For the percentage customer they are, we need to apply patient satisfaction-flow skills to address that part of their care.

Three key A-Team Behaviors (Table 3.1) and the elements of the A-Team Toolkit (Figure 3.5) are helpful in treating the customer service diagnosis.

Table 3.1: The Three A-Team Behaviors

Behavior	Actions and Reasons
Sit down	Patients and families will estimate you were in the room five times longer if you sit instead of stand.
Listen actively	Listen by repeating their words back to assure you have heard correctly. Ask them to repeat key information such as discharge instructions, test results, and possible diagnoses back to you to assure they understand.
Use open body language	Instead of standing across the room with arms folded across your chest (which projects a distant, closed body language), open your arms, use your hands to gesture, and touch the patient's hand or arm in an appropriate manner (which uses body language to establish contact, warmth, and concern).

Figure 3.5: The A-Team Toolkit:
Ten Highly Effective Tactics for Improving Patient
Satisfaction and Perception of Flow

---

1. Empowerment
      Point of Impact Intervention
      Service Recovery

2. Dealing with Difficult Patients
   Dealing with B-Team Members

3. Personal Patient Satisfaction Coaching

4. Rounding - Yours, Next, Sign Out

5. Key Words at Key Times

6. Hire Right - Screen for the Gene

7. Taking 4s to 5s

8. The Psychology of Waiting

9. Reward Your Champions

10. Leave a Legacy

How Do the Tools of Patient Satisfaction Improve Flow?

All the tools of patient satisfaction improve flow or the perception of flow through the system, which is why customer service and patient satisfaction skills are vital to effective flow leadership. Consider the concept of "expectation creation." Expectation creation combines several hardwiring principles, including negotiating skills, key words at key times, empowerment, and taking 4s to 5s (more later). It relies on an understanding that we intend to create an expectation, usually but not always around the axis of time, which we fully expect to be able to exceed. At Walt Disney World, the sign at a ride may read, "Wait from here is 40 minutes." Is the wait really going to be 40 minutes? As we learned when we benchmarked with Disney, in fact, 92 percent of the time the wait will actually be 32 minutes or less. But the Disney Corporation is the master of expectation creation, in that they have created an expectation (40 minutes) they fully expect to be able to exceed (Lee 2004).

How can we use this principle in healthcare? If a patient needs a chest radiograph in the ED and we expect (based on careful review of data) that the study will take 28 minutes or less, the art of expectation creation tells us that we should increase it to assure we can meet or exceed the expectation. Thus, we might say, "Your chest radiograph should take about 50 minutes to complete. I'll come back and discuss the results when it is complete." To be clear, this doesn't change the time required for the chest radiograph, but it nonetheless improves flow because it increases benefits by establishing a time frame in which the patient and family can expect the service to be provided— an example of using a key aspect of the Flow Toolkit: the psychology of waiting. All of the elements of the Flow Toolkit and the Studer approach to service, clinical, and operational outcomes improve flow by improving the patient's perception of the benefits received versus the burdens endured.

One of the most important of the Studer Group concepts is that of the acronym AIDET, which is a highly effective way of assuring there is consistently positive interaction with patients through effective language (which incorporates expectation creation in the "duration" area).

A—Acknowledge the customer by greeting them by name.
- Make eye contact.
- Sit down (our research shows the patient and family will estimate you were in the room five times longer if you sit down versus standing up).
- Make the patient and family feel you expected them. In the ED, we often say, "We knew you were coming; we just didn't know your name."

I—Introduce yourself, what you do, and how you are there to help them.
- Let them know your skill set, training, experience, and even certification.
- Manage up the skills of your team members.
- Manage up other departments and service transitions.
- Physicians should take particular care to manage service transitions and manage up their fellow physicians, particularly consultants or partners who will cover the service in your absence.

D—Duration of what you will be doing for them or how long you expect the service to take.

- Disney is the master of "expectation creation." (Remember the sign that reads, "Wait from here is 20 minutes"?) Use this concept by creating an expectation you expect to exceed; for example, if you think the wait will be 10 minutes, tell the patient 20, building in the possibility of unexpected delays.
- Break the service into discrete intervals and inform the patient of the time expectations for each interval.
- Let them know where they are in their healthcare journey and what to expect.

E—Explain in as much detail as necessary the important aspects of what you will be doing.

- Why are we doing this?
- What will happen next?
- What questions do you have?

T—Thank them for choosing your hospital or healthcare system.

- Be explicit in your praise.
- "I'm sorry you are ill, but I appreciate you choosing us for your care."
- No matter how profusely and how often you think you are thanking them, it is not enough—it is almost impossible to overdo it.

Applying AIDET has the advantage of both decreasing anxiety and increasing compliance, which work synergistically to improve clinical outcomes and patient satisfaction. Nationally recognized emergency physician and Studer Group coach Dr. Jay Kaplan says that AIDET is like baseball—just make sure you touch all the bases and you will hit a home run!

 A Word About Other Customer Service Skills:

Because patient satisfaction is so critical to the perception of effective and efficient flow, we have listed more depth on all of these tools at www.studergroup.com/hardwiringflow in a downloadable pdf titled "The A-Team Toolkit." There is also a separate pdf titled "Dealing with the Performance Gap."

LEAN MANAGEMENT

What Is Lean Management?

The terms *lean, lean management,* and *lean production* are virtually synonymous and refer to variations of the Toyota Production System (TPS), championed in Japan by Taiichi Ohno, former chief processing engineer of Toyota Motor Corporation (TMC), and Kiichiro Toyoda, the son of TMC founder Sakichi Toyoda. John Krafcik first coined the term *lean* at MIT's International Motor Vehicle Program and first described it in *The Machine That Changed the World: The Story of Lean Production* (Womack, Jones, and Roos 1990).

The TPS focuses all parts of the production system on eliminating waste in order to increase value, with value being determined from the customers' perspective (Spear 2009). (TPS, however, included no apparent road map for a detailed pathway by which to determine value, which we have tried to rectify with the burden-to-benefit ratio in our definition of flow.) Lean management is built on two main pillars:

---

1. Just in Time (JIT) Production: operating with the minimum resources needed to consistently deliver
   just what's needed in;
   just the right amount;
   just where it is needed; and
   just when it is necessary.

2. Jidoka: the intelligent use of people and technology wherein anyone involved in the production or delivery of the product or service can stop the system immediately upon any signs that a defect is present (Chalice 2007).

Typical programs that implement lean management also rely on two other tools:

1. Value-stream mapping: Examining and displaying in graphic fashion (using symbols) every system and its processes to identify those inflection points at which value is either added or waste occurs (Graban 2008).

2. The 5 "S" Approach to Waste: Five Japanese words that describe
    the elimination of non-value added processes (Black and Miller
    2008):
    1. seiri: sorting;
    2. seiton: simplifying access, or neatness;
    3. seiso: sweeping or cleaning;
    4. seiketsu: standardization; and
    5. shitsuke: self-discipline.

More recently, a white paper from the Institute of Healthcare
Improvement (IHI) noted (Institute for Healthcare Improvement
2005):

Simply put, lean means using less to do more.

These definitions help convey the concept of lean management, but in
our experience, asking bedside clinicians to make do with less while doing
more is, to state it mildly, a very tough proposition to sell. Because we think
that value must ultimately be delivered at the bedside in healthcare, we have
focused attention on the degree to which we are able to increase value by
increasing benefits and decreasing burdens.

How Does Lean Management Apply to Flow and Healthcare?

We clearly see the utility and importance of the fundamental concepts of
lean management and have built the elements of adding value and eliminating
waste into our definition of flow. This approach closely relates lean
management and flow in practical ways. In any given system or process, the
caregiver is able to assess value or waste through this ratio. Leaders are able to
use the Flow Toolkit to help guide the revision or design of processes with this
gold standard in mind.

Partially because its implementation requires less rigorous training and
infrastructure, lean management has been more widely adopted in healthcare
than programs such as Six Sigma (see below). Nonetheless, most authorities
caution that introducing lean thinking in an organization "is not for the faint
of heart. It cannot be done piecemeal, but must be a whole system strategy....
Those at the very top of the organization must lead it" (Institute for
Healthcare Improvement 2005). The lean system has been used in numerous

settings within healthcare, including Emergency Departments, Intensive Care Units, materials management, outpatient clinics, and logistics design, generally with good results (Dickson et al. 2008; Gelrud et al. 2008; Spear 2004).

A fully adopted lean system, however, includes several potential limitations. First, while the training and infrastructure requirements are not as time and capital intensive as programs like Six Sigma, they are nonetheless substantial. Second, we have noted that the heavy reliance on multiple words and symbols from another language are not always easily adopted, although the concepts themselves have substantial merit, in our view. Finally, value-stream mapping as a tool was designed for use in production systems. Healthcare involves critical aspects of production, but it is fundamentally not only a service industry but a service industry in which it is largely personal service that is being delivered through physicians, nurses, and other members of the healthcare team on a one-to-one basis. Value-stream mapping as a tool must be adapted to recognize, track, and allow improvements in value and elimination of waste at this key interface.

SIX SIGMA

What Is Six Sigma?

Six Sigma is a business management strategy targeted at identifying and aggressively removing errors and defects from systems and processes. Bill Smith originally developed it at Motorola, and it was quickly deployed at Honeywell and General Electric, the latter under Jack Welch's leadership (Smith 2003; Mayer and Jensen 2008). Technically Six Sigma is a registered trademark of Motorola, but the term's usage and the principles of Six Sigma have become widespread. In recent years, Six Sigma has been combined with lean manufacturing, resulting in the term *Lean Six Sigma*. While the principles share some similarity, it is certainly possible to adopt the principles of lean management discussed in the previous section without the structure of Six Sigma.

Six Sigma targets anything that can cause customer dissatisfaction as a defect through a defined series of steps using an infrastructure of trained experts within the organization. These experts are commonly referred to as

"Black Belts" (although some organizations have created additional hierarchy in the form of terms such as "Master Black Belts," "Champions," "Green Belts," "Gold Belts," etc.). Regardless of the terms used, the presence of a training program and a hierarchical infrastructure of quality is a common theme in Six Sigma programs.

In statistics, sigma (σ) represents the standard deviation of a statistical population; "Six Sigma process" represents the concept that six standard deviations from the mean of a process to the specification limit result in a massive reduction in defects. The widely accepted definition of a Six Sigma process is one that produces 3.4 defects per million. (Because of the recognized decline in performance of systems and processes in the long term versus the short term, the 3.4 defects per million actually corresponds to 4.5 sigmas, since this correlates to 6 sigmas minus the 1.5 standard deviations, which are a part of the system to account for the phenomenon of the inescapable long-term variation [Wears].)

Six Sigma generally utilizes two pathways toward improvement, one designed to correct existing but dysfunctional processes (described by the acronym DMAIC) and the other to help create a new process to achieve Six Sigma results (DMADV). Table 3.2 lists the components of these acronyms (Welch 2009).

Table 3.2: The Two Pathways of Six Sigma

Existing Process	New Process
DMAIC	DMADV
D-Define	D-Define
M-Measure	M-Measure
A-Analyze	A-Analyze
I-Improve	D-Design
C-Control	V-Verify

In order to give some perspective, let us look at the commonly used metric of patients with community-acquired pneumonia (CAP) receiving antibiotics within four hours of arrival. If 68 percent of patients with CAP receive their antibiotic within four hours, that is a two-sigma level of performance, whereas three- and four-sigma levels are, respectively, 93 percent and 99.4 percent performance. Six sigma would mean that only three to four patients per million patients with CAP would be treated outside the four-hour window.

How Does Six Sigma Relate to Flow and Healthcare?

The primary utility of Six Sigma in improving value is as a means of reducing waste, particularly through a very detailed approach to dealing with either existing or new processes through the DMAIC or DMADV constructs listed above. A number of healthcare institutions have used Six Sigma, with generally good results. Almost without exception, these successes have occurred in systems where Six Sigma has been adopted as an institution-wide program, with detailed training programs. These same organizations have created an aligned goal system, objective accountability system and offer specific leader training (EBL model).

The criticisms of Six Sigma focus on the need for a defined quality infrastructure, the large investment of time required, the difficulty in applying the 3.4 defects per million concept in healthcare, and the view that it is simply an extension of fundamental quality improvement and change management principles "dressed up in new clothes." Regarding the latter, Joseph Juran described Six Sigma as "a basic version of quality improvement" using "more flamboyant terms, like belts with different colors" (De Feo, Barnard, and Juran 2003). The proponents of Six Sigma acknowledge its roots in the work of many quality improvement scions, but stress the systematic and more advanced nature of the program. The requirement for a defined quality infrastructure has been criticized as having created a cottage industry of training, certification, and consultants. To be sure, a commitment to extensive training has been a necessity in Six Sigma, and there appear to be few shortcuts in this process. For most hospitals and healthcare systems, there has been a move away from "quality departments" toward training and development of all leaders and establishing accountability at all levels—among the most fundamental concepts of hardwiring. As others have noted, "The era when quality aims could be delegated to 'quality staff,' while the executive team works on finances, facility plans, and growth is over" (Reinertsen, Pugh, and Bisognano 2008). Based on these ideas, our view is that hospitals with existing Six Sigma programs may continue to use this methodology to accelerate the pace of change in eliminating waste and accentuating value. But the economic climate alone makes it less likely that the level of training required for full implementation of new Six Sigma programs will see widespread use, despite the potential attractiveness of its results.

HIGH RELIABILITY ORGANIZATIONS (HROs)

What Are High Reliability Organizations?

Karl Weick and Kathleen Sutcliffe, in their excellent work *Managing the Unexpected: Assuring High Performance in an Age of Complexity,* used the term *high reliability organizations* to describe those organizations that typically operate under stressful and trying conditions and yet have a very low rate of accidents, misadventures, or defective processes. Their examples included power grid dispatching centers, air-traffic control systems, nuclear power plants, aircraft carriers, hostage negotiating teams, and Emergency Departments, all of which face an excess of "unexpected events" in a way they described as "mindful," meaning those within the system were able to better notice the unexpected and halt its development. They found that "respectful interacting" and "heedful interrelating" are necessary antecedents to the mindfulness typifying HROs:

Respectful interacting is a social process through which one individual's interpretation is communicated to another individual, and, through this communication, a shared interpretation is generated. Respectful interacting requires the presence of trust, honesty, and self-respect.

While this description applies to all HROs, it fundamentally captures the sense of shared understanding so typical of excellence in all patient care activities. Indeed, without this shared mental model of the patient, success cannot occur and adverse events are extremely likely. "Trust, honesty, and self-respect" are also critical for and highly typical of A-Team members (high performers).

In addition to describing respectful interacting, Weick and Sutcliffe also noted that heedful interrelating is an essential part of HROs.

Heedful interrelating is a social process through which individual action contributes to a larger pattern of shared action and in which *individuals understand how their actions fit into the larger action.*

This ability to see how each member of the healthcare team's work contributes to the overall care of the patient is essential to improving flow. It is illustrated in an old tale:

In medieval times, a knight rode into the outskirts of a town and found three masons hard at work. To each, he asked the same question: "What are you doing?"

The first mason said, "I am putting a brick upon a brick."

The second mason said, "I am building a strong wall."

The third mason paused, looked directly at the knight, and said, "I am building a beautiful cathedral, which will inspire people for centuries!"

The point is clear—all three masons did the same work, but they viewed it in completely different ways. Only the third mason could see how his work fit into the broader endeavor. Once respectful interactions (creating a shared understanding) and heedful interrelatedness (with an understanding of how all interactions fit into the larger system.) are present, Weick and Sutcliffe found there were five characteristics of HROs:

1. Preoccupation with failure: Any lapse, large or small, is treated as a possible symptom of something wrong with the system that could lead to disastrous consequences.

2. Reluctance to simplify: Because their world is "complex, unstable, unknowable, and unpredictable," those in HROs put themselves and their entire team in a position to "see the whole

playing field." They encourage diversity of opinion and skepticism in service of the broadest possible view.

3. Sensitivity to operations: HROs are highly attentive to the front line and their view is far less strategic and more tactical, more drilled down to the operational level. Data are transparent on a real-time basis.

4. Commitment to resilience: They not only tolerate but respect the ability to acknowledge error and the ability to bounce back from worst-case situations and scenarios.

5. Deference to expertise: Dealing with the complexities that HROs routinely face requires recognizing expertise at various levels of the organization, which by nature is diverse and sometimes disparate. Experience may lead to expertise but is not necessarily a predictor thereof.

How Do HROs Relate to Flow and Healthcare?

As we noted above, the concepts of respectful interactions (creating a shared understanding) and heedful interrelatedness (understanding how all interactions fit into the larger system.) are highly accurate descriptions of the effective and efficient delivery of healthcare in an environment that improves flow by increasing value and eliminating waste. To extend an analogy we used in the previous chapter, in many respects, the description of operations on an aircraft carrier applies to what we see daily in our Emergency Departments:

Imagine that it's a busy day and you shrink San Francisco airport to only one short runway and one ramp and one gate. Make planes take off and land at the same time, at half the present time interval, rock the runway from side to side, and require that everyone who leaves in the morning returns the same day. Make sure the equipment is so close to the envelope that it's fragile. Then turn off the radar to avoid detection, impose strict controls on the radios, fuel the aircraft in place with their engines running, put an enemy in the air, and scatter live bombs and rockets around. Now wet the whole thing down with sea water and oil, and man it with twenty-year-olds, half of whom have never seen an aircraft close-up. Oh, and by the way, try not to kill anyone. (Weick and Roberts 1993)

Having had the rare privilege of spending 48 hours on the nuclear aircraft carrier USS *George Washington*, we can attest that this is an understated assessment of daily aircraft operations—and that the similarities to Emergency Department operations were readily apparent. In both settings, the organizational environment is constantly changing, there is a high level of interactive complexity, and there is a high interdependence of the multiple stakeholders involved in completing each task comprising the overall operation successfully. Other applications of the HRO concept are:

1. Preoccupation with failure: In healthcare, particularly in Critical Care and Emergency Departments, we constantly have to assume the worst and constantly assess, "How can we do this better? What have we missed?" When near-misses occur, we treat it as a near-disaster, not as a part of daily life.

2. Reluctance to simplify: Physicians at all levels rely on the input from nurses and other members of the team, since they spend so much more time with the patient. We spend a significant part of our delivery of patient care in issues like boundary management and stakeholder analysis. As Einstein said: "Simplify, simplify— but not too much!"

3. Sensitivity to operations: In healthcare, the front line is the key line and all else is in service of the front line. Knowledge is power and operational knowledge is the most important power. Data must be transparent at the bedside or lives can be endangered.

4. Cultivation of resilience: Very few cultures have as a part of their fabric the deep commitment to continually reassessing how we bounce back from failure or near misses. We have all been trained in a culture of morbidity and mortality conferences, case reviews, quality improvement, peer reviews, and continuing education examining how we can improve our care. We have also added after-action reviews (AARs) (*A Leader's Guide* 1993) and a high focus on risk prevention as a part of our culture of patient safety.

5. Deference to expertise: Medicine is imbued with a deep and abiding culture of seeking consultations in deference to expertise in any given area. The treating physician then synthesizes consulted opinions and arrives at a treatment plan integrating these various levels of expertise. Similarly, physicians seek the

knowledge and expertise of the nurses and other members of the healthcare team. For example, following a hip replacement, orthopedic surgeons routinely seek feedback from the physical therapist treating the patient, since he or she has a deeper level of information regarding the patient's progress, range of motion, and return of function.

It is apparent that the concept of HROs has many similarities to healthcare and we believe that this is a rich area for further study and development of strategies to improve our leadership in flow.

PATIENT SAFETY

What Is Patient Safety?

While the focus on patient safety is sometimes attributed to the justifiably influential 1999 report (Kohn, Corrigan, and Donaldson 1999) from the Institute of Medicine *To Err Is Human: Building a Safer Health System*, in fact the history of medicine is replete with efforts to keep our patients safe, dating at least to Hippocrates' dictum "Primum non nocere" (First, do no harm). Over the intervening centuries, physicians and nurses have had the desire and passion to do the right things—and only the right things—for their patients. But it has been only fairly recently that some of the more promising tools for assuring safety have been developed and made readily available to clinicians.

The origins of quality improvement and patient safety are distinctly different. The former arose in large part from the application of industrial methods to healthcare and include many of the flow teammates discussed here, including the teachings of Juran and W. Edwards Deming and programs such as lean management and Six Sigma. The critical thinking driving patient safety largely arose from the study of high-risk industries such as nuclear power plants, nuclear submarine and aircraft carrier operations, and chemical industries. Concepts such as HROs and the study of the psychology of error have given important insights to how we can most safely care for our patients (Weick and Sutcliffe 2001; Weick and Roberts 1993; Wears and Vincent 2009).

Despite the appropriately high level of focus on patient safety, it is a subject that resists simple definitions and solutions (Leape and Berwick 2005). As Wears and his colleagues have noted (Wears and Vincent 2009):

Patient safety is not easily defined; it represents an amalgam of ideas, or ideals, about optimizing care and avoiding harm. However, the path to safety is neither clear nor easy.

What is clear is that a massive amount of time, energy, and effort will continue to be expended in this effort and that the success of these endeavors will be judged almost exclusively by their ability to demonstrate successful implementation in the face of declining hospital operating margins. As the great psychologist Ernst Mach noted, "Knowledge and error flow from the same mental source; only success can tell one from the other" (Mach 1898). Rather than discuss the multitude of excellent patient safety efforts in detail, we list several of the most widely recognized and utilized concepts in Figure 3.6. These and undoubtedly many other efforts will continue to be trialed to discover which of the many efforts will provide the success to which Mach refers.

Figure 3.6: Representative Patient-Safety Programs

1. Evidence-based practice guidelines

2. Crew resource management (Wears 2004)

3. After-action reviews and failure-mode analysis
     (*A Leader's Guide* 1993)

4. Call-backs and call downs

5. SBAR: Situation, Background, Assessment,
     Recommendation (Weick and Sutcliffe 2007)

6. Information-transfer simplification—elimination
     of all but essential abbreviations, standardization
     of documentation, scribes, EMRs, and so on

7. Never events (Studer Group) (Never Events)

8. Inova Healthcare System Red Rules
     (Inova Fairfax Hospital)

9. A focused culture of safety

How Does Patient Safety Influence Flow?

Patient safety represents a paradox for several reasons. First, until very recently one of the fundamental tenets of medical education has been the assumption of trained perfectibility. In other words, all the years of training have been with the goal of training doctors to "get it right." A doctor who makes mistakes has been presumed to be "a bad doctor" at worst and at best, one in need of additional or remedial training. Rather than viewing mistakes as a chance for learning or for improving the system, they have, to a large degree, been stigmatized. But this educational approach dramatically fails to recognize that there simply is no doctor who can practice error-free medicine. As one of the first researchers to champion a fresh approach to patient safety noted (Leape and Berwick 2005):

Systems that rely on error-free performance are doomed to fail.
—Lucian Leape, MD

Healthcare is inherently a complex system and errors are therefore to be expected until we continually refine and reform the system. A major part of that is recognizing the sources of error and adopting a more enlightened and helpful approach to educating physicians and nurses in a culture of safety instead of a culture of blame. This is a key idea as we look at the link of safety and flow.

To be sure, many of the central tenets of patient safety may be viewed as taking more time, more effort, and more steps to accomplish. Handwashing to prevent the spread of MRSA and other pathogens, checking and double-checking armbands to assure we have the correct patient, marking surgical patients to assure correct-site surgery—all of these steps and more make our patients safer. But if they are not adopted in the context of flow, they not only slow the process down, but make it seem that flow is reduced from the patient's perspective. However, if these and other patient-safety initiatives are put in place with the appropriate focus on flow, they can actually improve the patient's perception of both flow and safety. For example, scripts or Key Words at Key Times can be highly effective in enacting safety strategies:

Mrs. Chen, let me double-check your armband to make sure we
have the right chart with the right information.

Mr. Ross, I'd like to examine you now, but let me thoroughly wash
my hands first and use this disinfectant for your protection.

Mr. Rodriguez, since we're going to be doing arthroscopy on your
knee, I am going to mark it with this black marker, so that everyone
on the team knows which side we will be looking at.

––––––––––––––––––––

If patients do not have these steps explained to them, they may appear as extra or even unnecessary steps, as opposed to a welcome part of the system designed to assure their safety. In this sense, patient safety may initially appear to be at odds with flow, since it may involve the extra time to get it right the first time—every time. But our experience is that, regardless of the framework used for patient safety, the adoption of the new culture of safety must be accompanied by a commitment to using the Flow Toolkit and the principles of hardwiring to assure that flow and safety are complementary teammates—and not competitive programs.

SUMMARY

Flow has many teammates, including patient satisfaction, lean management, Six Sigma, high reliability organization principles, and patient safety. All are part of the DNA of healthcare and no one program can ever be implemented without concerns for the other, including flow. As the "coach" of the healthcare team, the leader must learn which of these teammates to use, at what time, and how they interrelate to benefit the patient in the best possible way.

CHAPTER 4

LEADING FOR FLOW

"All happy families are alike; each unhappy family is unhappy in its own way."

—*Leo Tolstoy,* **Anna Karenina**

Tolstoy opened his legendary work with this insight and it is an appropriate one for a chapter on leadership for flow. There are certain highly consistent pathways in which we have observed leaders delivering on the promise of flow, while there are many, many ways in which flow fails. In this chapter, we will share with you the best ways in which flow can be successfully, consistently, and persistently delivered. We will also touch upon some of the many ways in which the capacity to deliver flow can fail.

LEADERSHIP: IT'S AS EASY AS 1, 2, 3...

Most of us recall hearing our parents, teachers, or coaches tell us, when referring to some talent or skill they wanted to impart, "C'mon! It's as easy as 1, 2, 3." The same is true of leadership. But the question is "*What* is 1, 2, 3?" If Tolstoy's view is correct, there should be a "1, 2, 3." Here are our thoughts on what they are. Getting your team to adopt the difficult changes necessary to enact successful flow strategies requires leadership skills, particularly because it requires change across the system, not just within a unit or smaller team. Three skills are essential.

Leadership Skill 1: What Is the "One Myth" for This Person?

The great Irish poet William Butler Yeats, in one of his most penetrating yet least quoted insights, offered this wisdom (1997):

There is some One Myth for each man, which if we but knew it
would tell us all that he thought and all that he did.

Yeats understood that each of us has some way of viewing ourselves that guides our fundamental approach to all that we do, most often in ways that we have never fully articulated or understood. In our experience, this way of viewing yourself comes to the fore in the most trying and stressful times, which is precisely what happens to the leader in the midst of a flow initiative. It doesn't take psychoanalysis to determine what the One Myth is, but it does take thoughtful reflection on what you have observed from a person or a group of people with regard to your perception of their One Myth.

By way of example, critical care nurses who work in the Emergency Department or the ICU typically view themselves as highly skilled nurses who have sought out the sickest of the sick patients and who love to save lives. Medical-Surgical nurses also value their roles as healers, but have chosen to care for patients who predominantly are not in life- or limb-threatening danger. Both are healers by nature and choosing, but they have chosen to work in areas of healthcare that fit their view of themselves. They have assessed their deep joy-deep need ratio and chosen their jobs accordingly.

The same is true of physicians. Trauma surgeons, emergency physicians, cardiologists, and intensivists have a fundamentally different myth for themselves than do pediatricians, internists, and family practitioners. The first group is often described as "adrenaline junkies," who delight in caring for the sickest of the ill and injured patients, while the second group have a more prolonged and patient view of their role in healing. Pediatricians enjoy taking care of patients with juvenile diabetes, managing their chronic needs deftly and skillfully, with an understanding that doing so helps limit the ravages of the disease over a long period of time. Emergency physicians and pediatric intensivists revel in the care of patients with diabetic ketoacidosis and the effective resuscitation of patients who present *in extremis*. (To be clear, the latter doctors don't want the patients to be in DKA—but they do want to be the one on duty if a patient with DKA presents.) In dealing with a flow initiative, which group do you think would more likely take the more patient, long-term view of progress toward flow?

Administrators and other healthcare leaders have their own One Myth. Some are highly data- and metrics-driven, while others effectively utilize and understand data but are more drawn to the effect on the patient's perception of the service, not the data themselves. If you can discern this through your observations of those with whom you work, you will have a very powerful tool at your disposal in leading flow. Note that the different people or groups of people aren't right or wrong, and the vast majority are guided by sound fundamental values. But they interpret the world and their role in it through the lens of their One Myth.

How can you discover the One Myth? Interestingly, Yeats doesn't say! But our experience is that a careful observer of human interaction who has the courage to ask can nearly always get a pretty accurate sense of the One Myth through those interactions with people over time. These are some of the questions that can help the discovery process.

What excites you most about this flow change we are considering?

What concerns you most?

To you, what would success look like as we pursue this initiative?

What role would you like to play as we move forward?

Paying close attention to the words, facial expressions, and body language will give you very important clues as to the One Myth. The most straightforward diagnostic tool is to simply ask them, "What excites you most about this job; what 'floats your boat'; what gets you up excited in the morning and what keeps you up concerned at night?" The answers to these questions go a long way to helping you understand those with whom you work and how they are likely to approach their role in leading flow. Finally, in the long view, people's One Myth may change over time. Be alert to this point and pay particular attention if you hear things that surprise you. When that occurs, either your "diagnosis" of their One Myth has been at least partially inaccurate, or they are changing their views based on the experiences they have had.

So the first leadership skill is asking, "What is the One Myth for this person and how will it affect the flow initiative we are proposing?"

Leadership Skill 2: What Is Their Intrinsic Motivation?

The great psychologist Abraham Maslow had many deep insights that are invaluable to understanding human nature and how those insights can be applied to leading people. While he is best known for his description of the hierarchy of needs, another of his pieces of wisdom is less known, yet deeply powerful (1999):

All meaningful and lasting change is intrinsically motivated.

Maslow and others have made the distinction between intrinsic and extrinsic motivation. Extrinsic motivation is forced upon us from others, usually those in positions of authority. The most common and classic example is when the Boss says, "Do it because I said so!" There are many variations to this theme, including these:

It's my way or the highway!

Get with the program.

You don't need to understand it—just do it!

For those who have children, here's an example of the futility of extrinsic motivation that's close to home. How's it going with the kids when you say, "Because I'm the mom, that's why!" Not too well, huh? It seems like it *ought* to work, but it never has and it never will....

What does occur with some regularity with extrinsically driven change is that there is temporary—and grudging—compliance for a brief period, followed by a decline in results. Intrinsically motivated change shifts the performance curve dramatically to the left, with faster and better results than the natural diffusion of ideas through the culture. The fastest way to get results (albeit temporary results) is through forcing extrinsic change, but those results erode after plateauing. This is a trap that ensnares many leaders, who are drawn to the lure of "the quick fix," instead of leading for the long haul. Figures 4.1 and 4.2 illustrate the dynamics of this process.

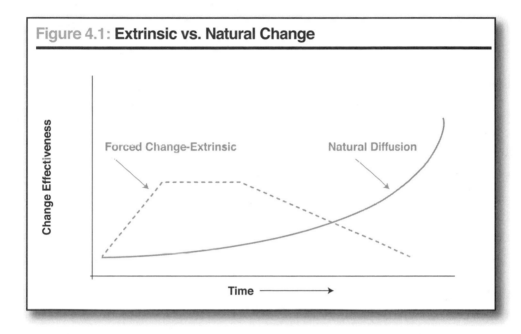

Figure 4.1: Extrinsic vs. Natural Change

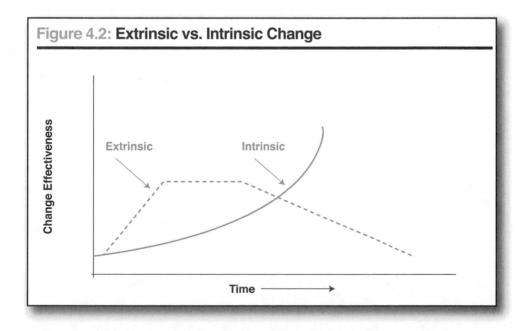

Figure 4.2: Extrinsic vs. Intrinsic Change

While some leadership lore advocates the effectiveness of extrinsic motivation, Maslow found that for change to be truly lasting and deeply meaningful, it must be fueled by intrinsic motivation, a self-driven epiphany that it is better to change than not to change. Without this aspect of a deeply felt desire to move from where we are to where we want to be, many change initiatives are doomed to either outright failure or only temporary success.

The most common intrinsic motivation in healthcare is the fundamental desire to help people, to discover worthwhile work in caring for others. But it is in the nuances of delivering that motivation that great leadership lays. Driving down to the details is critical in such circumstances. A great healthcare leader and close friend is Dr. James Adams, Chair of the Department of Emergency Medicine at Northwestern University Medical Center in Chicago. He tells the story of a flow initiative wherein patients who presented to the triage area with chest pain at times when there were no ED beds in the back had an electrocardiogram done at the triage area by the ED technician, who then was required to take it to an emergency physician. The emergency physician could then interpret it and determine whether the patient could wait or if she needed to be brought back immediately. It was referred to as the "cruise missile EKG program," since the intent was to get the EKG back and interpreted as rapidly as possible. As you might imagine, it wasn't always easy to get a busy emergency doctor to take a look at the EKG. The program was working, but not spectacularly, until one day when a tech took an EKG to an ER doc, who took one look at it and told the ED tech, "You just saved this guy's life!" (Adams personal communication). By tapping into the intrinsic motivation of the staff, the physician forever changed the lore surrounding the cruise missile EKG program. Now all the ED techs understood that they could play a role in the highest of human motivations—to save a life.

The second leadership skill is thus asking about your staff, "What is their intrinsic motivation?" and then putting it to work.

Leadership Skill 3: What Is in Their Self-Interest?

One of the most powerful tools to prepare leaders is a deep and abiding interest in history and biography. Studying the lives of great women and men and understanding the challenges they faced and the ways they dealt with those challenges will prepare you to face the difficulties inherent in leading flow. As President Harry S. Truman said, "The only new thing in the world is the history you don't know." One of the most interesting lives to study to glean leadership lessons is that of Winston Churchill. While Churchill is rightly honored for his almost unbelievable skill in leading Great Britain against Nazi Germany, he was equally challenged in many ways by his dealings with another foe, which later became an ally—and then a foe again—Russia. In one of his most cited quotes, Churchill said (1939):

Russia is a riddle wrapped in a myth inside an enigma.

Based on that quote, what are we to deduce regarding Churchill's view of the predictability of Russia? Most would say that Churchill was saying that we can't reliably predict what Russia would do. But that is not the full quote of what Sir Winston actually said. Here is the more accurate version:

I cannot predict to you what Russia will do. Russia is a riddle wrapped in a myth inside an enigma. But perhaps there is a key. *That key is Russian national interest* [emphasis added].

Taken in full context, now what is Churchill saying about predicting Russia's actions? He is saying that Russia's actions are in fact highly predictable, provided we can discern what is in her self-interest.

The same is true in our leadership skills. We must become highly skilled at reading the self-interest of the people and the groups with whom we work in our daily efforts. The more we know about their self-interest, the more closely we can predict their behavior.

Here's a simple example. A common problem in patient flow is boarding patients in the Emergency Department while they await assignment to beds upstairs. A careful study of the processes involved in discharging patients so that beds can be freed up for waiting ED patients shows some interesting facts. First, a rate-limiting step is the physician's order to discharge the patient. But does the internist or hospitalist have any self-interest in doing so in a timely fashion? (As we've noted before, most of us don't need a hospitalist; we need a "dischargist"!) Flow initiatives that recognize the importance of self-interest have created pay-for-performance programs for hospitalists, rewarding them for earlier discharges or faster "bed turns." These programs help align the strategic incentives and self-interests of the hospital and the hospitalists. It is also in the interests of the patient, who is able to get home earlier in the day. Once the patient is discharged, who informs housekeeping that the bed needs to be cleaned? Who informs the bed board once the bed has been cleaned and is "back in service"? In many systems it is the nurse on the unit who does so. Does the nurse have any self-interest in getting the bed filled with another patient as quickly as possible? Isn't that just "more work"? Some forward-thinking hospitals are beginning to create systems that measure the time from patient discharged to bed back in service and then reward those teams that achieve high-level metrics.

None of this means that the physicians and nurses are anything less than honest and well-meaning professionals, dedicated to the care of their patients. But it does mean that the system has been designed so that it is not in their self-interest to get the patients discharged and the bed filled as fast as possible. These sorts of insights are critical to understanding how people are likely to react in the midst of flow initiatives that change their daily work processes, particularly if their views and self-interests are not considered as a fundamental part of leading flow.

So the third flow-leadership skill is considering, "What is in this person or group's self-interest?" and finding ways to take advantage of that self-interest.

Mastering these three leadership skills is essential to effective flow leadership.

LEADERSHIP VERSUS MANAGEMENT

An additional key insight is that leadership and management, while closely related, are not the same. Equally important, the challenges we face in successfully improving flow require both sets of skills, as some of those challenges are primarily leadership-based, while others require management techniques. The great leadership scholar Warren Bennis recognized this when he said (2009), "Managers do things right. Leaders do the right thing." Stephen Covey made the same point in a different way when he noted (1992):

Managers do a great job of assuring that the team is making great progress at cutting their way through the jungle. Leaders climb a tree, survey the landscape and say, "Wrong jungle!"

Covey's point is that there is no sense doing well that which we should not be doing at all! Both recognize that leadership and management challenges—and the skills required to successfully address them—are simply different. Harvard professor John Kotter has written extensively on this issue, and we turn to his work to help further delineate the issue. Here is his succinct statement of the differences (1999):

Leadership is the development of vision and strategies, the alignment of relevant people behind those strategies, and the empowerment of individuals to make a vision happen, despite obstacles. This is in contrast to management, which involves keeping the current system operating through planning, budgeting, organizing, staffing, controlling and problem-solving.

In different terms, management deals with *what is*—the cold, hard realities of making budgets, hitting targeted metrics, dealing with the vagaries of teams, and making course corrections. Leadership deals with *what our future will be*—the place to which we aspire to be over time. In some respects, it is the difference between *focus* on the issues in front of us versus the *vision* of what lies in a future the leader must help make real. Let's be clear—put in these terms, most members of the team hear this distinction and say to themselves, "I'd much prefer to be a leader than a manager! Making budgets and hitting targeted metrics is for someone else!" The fact is, healthcare organizations require both leadership and management skills to succeed. One without the other is a recipe for either a poorly run ship or one without a rudder. What is important is to recognize which of the challenges we are facing require leadership skills and which require management skills—and use the right skills in the right mix to create the conditions for success.

If managers do things right and leaders do the right thing,
in healthcare we have to do both well.

—Thom Mayer, MD

Healthcare teams are fundamentally "flat" enough that we cannot afford a management team and a separate leadership team—our teams have to be trained for both. (To be sure, the CEO of the hospital or healthcare system is charged to a substantial degree with leadership as opposed to management challenges. But the path to the CEO's office is full of both leadership and management challenges, as we learned from our colleague Reuven Pasternak, MD, the CEO of Inova Fairfax Hospital. In addition, one critical role of the CEO is mentoring both the leaders and managers of the team, so an articulate understanding of both is necessary.) Figure 4.3 shows some of these differences between leadership and management.

Figure 4.3: Differences between the skills of leadership and management

Leadership	Management
• Envisioning	• Planning
• Strategies	• Budgeting
• Alignment	• Organizing
• Empowerment	• Staffing
• Direction Setting	• Controlling
• Execution	• Problem-Solving

Kotter examines the leadership-management dichotomy further:

> Leadership works through people and culture. It's soft and hot. Management works through hierarchy and systems. It's harder and cooler. *The fundamental purpose of management is to keep the current system functioning. The fundamental purpose of leadership is to produce change, especially non-incremental change* [emphasis added].

Thus, there is a basic dichotomy between keeping things stable in management versus actively seeking change in leadership. Chris Argyris (1993) noted this in slightly different terms in his discussion of first-order change (changes *within* a system) versus second-order change (changes *of* a system). The sociologist Kurt Lewin, among his many penetrating insights into human interaction, noted in his model of change that it comprises three discrete steps (Lewin 1948):

1. *unfreezing* the status quo, including highlighting the disconfirming data showing that the current system is broken and not working;
2. *moving* the system in ways likely to produce better results; and
3. *refreezing* the system with rules and reduction of variation, so the new system is adhered to.

Roughly speaking, Lewin's first and second elements speak to leadership, and the third speaks to management skills in refreezing the system and maintaining the new status quo.

Let's consider a simple example of leadership and management skills from the flow experience. It is also a great example of not doing well something we shouldn't be doing at all. The concept derives from redesigning the triage processes in the Emergency Department to improve the benefit-to-burden ratio and therefore increase value.

Recall from our discussion in Chapter 2 that in the mid-morning hours, if five people walk into triage, our typical processes "make them wait" while the triage nurse processes them sequentially, one by one. At that time of the day, each patient is going to the same treatment area to see the same nurses, see the same doctors, and use the same resources. Why not skip the line and take them directly back to the rooms? They can be triaged there by the primary-care nurse, thus avoiding the step at triage. But what about registration (where they usually go after triage)? In-room registration is the answer to that question, where the registration personnel go to the room and capture the same information they would have obtained at the registration area. The possibilities created here are part of what we have referred to as the "Triage Cascade," all of which were first developed and implemented at Inova Fairfax Hospital and which include a portfolio of new processes including:

1. *Direct to Room*, in which patients bypass triage and are taken directly to available rooms, where they have in-room registration (also known by other names, including "Quick Reg-Triage," "Pull 'til You're Full," "Direct to Room," "Direct to Doc," and other

terms, all referring to the central concept of using available rooms immediately instead of making patients "go through the maze";

2. *Advanced Triage–Advanced Initiatives*, during times when all the ED rooms are full, in which standing physician orders are written for specified clinical entities, so their diagnostic and therapeutic interventions can begin at the triage area—clearly a combination of the evidence-based medicine and evidence-based leadership approach, in that it marries clinical guidelines with a team-based approach to the implementation of those guidelines; and

3. *Team Triage*, utilized when there are predictable times when there will be no rooms available for several hours and deploying a team of a doctor, nurse, technician, registrar, and scribe at the triage area, which begin (and in many cases, complete) ED care at the triage area.

All of these concepts (and many others) are discussed in more detail in Chapters 7 and 10. The point to be made here is simply this:

Is the development and implementation of these flow initiatives a leadership issue or a management issue?

The answer is that it involves both, depending upon which aspect is being considered. The envisioning of a different process across the boundaries of the team is clearly a leadership issue. A deep understanding of the skills of boundary management and stakeholder analysis will be key to successful implementation of the new processes. All of these changes require leadership skills. However, the details of the key process changes and the ability to monitor compliance (preferably in a metrics-based fashion) with the new protocols and systems (refreezing in Lewin's formulation) are the province of management. Getting the various members of the team to collaborate in the difficult process of change is a leadership issue, as is the process of deciding which data will be used to monitor progress. Interpreting that same data to determine progress toward the overall goal and assuring staff members are complying with the newly designed system is a management function. To restate Kotter's distinction between leadership and management, *envisioning* the new system is a leadership issue, while keeping the newly devised system *functioning* is a management issue. To be sure, "toggling" back and forth between these functions may be dizzying, but it is essential if our flow initiatives are to be successful.

Perhaps one of the most powerful insights is one that has been made by many in healthcare:

Most companies are overmanaged and underled.

Is that true of your organization? If so, it is time to get to work, unit by unit, department by department, and, yes, patient by patient, assuring that we put the principles of EBL to work for the good of the patient—and for the good of those who take care of the patient. Finally, the Marine Corps makes clear to its officers a bright-line insight, a saying that is the focus of the next section.

All Marines are riflemen, but not all Marines are ideal for every firefight. Marine officers must choose their teams well.

GETTING THE RIGHT PEOPLE ON THE BUS AND IN THE RIGHT SEATS

Leadership researcher James Collins has made a life's work of studying which companies have been successful and why—and which companies have failed to achieve or sustain their potential and why. His three seminal books, *Built to Last*, *Good to Great*, and *How the Mighty Fall*, have great insights for leaders and managers in all fields, but we will summarize several particularly pertinent to healthcare here. In describing the progression of leaders to the highest level (from 1, the lowest, to 5), Collins differentiates Level 4 leaders from Level 5 leaders in the way shown in Figure 4.4.

Figure 4.4: The Difference between Level 5 and Level 4 Leaders

Level 5 Leaders	Level 4 Leaders
First who • "Get the right people on the bus" • Build a superior team	First what Set a vision • Road map for driving the bus
Then what • Get the right people in the right seats	Then who • Enlist "helpers"
Then, the path to greatness	

Collins's studies found that great companies focused on recruiting and retaining the best talent—the high performers or A-Team members—as an absolute priority and then, and only then, focused on the specifics, based on the talent assembled. In contrast, Level 4 leaders focus first on the "What" and only secondarily on the "Who." Getting the right people on the bus—and assuring that the right people are in the right seats—is an essential priority for leaders. Because leading flow requires team support and a core group of leaders who can envision change and empower others to create that change, this is a critical insight.

For example, when we teach leadership at the American College of Emergency Physicians (ACEP) Emergency Department Directors' Academy, we tell those directors:

> Frankly, we don't care how your Emergency Department runs when you are there. We *know* it runs well when you are there. What we want to know is how it runs when you're *not there*.

In other words, have you gotten the right people on the bus in the right seats, so that your department will run well 24/7/365? Is it *hardwired*? Mike Krzyzewski, the basketball coach for Duke and for the U.S. Olympic Team, makes the same point in a different way in his book *Leading with the Heart*:

> It's not what I know that matters. It's what they do on the court that matters.

The most talented leader in the world is of little use if she hasn't surrounded herself with people, any one of whom can outperform her in a given area of expertise. Indeed, when the right people are on the bus in the right seats, the entire organization gets stronger and more resilient. In his follow-up study examining why organizations fail, Collins noted:

If I were to pick one marker above all others to use as a warning sign, it would be a declining proportion of key seats filled with the right people.

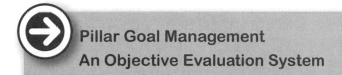

Pillar Goal Management
An Objective Evaluation System

If...you do only one thing aimed at taking your department or entire organization to the top, make it this: Establish an objective evaluation system to hold leaders accountable.
— *Quint Studer,* Results That Last

Perhaps the most important insight from Studer Group is to hold leaders accountable for defined measureable organizational outcomes. This can occur only when leadership evaluation is constant, consistent, and embedded in the culture of the organization. Without accountability for measurable results, the organization simply cannot progress.

An objective evaluation system allows leaders and physicians to track and reach *organizational goals* and achieve excellence. First, the leadership team needs to define the organizational goals that are to be used—and measured—to gauge progress toward success. The goals should be built within a framework. Studer Group uses the pillars (service, quality, people, finance, growth, and sometimes community) as the foundation for organizational goals. The pillars are populated with the highly specific measurable goals underneath them (Figure 4.5).

Figure 4.5: Pillar Management: Populating the Pillars with Defined Goals

The 5 Pillars of Healthcare Success™

Service	Quality	People	Finance	Growth
• Delighted patients	• Improved clinical outcomes- decreased noscominal infections	• Reduced turnover	• Increased bed turns	• Higher volume
• Reduce legal expenses		• Reduced vacancies	• Reduced vacancies	Increased • revenue
• Reduced malpractice expense	• Reduced length of stay	• Reduced agency costs	• Reduced agency costs	Decreased left • without treatment in the ED
	• Reduced re-admits	• Reduced PRN	• Reduced PRN	• Reduced outpatient no-shows
	• Reduced medication errors	• Reduced overtime	• Reduced overtime	
		• Delighted A-Team members	• Reduced physicals and cost to orient	• Increased physician activity

For sample organizational and leader goals, go to www.studergroup.com/hardwiringflow.

Once the goals are agreed to, widely communicated metrics toward progress support at least three important areas. First, they support the organization's goals and align desired behaviors. Second, establishing the metrics excites the organization. Healthcare professionals are by nature competitive and love the challenge of managing the metrics, particularly when the metrics matter—meaning that changes in the metrics have improved the lives of patients and those who take care of patients. Third, measurement across the goals by pillar provides a clear and unmistakable framework for holding ourselves accountable. This framework not only enables leaders to hold their teams accountable, it helps create an atmosphere where every team member takes pride in their own accountability as well.

This is why leader evaluation, leader development, and dealing with the performance gap are so critical to the process of hardwiring. Without them, we will have too many key seats filled with the wrong people. How does a leader distinguish the right from the wrong people? Clearly stated pillar management goals are the foundation from which we evaluate our team and their ability to lead teams in pursuit of those goals, followed by Monthly Report Cards and 90-Day Plans. Quint Studer offers a critical distinction between "owners versus renters" (2008); high performers feel they "own" their piece of the organization and hold themselves deeply responsible for not only their performance but that of the entire team. They are engaged and engage others in purposeful, worthwhile work that makes a difference in their patients' lives. Renters are just "hanging out" at work, often seeming to have "retired on the job." They occupy space and drain resources, but contribute little to the organization's purpose. Collins states it this way:

One notable distinction between wrong people and right people is that the former see themselves as having "jobs," while the latter see themselves as having *responsibilities*. Every person in a key seat should be able to respond to the question, "What do you do?" *not* with a job title, but with a statement of personal responsibility.

When the answer to "What do you do?" is, "I make x and y *happen!*" you know you have the right person, who not only accepts but embraces responsibility. The high performing, A-Team members bring not only energy to the team but passion as well.

Leader development and evaluation, including getting the right people in the right seats, is an ongoing process, full of the dynamic tensions typical of the change embodied in flow initiatives. For this reason, leaders must continually reassess and adapt to changing circumstances and the changes in the talent pool, since turnover in healthcare is a reality. (Indeed, if you are successful in leading a team of talented change agents, they will be offered career advancement in the organization, which is a testament to your ability and that of your colleagues to develop talent.)

The legendary basketball coach at UCLA, John Wooden, who won 10 national titles, made this point in discussing the changes he made personally as a coach when he went from coaching Lew Alcindor (later Kareem Abdul-Jabbar) to Bill Walton. He noted that Alcindor was very attentive to his coaching and suggestions and directive leadership was highly effective with him. Walton, on the extreme other hand, was highly resistant to direct leadership methods. Indeed, a self-described free-thinking child of the '60s, Walton truly "answered to the beat of a different drummer," as Emerson said. To coach Bill Walton well, Coach Wooden adapted his coaching style.

It wouldn't have worked with Bill and me if I hadn't found
better leadership skills. It would have been a shame if I hadn't
been a good enough leader to work effectively with Bill Walton.
(Wooden and Jamison 2007)

Think about Wooden's insight for a moment. Here is the greatest coach in college basketball history, who had already won seven national titles, who instead of insisting that his player adapt to meet the coach's style adapted his own style to his player's. Why? *Because it made the team stronger.* Indeed, during Walton's years at UCLA, the team went to four straight Final Fours, winning three national championships. The power of leaders having the ability to adapt cannot be better illustrated.

Contrast this with Winston Churchill's comment about directive leadership during World War II (1951):

All I wanted was compliance with my wishes after
reasonable discussion.

Clearly, both Churchill and Wooden are examples of great leaders, but the basketball coach teaches the better lesson about the need for the leader to adapt to the needs of his team.

LEADERS AND ROUNDING

Leader rounding is an important part of hardwiring and evidence-based leadership. However, it is particularly important to leading flow. Leading flow involves the ability to maximize the deployment of resources that are:

- scarce;
- capacity-constrained;
- functionally siloed; and
- often recalcitrant to change.

If the resources available to us were not scarce and capacity-constrained, there would be no imperative for flow. Unfortunately, our staffs often feel they are "outmanned, outgunned, and outrun" as the saying goes—there seldom seems to be enough staff and other resources to go around. Functional silos abound in healthcare and we hear these kinds of comments too often:

That's not a doctor problem; it's a nursing problem.

That's not a nursing problem; it's radiology's problem.

That's not an ICU problem; it's the medical-surgical floor's problem.

The list seems endless and the comments go on ad infinitum. All are good people, but they do not have the fundamental insight that if it is a problem for the patient, it is our problem. The fragmentation of work into functional silos makes the work frustrating and, in large measure, helps account for what seems on the surface to be a set of recalcitrant resources that have difficulty coming together for the good of the patient.

Rounding on your units and "rounding on next" (meaning rounding with your leadership colleague on whatever units your patients go to after they leave your span of influence) is a very powerful tool for flow detectives. Take a tour of your own department, but do it from the patients' perspective, seeing it through their eyes, not yours. What is it like for them? Are their expectations assessed and met? Are call lights answered? Better yet, are call lights preempted by anticipating the patients' needs? How does it feel for them to go to Radiology and wait in the hallway? How long does it take to get their questions answered? This is not "MBWA" or management by walking around. It is a disciplined effort to dive deeply into the patient experience and learn how we can offer an improved ratio of benefits to burdens. It requires observational skills of the highest order and a keen insight into details. For most of us in healthcare, we see snapshots of patients' care, in that we see them for a circumscribed period of time in a specific framework, with certain expectations, and, increasingly, through the lens of the data that will determine "whether we have done a good job." All of this is both necessary and, to a certain extent, reasonable as we need to measure progress in pillar management. But leader rounding requires a finer eye, attuned to the nuance of not just data but wisdom. Part of our job is taking these snapshots and turning them into a motion picture of flow, which better tracks their movement—or lack thereof—through our system.

Truly great healthcare leaders observe with a scientist's mind and a servant's heart.

—Thom Mayer, MD

We get ample training in "the scientist's mind," but we could all use some help in further developing our "servant's heart." One of the best tools is rounding with a servant's heart, viewing flow from the perspective of the patient, not just the provider. One of the great benefits of rounding with this lens is that it helps to effectively tell the story of flow through the story of our patients. As Mark Twain said, "If you want to rise to the heights of literary greatness, don't write about Man—write about *a* man" (2007). Telling the stories of our patients is one of the most effective tools for healthcare leaders, precisely because flow requires change and change is difficult. Our experience is that people rarely undertake difficult things unless they understand how it helps others (since part of the One Myth for those in healthcare is serving others) and themselves (what is in their self-interest?). The great Danish writer Karen von Blixen (whose pen name was Isak Dinesen) put it this way (1957):

All sorrows can be borne if you can put them into a story or tell a story about them.

An important part of our jobs as healthcare leaders is to tell our patients' stories in such a way that the rest of the healthcare team will not only understand it and what it means but also in a way that helps them reconnect to their servant's heart. Here's a simple example.

We had a serious and ongoing problem with patients boarding in the Emergency Department, waiting for beds upstairs. It had gotten to the point that nearly all of the treatment rooms were filled with boarders and we were seeing all of the incoming emergency patients in the hallways, including elderly patients with complex problems. I was just finishing rounding and we had a lovely lady—let's call her Ida Smith—who had been in our hallways for over six hours during her work-up. She had no privacy, was in her patient gown, and was able to get little or no rest from the noise and confusion in the ED. As fate would have it, just after rounds, I was scheduled to meet with the CEO, with whom we had been working on the boarding problem. When I went in his office, I said, "Steve, indulge me if you will, but how about we have our meeting while we walk through the ED? There is someone I'd like you to meet." Being a positive, people-oriented CEO, he readily agreed. When we got to the ED, I introduced him to Mrs. Smith, who was still in the hallway, her husband now anxiously standing at her side. We apologized to them both and explained the reasons she was in the hallway. Her response was typical of "The Greatest Generation": "Oh, don't worry about me. You have plenty of people much sicker and in need of help than me. I've been watching them!"

Steve, the CEO, is truly a kind and generous man. But he admitted that he didn't truly understand the boarder issue *from the patients' perspective* until he met Ida Smith and her husband. Immediately thereafter, we began to see a much more rapid pace of change on boarder issues.

We certainly can't meet all of the patients whose care we supervise, but the more of them we meet and the better we become at telling their stories, the more we can motivate our team to enact the sometimes difficult changes necessary to improve flow.

It is these stories that can help break down functional silos and help our team reconnect to purpose. One of the most powerful elements of the Flow Toolkit is systems thinking and an appreciation of the fundamental systems nature of healthcare. The problem is that much of healthcare doesn't even recognize its "systemness," meaning the fact that each process and unit is connected to others that precede or follow it. More importantly, as we've noted in Chapter 2, improvements in one unit or process may actually cause a negative reaction in the next unit or to the system as a whole. For example, a focus on decreasing ICU length of stay may well be a worthy flow goal, but if a substantial number of patients "bounce back" to the ICU because they deteriorate on the medical-surgical floors or the step-down units, the data for the ICU may look good, but the system is failing these patients.

Stories are also important in making progress in another aspect of the Flow Toolkit—managing demand-capacity mismatches (DCM). The problem with DCMs is rarely recognizing that there *is* a DCM. That's painfully obvious. What is usually missing is *why* the DCM is there and *what* needs to be done to correct it—both now and preventing it in the future. Powerfully telling the story can be very effective in highlighting high-leverage strategies.

Our Emergency Department was a case-study in overcrowding, boarders, and ED diversion. It was also deeply committed to innovative flow solutions, such as Direct to Room, AT/AI, Team Triage, and moving patients up to beds upstairs at the earliest possible time. Even with all these highly creative programs, we were still facing the fact that we were seeing over 80,000 patients a year in a space that was designed to see no more than 40,000. In the midst of this, I was summoned to make a presentation to the hospital board. Subject? "Why it takes so long to be seen in the Emergency Department."

I was given a very strict instruction that under no circumstance was I allowed to mention space or the fact that our ED was too small in my presentation, since management was not prepared to recommend construction of a new ED in the budget. Well, this was a bit of a dilemma, to say the least.

The appointed day and hour came and I was introduced to the board. Here's what I said, "Thank you very much. A guy is driving down the interstate highway and is following a white semi-trailer truck with no markings. Every five miles, the truck driver gets out and beats the side of his trailer with a stick, tosses the stick back in the truck, and heads on down the road. This happens four times. Finally, the truck driver pulls into a rest area. The guy follows and parks beside him. As the driver gets out of the truck, the guy who has been following him says, 'Say, I know it's none of my business, but I couldn't help noticing that you get out of your truck every five miles and hit the trailer with a stick. Just out of curiosity, what's that all about, if you don't mind my asking?' The truck driver smiles and whispers, somewhat conspiratorially, 'Well, you see, I'm carrying 80,000 pounds of canaries in the back of that truck. I'm licensed to carry only 40,000 pounds. So I've got to keep half of them flying all the time!'"

And then I sat down. That was the sum total of my presentation to the board. I returned to work, fully expecting to get a call telling me to clean out my desk. Instead the chairman of the board called and said, "Okay, we get it. We approved the funds for expanding the ED."

While we might not recommend this precise approach in every circumstance, it nonetheless illustrates the power of the story on behalf of improving flow for our patients. It is always the job of the leader to use both their scientist's eye and their servant's heart to astutely observe—and then to tell the story of their patients and the people who care for them.

CHAPTER 5

SHOW ME THE MONEY: MAKING THE BUSINESS CASE FOR IMPROVING FLOW

If you ask anyone working in healthcare what our chief task is, the answer is likely to be serving patients and communities. True enough, but the idea of *service* has an important implication: Being in a service business means we compete for customers and resources. Improving flow has twin purposes—to provide better service and to attain financial goals. Teaming those two components—not competing between them—will get your hospital system across the finish line. If the service we provide (in business terms, a *product*) is poor, then our business will decline; if our business falls off, we may be unable to achieve our goal of providing service to our patients. To provide better service, we need to follow sound business principles.

Today the need is even more pressing than in the recent past. Historians will no doubt record 2008 as the year an extraordinary global financial crisis invaded our lives. Bankruptcies, foreclosures, tight credit, tumbling stock prices, rising unemployment, and evaporating 401(k)s were reported hourly. On top of the economic crisis, increasingly the concept of "pay for performance" (P4P) has come into play: Most of our patients have choices about where they can get their healthcare—and they're not reluctant to exercise those choices. To attract their business, healthcare systems increasingly will have to find ways to satisfy customer expectations for service. If ever there was a time to define and defend the business case for improving patient flow, that time is now. When you consider your current financial pressures, the economic benefits of improving flow create their own convincing argument: increased revenues, reduced costs and waste, and improved service, safety, and satisfaction. Taking steps to enhance patient flow can empower administrators and medical directors to effectively address shrinking margins and increased competition. The business case for hardwiring patient flow is compelling.

EARNING AN MBA IN FLOW: THE BUSINESS PERSPECTIVE

A healthcare system's reputation is based on perceived quality of care, patient satisfaction, and financial performance, and as we've noted, these components are related. Elsewhere we've used the terms "hard green dollars" and "soft green dollars" (Jensen et al. 2007) in referring to the two sources of increased revenue for healthcare systems: hard green dollars from concrete operational factors, such as increasing admissions and managing diversions, and soft green dollars from intangible factors, such as patient satisfaction and staff satisfaction. In building the business case for improving flow, you need to relate such improvement to these sources of revenue. In simple terms, improved patient flow leads to increased capacity, increased ED revenue, increased surgical volume, and increased hospital revenue. When you make the case effectively, administration should support the project to improve flow. The approach should be businesslike; develop a business plan complete with objectives, anticipated costs, and expected revenues. Explain the metrics you will use to determine the success of your improvement plan. To make a strong business case for your plan, focus on clinical excellence, operational quality and effectiveness, customer satisfaction, and sound financial management.

CLINICAL EXCELLENCE

If you remember your Flow Toolkit from Chapter 2, one of the important tools was teamwork. Thus, emphasize hiring the right people and building an effective team. Doing so leads to well-flowing operations and staff satisfaction. From a business perspective, you can provide some concrete projections in regard to the benefits of a high performance team. To begin with, determine what your break-even points for personnel costs are, using the following factors:

1. Cost per hour of physician staffing;
2. Cost per hour of nursing staffing;
3. Cost of overtime (hours of overtime x staffing costs per hour = overtime costs per day [or week, month, or year]);
4. Cost of extra physician coverage and overtime; and
5. Cost of extra nursing coverage and overtime.

You're now ready to illustrate how having an effective team translates into financial terms. Before we provide a couple of examples, though, we'll introduce two useful concepts in business management, net patient revenue (NPR) and contribution margin (CM). For purposes of this discussion, we will define NPR as the average expected payment for a patient service. Once direct expenses incurred to deliver the respective service are subtracted from the NPR, the resultant difference is the CM. In healthcare, the NPR comes from patient visits and related procedures, and the cost represents expenses incurred in providing these services. Another concept we'll use in this chapter is "patient velocity" (PV), a calculation of the number of patient visits divided by the unit of time for the relevant critical server—physician hours, nursing hours, critical-care-bed hours, OR hours, and the like; in other words, patients served per unit of time for the key server being studied or utilized. While it is a "patients per hour" figure, in reality it is much more than that. It is a critical measure in healthcare of revenues (patients) to costs (the labor cost of the providers).

Graphically it is expressed as:

$$\text{Patient velocity} = \frac{\text{Patients seen, treated and billed}}{\text{Hours of service coverage}} \quad \text{or} \quad \frac{\text{Revenues}}{\text{Costs}}$$

To convey the financial implications of a stable, satisfied workforce, here are two examples. The first shows the costs of high turnover, specifically what hiring a new ED physician might cost, and thus illustrates saving money by avoiding recruitment costs:

Recruiting Costs
- recruiting fee—$20,000;
- ancillary costs (time, dinners, travel)—$5,000;
- signing bonus—$5,000–$10,000;
- moving expenses—$2,500–$10,000;
- time, effort, energy—unmeasured but true costs;
- **Total recruiting costs = est. $40,000.**

Assimilation Costs
- productivity (e.g., six months at a PV of less than 1.0 patient per hour [or less than .5 or .25] x NCR per patient = decrease in patient flow dollars—an opportunity cost);
- teamwork building.

You can fine-tune these estimates based on your own system's experiences; at a glance, you can see that the cost to a system of recruiting a new physician can be substantial. Compounding these recruitment costs are associated costs that may not be as visible but are nonetheless real: the added stress imposed on other team members making up for the current shortage, for example—potential burnout. Staff satisfaction decreases during staff-shortage periods that extend indefinitely, even beyond four to six months—a particularly challenging problem in that the average time period a hospital experiences from identifying the need to add a physician to having that new physician working a schedule is more than nine months.

The second example illustrates the potential revenues associated with retaining an effective, satisfied, stable ED staff in a well-flowing operation:
- The average NPR (or facility fee) for an ED visit is $400 per visit.
- With a moderate flow-improvement initiative successfully implemented, a PV can increase from 1.75 to 2.0.
- 1.75 x $400 = $700 of hourly NPR;   2.0 x $400 = $800 of hourly NPR
- Every .25 increase in a physician's PV = a $100 hourly increase in NPR.
- Every one-hour decrease in physician staffing costs = $150 in savings.

- So every one-hour change in physician coverage per day = a direct expense reduction of $54,750 per year *or* a CM improvement of almost $55,000!

Your system can reduce personnel costs without staff changes by using the principles outlined in the Flow Toolkit in Chapter 2. Figure 5.1, for example, shows how improving flow reduces relative wage costs and thus saves money and increases profits.

Figure 5.1: Reducing Wage Cost per Admission from a Flow Perspective

Component	Flow Intervention
Average hourly wage	Predicting demand to optimize staffing (reducing overtime pay and agency fees)
Hours per patient day	Predicting demand to optimize staffing (adhering to staffing budgets)
Length of stay	Using multidisciplinary rounds, cooperation with extended-stay facilities, care pathways and protocols, and utilization criteria for patient placement (resulting in fewer patient-days to cover per admission)

Another benefit of a clinically excellent, effective team in a well-flowing operation is that it mitigates the risks of medical malpractice. The potential savings of reducing those risks should be obvious.

OPERATIONAL QUALITY AND EFFECTIVENESS

Readers of a certain age probably remember the sign that used to be outside every McDonald's restaurant, giving the total number of customers served by the chain. This statistic wasn't just a marketing gimmick; it reflected the principle well known by fast food restaurants: The faster tables turn over, the more customers are served, and the more profits increase. For owners of restaurants, financial gain is indicated more by table turnovers than by the number of tables occupied at any given time. The same principle applies to healthcare. The best way to increase profit is to serve more customers for the same fixed costs, keeping the increase in variable costs to a minimum. For Emergency Departments, serving more customers equates to improving throughput so that PV increases, with PV measuring the number of patients seen (or treated or processed) per hour. For the hospital as a whole, serving more customers equates to increasing the number of bed turns—inpatient, specialty-unit, and OR beds (table turnovers for our fast food restaurant), again through improving patient flow (as discussed in Chapter 2, particularly in the section on managing bottlenecks). Figure 5.2 offers some concrete ways of calculating how increasing the number of bed turns can affect your system.

Figure 5.2: Increasing Bed Turns

Number of patients seen per bed per day =
the number of hours per day (in ED, PACU, or ICU)
or days per year (inpatients) bed is available divided
by the average throughput time per bedded patient; e.g.,
- If ED LOS = 4 hours, then each bed serves
  6 patients per day.
- If hospital LOS = 4.5 days, then each bed serves
  81 patients per year (365/4.5 = 81).

To quantify the impact of throughput reduction through
improving flow: reducing throughput time by 11 percent
per bed = improvement of hospital LOS from 4.5 to 4.0;
the impact of this improvement translates to
- 91.25 patients per bed per year *or*
  10.25 additional patients treated;
- at an average NPR of $7,500 per admission,
  $76,875 NPR annually per bed;
- in an average hospital LOS improvement experienced
  in 50 beds representing the medical floors, therefore,
  an achievement of an annual NPR improvement
  of **$3,843,750**

Again, considering what seems to be a very modest increase has a dramatic effect, as you can see from this calculation of the impact of admitting one more patient each day through the ED:

- 20 admissions per day x $7,500 per admission on average = $54,750,000 per year NPR;
- 21 admissions per day x $7,500 per admission on average = $57,487,500 per year NPR;
- 1 more admission per day = $2,737,500 per year additional NPR for your system.

When you make the business case for improving flow, you need also to illustrate the flip side to demonstrating the impact of increasing admissions and bed turns—what we call *opportunity cost*. That cost is the potential revenue you lose through lost admissions, that is, walk-aways and diversions. Walk-aways fall into several categories, generally seen in the ED. Those categories comprise patients who leave without being seen (LWBS), leave without being treated (LWOT), or leave against medical advice, without completing recommended treatment (AMA). Here is a calculation of the opportunity costs of walk-aways:

- NPR for physician services (e.g., $100 per patient) x the number of patients leaving per year = the opportunity cost per year for physician services.
- NCR for hospital services (e.g., $400 per patient) x the number of patients leaving per year = the opportunity cost per year for the hospital.
- NCR for an admitted patient (e.g., $7,500) x the number of patients leaving per year x the admission percentage = the opportunity cost per year for the hospital.
- Using a conservative estimate for lost admissions of 5 percent of walk-away patients, the opportunity cost = $7,500 in the contribution margin per patient for admissions x the number of patients not seen x 5 percent = the potential revenue from lost admissions.

Using this formula with the example amounts for various services, a hospital system with an ED averaging 50,000 patient visits per year would realize $50,000 in new physician revenue without any increased overhead for reducing the number of walk-aways by 1 percent; similarly, the system would realize $387,500 in new NPR for that 1 percent reduction. As with the impact of an hour in our earlier example, a seemingly modest 1 percent change leads to significant financial results.

Diversions to other hospitals because of limited capacity entail similar opportunity costs of lost revenue. Continuing with the example of 50,000 annual ED visits, on average six patients are being treated per hour, and one of those six gets admitted each hour (a 16 percent admission rate). Using our average figure from above of $7,500 NPR from an admitted patient, 6 visits x $400 NPR + 1 admission x $7,500 lost NPR = $9,900 lost NPR per hour of diversion. Each hour your ED is on diversion, you are turning away almost $10,000 of NPR—if that isn't enough to bring you to the attention of the CFO when pointed out, add to that amount the direct expenses you are still paying for staff to treat those patients you are diverting! Having this in turn pointed out may bring your CFO to the Emergency Department—as a patient! As with our other examples, you can see the impact a single hour makes when you calculate the cumulative amount of lost revenue per hour of diversion based on your system's average number of diversions. Additional factors that go into calculating opportunity cost are the labor hours spent diverting and the cost of processing lost patients within the ED.

Improving flow by streamlining processes through the benefit-burden ratio also has dramatic financial impact. Recall the example in Chapter 1 where eliminating the use of oral contrast in abdominal CTs resulted in creating capacity for 10,000 additional Emergency Department patients. Now consider the financial impact: 10,000 patients times an NPR of $400 is $4 million.

A different type of opportunity cost results from the "burden of boarding." If you have inpatients taking up outpatient beds, in the ED or OR for example, your system is losing potential revenue from the blocked capacity. Think of an analogous situation: jets sitting in a queue on a runway awaiting takeoff. The flight for Atlanta is ready to go, but it can't leave until the flight for Orlando takes off—but that one can't leave until the flight for Boston gets clearance, and so on. Again using the average figures for your system, you can calculate what this opportunity cost is per day, per month, and per year.

Keep in mind that *quality* is an integral factor when working to improve flow for operational effectiveness. Simply working to increase PV and bed turns to make money is not the goal; working to implement measures to improve flow, which then leads to increased PV and bed turns and ultimately more revenue in conjunction with increased quality of service and shorter stays, is the goal. A restaurant that concentrates solely on turning tables as quickly as possible and neglects the quality of its food and service won't stay in business long.

> Another helpful tool in understanding the economics of flow is the concept of ROI or return on investment of our flow efforts. Studer Group provides a very helpful tool that helps quickly calculate the ROI of emergency department flow through the use of "The ED Calculator," which is available at www.studergroup.com/hardwiringflow.

CUSTOMER SATISFACTION

As we've just noted, improving flow in an ED and a hospital system as a whole results in smoother processes that lead to increased PV but also better service and shorter stays. Patients aren't going to mind being turned out of bed, so to speak, more quickly when they're receiving high quality care and attention and being treated efficiently. The good thing about improving patient flow is that the various components affected are interconnected, and improving one improves the others as well. When your initiatives work to improve flow, you improve throughput time, and when you do, the result is more satisfied patients. Improved patient satisfaction has two results: The patient who is happy with the service is more likely to return to the hospital again and is more likely to recommend the hospital to friends, relatives, and associates. Conversely, poor service is an opportunity cost: the loss of repeat patronage and the loss of prospective business from others who hear from dissatisfied patients.

The benefits of improved flow in regard to customer service can be seen as an increase in visits and a decrease in complaints. Both lead to increased inpatient and outpatient PV. Handling patient complaints can be seen in one sense as the reverse of an opportunity cost—it's having to spend money (in processing costs and staffing time) that could be saved in a system with better flow.

We noted earlier the potential financial benefit of reducing the risk of medical malpractice. Statistically, hospital systems experience one lawsuit for every 20,000 to 30,000 patient visits. If improving flow raises the number of visits in that equation, the savings can be significant.

SOUND FINANCIAL MANAGEMENT

Improving patient flow involves several components of effective business management: managing costs; increasing PV and NPR per patient; handling documentation, coding, and billing more efficiently; and dealing with "chart stragglers." Use of several innovative techniques has proven beneficial in implementing better management:

- template charts;
- scribes;
- a checkout registrar;
- discounts offered for onsite processing of patient bills; and
- onsite credit card processing.

Let's take a look at one of these techniques: using scribes, college students who document patients' medical treatment for nurses or physicians. Remember our discussion of the theory of constraints and managing bottlenecks in Chapter 2? One of the implications of that discussion was to use resources effectively, having physicians perform duties only they can do, for example. Using scribes fulfills this principle, freeing nurses and doctors to concentrate on their core responsibilities. (And scribes should not be difficult to recruit; go back yet again to our example of fast food restaurants—do you think the average college student would prefer flipping burgers to maintaining charts?) Here are three reasons for allowing scribes to document:

1. They often improve the legibility of charts. This factor will benefit not only current medical personnel who read the charts but also anyone who may need to read them in the future. It also has a positive impact on patient safety.
2. They increase the ED's efficiency. Staff can see more patients, and the ED can decrease the number of walk-aways. Scribes also help track labs and X-rays more effectively.
3. They correctly document the medical record. Reducing incorrect or incomplete documentation increases hospital reimbursement levels. One hospital, for example, recovered its investment in scribes in two months and subsequently hired scribes for PAs as well.

Use of scribes is thus a sound business practice that also improves flow, alleviating workloads of highly stretched nursing teams—and so increases staff satisfaction as well. Once again, you can see how interrelated the components we've been emphasizing are. Improve one and you're likely to improve others as well. Table 5.1 illustrates concisely and vividly the financial benefits of using scribes.

Table 5.1: The Benefits of Using Scribes

Indicator or Measure	With Scribe	Without Scribe	Percentage Increase
Patients per physician per hour	2.52	1.98	27
Average relative value unit (RVU) on charges	251	223	17
Ratio of compliments to complaints per 1,000 patient visits	9:1	5:1	56

Sound financial management implies a caution about some efforts to improve flow. One innovation that might be attractive and promise improvements in efficiency is switching from paper documents to electronic medical records (EMR). And it very well might result in such improvement. But here's a look at the dramatic impact of just five minutes:

- A hospital treats 100 patients a day, using staff hours of five 8-hour physician shifts and one 10-hour physician shift per day.
- Current throughput for patients is an average 180 minutes.
- Daily cost of coverage is $7,500 (for each physician's salary and benefits at $150 per hour).
- Increased time required to implement EMR, using 5 minutes per patient per physician, is 100 patients per day x 5 minutes per patient = 500 minutes—or 8.33 hours of increased physician work per day.
- The additional physician cost to maintain patient throughput at the current level for 8.33 hours x $150 per hour = $1,250 per day or $456,000 annually (Bryan Vineyard EM News).

Does that mean you should keep medical records the old-fashioned way, on paper? No. But it does mean you should keep all the principles from the patient-flow toolkit—such as use of scarce resources in managing bottlenecks—in mind when working to improve flow and your business practices.

CHAPTER 6

ENGAGING PHYSICIANS IN FLOW: THE RATE-LIMITING STEP

"Give me a long enough lever and I can move the world."

—*Archimedes*

Peter Senge famously began his groundbreaking work describing learning organizations with this quotation (Senge, 2006). The principle of using high-leverage strategies and techniques to effectively accelerate the pace of learning and change in organizations is one that has become widely accepted. But what are the highest-leverage strategies with regard to change in the healthcare arena? Of all the things we could do, which are the ones we should do to help maximize flow? Effectively and successfully engaging physicians would certainly be among the items at the top of any list. In this chapter we will describe some of the unique relationships represented by dealing with physicians, as well as distinct aspects of the training and mind-set of this group. We describe here one model of engaging physicians, bringing in insights from multiple sources to build a platform from which to begin to align strategic incentives between physicians and healthcare institutions.

ALIGNING STRATEGIC INTERESTS OF PHYSICIANS AND HOSPITALS

Some of you may recall an ad run during Super Bowl XXXIV in 2000, the theme of which was the story of a group of grizzled cowboys—who herded cats. One of them says, "Herding cattle is nothing compared to herding cats! I'm living my dream." For those who have tried to lead physicians, you might well feel that trying to lead them is like herding cats. As physicians ourselves, we of course are deeply offended by this— not because we are physicians, but because we have cats. While many people recall the herding cats commercial, however, very few can tell you what company ran the ad or what it was for—EDS. That's largely because the message was inefficiently tied to the company—a good lesson for leading flow.

The fact is that leading physicians in the teams required to create and sustain the conditions for flow *can* seem like herding cats and there are some very important reasons for this phenomenon. First, we are aware of no other business model structured like healthcare, where, in the vast majority of cases, the primary driver of utilization and therefore cost is a group of people (physicians) who are only loosely affiliated and scarcely under the control of the entity charged with enacting the orders (the hospital or healthcare system).

Second, in our current system, nothing or very little occurs without a physician order—that is the rate-limiting step in the vast majority of healthcare processes and systems. This step is not only a practical necessity but a legal mandate in that most of the care we provide derives from physician decisions and recommendations. For a simple example, the next time you are on a clinical unit, flip through the chart to the place where we enter what will be done for the patient. At the top of the page you will see, in bold letters:

PHYSICIAN ORDERS

It doesn't read "Physician Suggestions," "Physician Thoughts," or "Physician Recommendations." It is a highly directive and even authoritarian process. The orders are typically timed and notations are made to indicate not only that they are taken off but when they are taken off and when they are enacted, all with military precision. A corollary to the physician ordering what occurs in healthcare is the very process by which we select medical students. We don't select medical students because of their ability to effectively "play in the sandbox with others." We don't select them because of a demonstrated ability to play on teams with others or lead teams successfully. We typically select them because of their ability to score highly on tests and crawl over the backs of their fellow students to get good grades. (Our colleague Dr. Leighton Smith, the Chief Medical Officer (Smith, 2009) at Northwest Community Hospital in Arlington Heights, Illinois, shared the penetrating insight that the best physicians—and especially the best physician leaders—are usually those who have played competitive sports at the high school or college level. This ability to "play well with others" is a key aspect of successful physicians.)

Third, this authoritarian relationship derives from the earliest days of physician training. As Table 6.1 shows, doctors and nurses are selected and trained in fundamentally different ways.

Table 6.1: Differences in the Education and Training of Physicians and Nurses

MD Characteristics	RN Characteristics
Autonomous	Dependent
Authoritarian	Collaborative
Hierarchical	Communications
Intense, focused time	Expanded time
Outcomes driven	Process driven
Technical expertise	Interactive service
Problem solver	Critical thinking skills
Linear perspective	Circular perspective

The education and training of physicians is hierarchical in nature and nearly always authoritarian as well. Physicians are trained to be autonomous in that, despite the team nature of rounds, it is drilled into their heads that they are ultimately responsible for the care of patients. Physicians spend intense focused time with patients, and are very interested in the specific outcomes such as whether the oxygenation improved, what are the vital signs, what are the results of laboratory and imaging studies, and so on. They tend to be driven by a high level of technical expertise and view themselves as problem solvers. Finally, physicians tend to have a linear perspective, engaging with individual patients in their journey from disease to health.

This profile is in contrast to nurses, who are driven by a much higher level of communication and spend far more time with patients. Nurses are certainly interested in outcomes, but they tend to be more process-driven in the manner in which they are educated and trained. While they have a high level of technical expertise, nurses are trained far more in the interactive service skills, probably because they spend such extended time with patients compared to physicians. Nurses are used to working in teams in a collaborative fashion, and the curricula of nursing schools reflect this. Whereas physicians tend to look at themselves as problem solvers, the term most often used in nursing schools and training programs for nurses is "critical thinking skills," by which is meant the ability to reason in context with patients' overall needs, not strictly with individual problems. Finally, nurses tend to take a more circular perspective and incorporate the data within a broader perspective than perhaps the physician is trained to do.

Fourth, given the above conditions, it is perhaps not surprising that physicians truly feel ultimately responsible for the care provided to their patients. Until recently, most physicians truly felt that they were expected to have all of the answers to patients' problems. In our travels, we have repeatedly heard physicians say variations of the following:

My license and my name are on the line in caring for this patient!

If I'm wrong, people will get hurt.

I appreciate all of the input, but ultimately I have to make the decision.

To be sure, the emergence of the Internet and the rise of evidence-based medicine have helped physicians feel that they *don't* truly have to have all of the answers. Nonetheless, physicians tend to view themselves as the ultimate decision makers in the course of the care of individual patients. An unfortunate corollary to this view is that many physicians have a deep fear that what they do may potentially harm a patient. Very few physicians commonly offer up this thought, but many of them harbor it deeply:

Will I do the wrong thing and harm a patient today?

An additional corollary is that physicians tend to vastly overestimate the malpractice risk to which they are exposed. Surveys have shown that physicians commonly overestimate their malpractice risk by at least a two-fold and more typically a three-fold factor (Hickson, 2002).

Fifth, traditionally, physicians have been trained with a healthy respect for autonomy among other physicians. This is a critical insight to keep in mind with regard to the process of change and particularly the systems and processes necessary to improve flow. As Dr. Joseph Bujak has noted:

Physicians will not interfere with an individual's right to go off
in his own direction, but they would resent an expectation that
they follow. (Bujak, 2008)

A common refrain that is often heard is, "I wouldn't do it that way, but I respect your right to do so."

Sixth, as we begin to engage physicians in flow, it is important to remember that many of them have had previous experience with change initiatives, so this will not be "the first bite of the apple" for many of them. We recently asked the president of a medical staff at a major teaching institution if he had experience with previous change initiatives. His answer was:

"Oh, yes, I have a lot of experience with change initiatives—
some bad, some very bad!"

Famous Major League Baseball manager Casey Stengel phrased it this way: "I don't have any experience with that—and it's all bad" (Stengel, 2006).

This is certainly not to say that every physician will have had nothing but negative experiences with regard to change initiatives, but the progression through previous initiatives such as continuous quality improvement, total quality management, bundled payment, purchase of physician practices, and other such changes has not always been spectacularly successful. The good news about this experience is that it creates an opportunity for us to be able to say, "I understand you've been through this before. But let us show you what will be new about this time."

Finally, like it or not, many physicians feel they could wake up tomorrow and, with little or no training, do the CEO's job better than it is currently being done. This is more than arrogance on the part of these physicians—it is a fundamental lack of understanding of current-day healthcare operations, as well as a difference in mind-set, training, and worldview. Dr. David Eddy refers to this as "The Problem of the Apostrophe" (Eddy, 1996). He notes that physicians are part of and trained in an expert culture in which they have an ethical imperative to serve as the patient's advocate. Hospital administrators and non-physician healthcare leaders are trained in an affiliate culture where they are expected to serve as the patients' advocate. The issue is significant and deep, but, in our experience, can be overcome through recognition of these differences and a deep and ongoing dialogue aimed at bridging these views. Stated differently:

Physicians focus on "Fires!"

Administrators focus on "Fire Stations!"

In the face of these inherent difficulties in engaging physicians in flow, there are some extremely bright spots as well. First, physicians typically value collegiality, which has been instilled within their training programs. The process of obtaining consults, sharing ideas, and participating in carefully structured morbidity and mortality conferences is one that all physicians have been through, regardless of specialty. It is incumbent upon us to help these physicians recall this collegiality. (Here we accentuate the concept of *re-call* to mean returning to those roots in our training program that emphasized this collegiality.)

Second, credible evidence usually does prevail with most physicians, even if it means inconvenience for the physician to comply with that credible evidence. To increasing degrees, evidence-based medicine triumphs over "eminence-based medicine." Physicians enjoy working within an evidence-based format if they have had a voice in generating that format. (More on this in the next section.) Finally, in our experience, the vast majority of physicians are honest and straightforward providers who simply want to provide the best possible care they can for their patients. They certainly may differ with regard to their concepts of what the best care consists of, but this common dedication to the patient is a theme that can help engage physicians.

One concept we have found to be critically important in engaging physicians in flow concerns *waste*, or non-value-added activities. Without question, physicians believe a high percentage of their time is wasted on activities that do not produce value either for them or for the patient. In order to maximally engage these physicians, we need to help them understand the benefit-to-burden ratio and our efforts to leverage that concept to improve the use of their time. Indeed, the following questions are important to pose to our physicians:

What can we do to make better use of your time?

What would the "no waste practice of medicine" look and feel like to you?

Framing the question with regard to the "no waste practice of medicine" can be very helpful in changing the mind-set of physicians toward the reality that, in fact, this time the hospital is serious about the improvement initiative driven by flow as defined in the benefit-to-burden ratio. In fact, if we were to give you one piece of advice regarding how best to engage physicians in flow, it would be to continually engage them in a dialogue of what, in their view, the "no waste practice of medicine" would be like. Listen to their answers carefully. Don't be surprised if they are a bit stunned by the question at first. In all likelihood, they've never been asked it before.

In many cases they will answer that they would like the nurse to have the chart and all pertinent information available when he calls the physician. Others will say they would like physician preference cards instituted so the staff can proactively know their practice patterns. Emergency physicians may answer that they would like to institute the use of scribes, who document the medical record and assist with organizing laboratory and imaging results. As experience with the concept increases, physicians typically become more detailed in their descriptions of the "no waste practice of medicine."

Two additional thoughts are important. First, expect that each physician will have her own answers, although there will undoubtedly be similarities within practice specialties. Cardiologists' view of the "no waste practice of medicine" will be different from the view of orthopedic surgeons. Don't be surprised if procedure-based practices (cardiology, gastroenterology, and surgeons) have differences from primary-care physicians (pediatricians, family medicine, and internists) in their views. Second, expect that the definitions will change and develop more focus over time, as they adapt and think about their response. Indeed, your most thoughtful—and valuable—physicians will continue to reflect on wasted time and effort and will come back to you, often beginning this conversation with:

Listen, I've been thinking about your question about the "no waste practice of medicine" and I've had a few thoughts....

A MODEL FOR CREATING PHYSICIAN ENGAGEMENT WITH FLOW INITIATIVES

Perhaps because of the recognized importance of engaging physicians in hospitals' and healthcare systems' initiatives, there has been a recent increase in the number of resources discussing how best to engage physicians. Each model has its own strengths, as well as areas that perhaps need to be strengthened. Recognizing the importance of physician engagement in quality improvement efforts, Reinertsen and his colleagues with the Institute for Healthcare Improvement (IHI) developed a six-step "Checklist for Engaging Physicians in Quality and Safety" (Reinertsen, 2007).

For those interested in more details, the document is available online at http://www.ihi.org/IHI/Results/WhitePapers/SevenLeadershipLeveragePointsWhitePaper.htm.

Similarly, Dr. Joseph S. Bujak has developed a model for physician engagement for the American College of Healthcare Executives titled "Understanding and Influencing Physician Behavior: The Strategic Imperative." The fundamentals of that course are delineated in his book *Inside the Physician Mind: Finding Common Ground with Doctors* (Bujak, 2008). However, the most effective model we have seen for engaging physicians comes from our colleague Stephen Beeson, MD, of Studer Group, whose book *Engaging Physicians: A Manual to Physician Partnership* (Beeson, 2009) is a terse and excellent resource with a very helpful structure to sustain an effective dialogue with physicians. Each of these formats is listed in Table 6.2.

Table 6.2: Three Models for Obtaining Physician Engagement

IHI Format (Reinertsen et al.)	ACHE Format (Bujak)	Studer Format (Beeson)
Discover common purpose	Understanding physicians' culture	Create and communicate organizational vision and goals
Reframe values and beliefs	Physician response to change	Leadership development and accountability for performance
Segment the engagement plan	Specific approaches to influencing physician behavior	Establish physician confidence and trust
Use "engaging" improvement methods	Structural changes to align physicians and healthcare organizations	Building physician leadership
Show courage	Physicians as barriers to improvement	Training physicians
Adopt an engaging style	Engaging physicians	Physician measurement and balanced scorecards
	Eliminating distrust	Implementing physician behavior standards
	Healthcare leader as change agent	Managing the disruptive physician
		Recognizing physicians- reward your champions

Stage 1: Create and Communicate Organizational Vision and Goals

---

If you do not know where you are going, no wind is the
right wind.

—Seneca (Seneca, 1996)

No initiative involving people of any kind can hope to be successful without a clear and concise statement of "where you are going" as Seneca said. With physicians in particular, it is important to remember this advice: "If they are not with you on the takeoff, they will not be with you on the landing." The ultimate goal of communicating vision and goals is to assure that everyone at every level of the organization has a clear and consensually shared sense of purpose. You should be able to walk up to any team member—physician or otherwise—and ask, "Why are you here and what are you trying to accomplish?" and get the same or a very similar answer, 24/7/365. As Dr. Beeson has noted: "What good is a vision if it has little impact on those who are tasked to execute it? *Does a vision even exist if it does not guide the daily actions of each member of the team?*" (emphasis added) (Beeson, 2009). Not surprisingly, if we ask physicians to "engage," they will undoubtedly say, "Engage in what?" In the past, hospitals and physicians have tended to stare at each other across fences each asking a similar question, "How do we get *them* to engage in *our* agenda?" The answer quite simply is to create the agenda by assuring that everyone has a clear understanding of vision, mission, goals, and strategies in a consensus-based fashion. If we want physicians to join the hospital's quality agenda, we should first seek to understand this agenda.

Seek first to understand, then to be understood.

—Stephen Covey (Covey, 2004)

He who has a strong enough "Why?"
Can bear almost any "How?"

—Friedrich Nietzsche (Nietzsche, 2004)

As Nietzsche advises us, given the right vision (why) we can get there through many different strategies and goals (how). What does this point mean for flow? It is incumbent upon leaders to help craft a clear vision, mission, and strategies, in concert with their physicians with regard to improving flow and what it means for the patient, the physician, and the healthcare institution. The beauty of the flow definition as increasing value while eliminating waste through increasing benefits while eliminating burdens is that it provides a fairly simple calculus for time flow to the overall vision, mission, and strategies of both the physicians and the healthcare institution in which they practice.

What other features will likely typify the organizational vision and goals? To an increasing degree, physicians are "metrics motivated," meaning that data help drive decisions for most physicians and physician groups. As one chief medical officer recently noted,

---

We like to say that our improvement work is "Physician-Led, Evidence-Based, Data-Driven," but what we're really saying is that we believe that physicians have a deep-seated need to learn together, with evidence and data at the foundation of the learning. (Reinertsen, 2005)

The adage that "Physicians love data!" is generally correct. However, in our experience we have noted that physicians love what Kurt Lewin called "confirming data," data that confirm their view that they are doing a good job or generally moving in the right direction. It is always of concern to physicians when they face "disconfirming data," data showing that they are either out of compliance or that the results of the combined efforts have been disappointing. (Lewin, 1997) The key when disconfirming data appear is to help craft a consensus-based, evidence-based pathway to improved flow.

Finally, it is essential that telling the story of vision, mission, and goals for flow be done as succinctly and tersely as possible. As we have noted previously, "If I can't say it to you in 30 seconds and you can't remember it and repeat it back to me in 15 seconds, it's time to go back to the drawing board." Too often, we attempt to explain the why, what, and how of healthcare in terms that are far too long. Simply stated, if you can't fit your vision, mission, and goals on one page, it's time to revise. Here's one of the best we've seen, from one of the best CEOs with whom we've worked, Bruce Crowther of Northwest Community Hospital, just outside Chicago:

Big city smarts—small town values.

Once the vision is clear, concise, and consensus-based, tie it to the pillar goals of the organization and communicate it broadly with a "multichannel" approach, including leader rounding, department and section meetings, phone calls, e-mails, and mailings. A good rule is you should figure out how much communication you think is enough—then multiply it by five. It is virtually impossible to over-communicate when it comes to the vision, mission, strategies, and goals.

Stage 2: Leadership Development and Accountability for Performance

Once the vision, mission, and goals/strategies are established and agreed to in a consensus-based fashion, leaders should be trained in the principles of hardwiring, evidence-based leadership, and leading flow, as delineated in Chapters 1, 2, and 4. Tacitly or explicitly, every organization has a "language of the realm," or a lingua franca, through which leadership principles are discussed.

Creating and maintaining a high-performance leadership team requires assuring that this language is well known to those who have been asked to lead in the flow efforts, particularly physicians. Because of their problem-oriented approach, once physicians know what the common purpose is, they then want to know how the flow concepts will be deployed and what their place is within the leadership thereof.

In addition to the hardwiring and evidence-based leadership approach, an additional piece of leadership training can be helpful for physicians. In our view, all effective change requires both a *wedge* and a *magnet*. A wedge is something unpleasant or less than satisfactory that drives us off of our current status. In Lewin's terms it is disconfirming data, which tell us that there's a metrics-based way of showing our performance is not meeting the vision and mission we have laid out. Lengthy turnaround times, lengthy infection rates on central venous lines, surgical infections, inability to meet CMS guidelines and core measures, and inappropriate utilization are all simple examples of the disconfirming data that act as a wedge to drive us off the current status quo. However, in our experience there also must be a magnet, which is a sense of what a preferred state would look like, and at least a general sense of how that status may be approximated. Thus, the wedge is rarely enough alone to cause change, unless there is a magnet that helps pull us toward a better status. Indeed, accomplishing flow requires leadership to assure that, at each stage of the healthcare experience, we are not *pushing* patients through the system as much as we are helping our staff *pull* them into the next stage of care in a flow-directed fashion. An important part of physician leadership is to assure a clear understanding of this wedge and magnet phenomenon.

As we mentioned previously, many physicians have had previous experience with change initiatives that were less than satisfactory. It's important to assure credibility by obtaining at least small results in the early stages of flow initiatives. Building upon these small successes helps build physician credibility and trust that the organization is truly committed to the goals that it has laid out. This initial credibility is critical and leads to an exponential acceleration of later progress, particularly as physician confidence in the process further develops.

An effective tool for developing physician leaders and building accountability is through the use of Leadership Development Institutes or LDIs, a series of educational sessions with clear curricula geared toward educating physicians in the principles of hardwiring.

Stage 3: Establishing Physician Confidence and Trust

One of the best ways to establish physician confidence and trust is to assure that members of the leadership team have as a central goal creating a hospital or healthcare system that is the "facility of choice" of physicians. In other words, healthcare leaders understand that many physicians have a choice of which institution in which to practice. Flow initiatives, particularly by eliminating the waste of time for their physicians, develop a competitive edge by setting the stage for physician partnership through the institution's commitment to becoming the easiest place to work.

Building confidence and trust among physicians begins by surveying them with regard to what their needs are. An extremely powerful question centers around discovering what the "no waste practice of medicine" would be like at your hospital. While written surveys can be valuable in this regard, leaders should round on their physicians as much as possible, seeking open-ended responses to questions about how flow can be improved by increasing value and eliminating waste, both for the patient and for the physician. One of the most satisfying responses comes when physicians begin to ask, "What about the nurses? Can't we focus more on increasing value and eliminating waste for them?" When this occurs—and it will occur, predictably—it is a symbol that the physicians have not only bought into the system and its mission and vision but that they understand the fundamental team nature of the provision of healthcare. In our work, we have stressed repeatedly the following insight:

> The most important sign of the health of a healthcare organization is the relationship between the physicians and nurses.

Using the principle of active listening we discussed in Chapter 3, once the physician responds with suggested initiatives to improve flow, it is a wise idea to follow up with this question:

> So if we were able to_____, [fill in her suggestion here] that would be a sign that flow was working?

An additional follow-up question is:

> How would we measure that as a sign that flow was working?

Stage 4: Building Physician Leadership

As we select and recruit physician leaders, many talents and abilities are important. However, if we were forced to summarize them in two categories, they would be *courage* and *social leadership skills*. Change is never easy and the status quo often seems like the warmest blanket in which to wrap ourselves. Successful physician leaders have the courage to generate change— particularly non-incremental change. This is often simply the courage to speak one's mind before those who may not agree with the tenets of the flow initiative under discussion. This is a critical if uncommon virtue. As Frederick the Great said:

> Courage in battle is exceedingly common, but courage in everyday life is rare.   (Frederick the Great, 1998)

How can we know which physicians are likely to show courage? Many psychologists have noted that the best predictor of future behavior is past behavior; therefore careful reflection upon your experiences in dealing with physicians in past endeavors is the first guide to discovering whether they will have courage in the future. However, equally important is assuring them that you will support them, and, more importantly, the team will do so as well in the face of the "white water of change," which will inevitably include dissension among certain parties regarding the change involved in the flow initiative. Selecting physician champions is a concept illuminated by Rogers' work on change. (Rogers, 1995) Figure 6.1 illustrates Rogers' insight that people's response to change can be predictably classified according to the following general categories:

1. **Innovators**—These are the 2.5 percent of the people within an organization who are constantly "pushing the envelope" with regard to new, creative means of changing processes and systems.

2. **Early adopters**—This group of people, which comprises 13.5 percent of the team, quickly sees the advantages of proposed change and commits their resources (including mental, physical, and psychological resources) to the effort.

3. **Early majority**—This group of roughly 34 percent of the team will commit, but not quite as carly and not quite as enthusiastically as either the innovators or early adopters. However, their contribution is essential to effective change.

4. **Late majority**—These team members also constitute roughly 34 percent of the group, but are more "fence sitters," in that they want to see what the results are from the change effort before committing themselves to it.

5. **Laggards**—This group may be said to fundamentally disagree with the change effort altogether and are unlikely to be effective either in the early or late stages of the change effort. Fortunately, they comprise only about 16 percent of the team.

There is an understandable tendency for many of us to consider ourselves as innovators or, at the least, early adopters. The most successful of physician leaders are those able to adapt and understand leadership, change, and principles exemplified in the evidence-based leadership approach. To be sure,

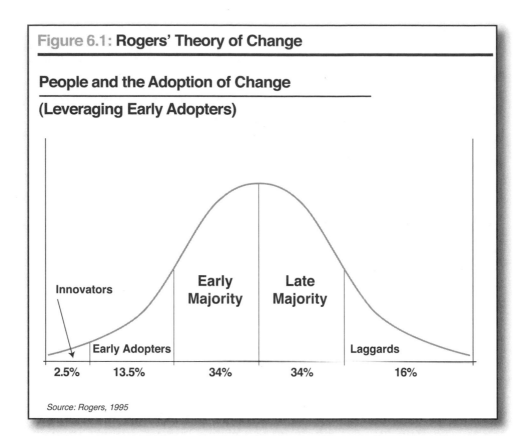

Figure 6.1: Rogers' Theory of Change

People and the Adoption of Change

(Leveraging Early Adopters)

Source: Rogers, 1995

not every physician proves to be an effective physician champion during the course of change. However, careful selection and rigorous training around the hardwired and EBL principles are essential to assuring that there is a common means of operating successfully within the system.

Stage 5: Training Physicians

All of the concepts listed in Chapter 1 and Chapter 4 need to be further developed in the course of training physicians. This is also a time to help them focus their efforts and discover their passion both for leadership and followership in flow initiatives. As we'll discuss in the next section, a metrics-based, evidence-based approach is extremely important to successful physician leadership. The approach requires a deep focus on doing what matters and measuring what matters. Focus requires being specific as to what we target, what we measure, and how we measure. There are important sports medicine analogies that can be helpful in this regard. What may seem like focus to one person may be unacceptable confusion to another. In general, the more highly trained the leader or athlete, the more laser-like their focus is. For example, Trevor Matich, one of the National Football League's best long snappers (the guy who hikes the ball to the punter or placekicker) was asked whether he focused on the punter or holder's hand when he snapped the ball. His response was classic:

> Absolutely not! If I did that, I'd never get the snap where it's supposed to be. I focus on the pad of the thumb of the holder or punter's hand. That way I have a very clear focus on precisely where the ball is supposed to go. If I don't hit the pad of the thumb, I consider it a bad snap.

One of the best lacrosse players in collegiate history, Duke's Matt Danowski, the winner of the 2008 Tewaaraton Award for the best collegiate player, made the same point in another way.

> I don't aim at the goal or the net; I aim at a specific one-inch square in a specific part of the net when I shoot.

Danowski's focus led him to the career record for points scored in NCAA men's lacrosse history. Similarly, our focus as physician leaders needs to be on highly detailed results, as it is only by that focus that we can assure that our activities are successful. Whether training in physician rounding, AIDET, use of Key Words at Key Times, or any other elements of the principles of hardwiring, attention to highly focused goals is essential.

Helping physicians discover their passion for leadership in the development of flow initiatives is also critical, by which we mean the fundamental focus on those aspects for which they have passion, energy, and enthusiasm.

> This is the true joy in life, the being used for a purpose recognized by yourself as a mighty one: the being thoroughly worn out before you are thrown on the scrap heap; the being a force of nature instead of a feverish selfish little clod of ailments and grievances complaining that the world will not devote itself to making you happy.
> —George Bernard Shaw (Shaw, 2003)

Stage 6: Physician Measurement and Balanced Dashboards

All current approaches aimed at engaging physicians have as a central thread the importance of metrics-based management, which focuses on discrete improvements in mutually agreed-to data points. The question is, "What should be measured?" The simplest answer is, "Whatever the organization values, whatever matters to the success of the endeavor." In other words, the metrics should be intimately tied to the vision, mission, strategies, and goals identified in Stage 1. Properly identified and communicated, they should permeate the organization and its quality improvement and safety efforts—including flow initiatives. We strongly encourage the use of a balanced dashboard approach directly tied to the organization's vision and mission. (While most institutions use the term "balanced scorecard," we think physicians react better to the concept of a dashboard. Just as you can't fly an airplane without a real-time dashboard, which updates the pilot with critical information, so too must physicians—particularly physician leaders—have a dashboard to navigate their progress and that of the team.)

One of the fundamental precepts of evidence-based leadership is the concept of pillar management, or stating specific goals across the five pillars of Service, Quality, Finance, People, and Growth (Figure 6.2). (Not-for-profit healthcare systems sometimes add a sixth pillar—Community.) Because physicians are such a key part of attaining the organization's goals, their dashboard should be integrated into the pillar management goals. Without clearly stated and measurable goals, progress is difficult or impossible. Even if the five pillars themselves are not used in your organization, metrics-based management and the use of dashboards is essential.

As an example, the vision statement—the "Why we exist"—of our organization, BestPractices, Inc., which provides Emergency Department solutions for leadership, training, and staffing, stresses three fundamental issues: the Science, Art, and Business, all of which must occur in the setting of leadership and innovation. In order to measure progress against these goals, we use a 4S Balanced-Dashboard.

Figure 6.2: **Pillar Management with Discrete Goals in Each of the 5 Pillars**

Pillar Management for Progress

(Balanced Scorecard)

Service	Quality	People	Finance	Growth	Community
· Reduced claims	· Improved clinical outcomes – decreased riosocomial infections	· Reduced turnover	· Improved operating income	· Higher volume	· Increased philanthropy
· Reduced legal expenses		· Reduced vacancies	· Decreased cost per adjusted discharge	· Increased revenue	
· Reduced malpractice expense	· Reduced medically unnccessary days and delays	· Reduced agency costs	· Improved collections	· Decreased left without treatment In the ED	
· Physician satisfaction		· Reduced overtime		· Reduced outpatient no-shows	
· Patient satisfaction	· Reduced re-admits	· Reduced physicals & cost to orient	· Reduced accounts receivable days	· Increased physician Activity	
	· Reduced medication errors		· Reduced advertising costs		

The 4Ss are science/safety, service, sustainability, and superior leadership. Note the strong similarity to the five Studer Group pillars: Service, Quality, People, Finance, and Growth. *Science/Safety* measures progress towards 100 percent compliance with evidence-based protocols for the presenting complaints and diagnoses seen in our Emergency Departments. It is guided by two evidence-based clinical-protocol programs geared for the emergency physician (Creating the Risk-Free ED™ and The Pediatric Risk-Free ED™) and one for the nursing staff (The Nurses Guide to the Risk-Free ED™). *Service*, not surprisingly, tracks patient satisfaction scores by individual physician, patient complaints, and patient compliments. *Sustainability* tracks specific flow metrics, including patient velocity (the number of patients seen per hour of coverage) as well as turnaround time, broken out by discrete intervals. Finally, because of our relentless focus on leadership, we include *superior leadership*, as we believe that the clinical aspect of leadership in the

Emergency Department is every bit as important or more so than administrative leadership.

Your dashboard will undoubtedly be different and will reflect what your organization values and how you measure flow by increasing value and eliminating waste through the benefit-to-burden ratio as your patients move through the service-transitions queues and bottlenecks of your healthcare system. Using a dashboard tied to pillar management goals is a highly effective way of linking physician performance to results.

In implementing your dashboard, several items are important. First, measurement must be frequent enough that clinicians can connect actions to effects. The ideal system tracks metrics daily, although weekly and monthly systems are sometimes necessary as the process begins. Second, the data must be transparent. We live in an era where public reporting is transparent, so we need to be able to make these data readily available to those whose actions generate such data in the first place.

Perhaps the most powerful method of channeling leadership
attention is to harness the power of transparency.
(Reinertsen, 2007)

Margaret Wheatley eloquently spoke to this issue in her elegant book: "When people who have shared purpose are given access to relevant data and are allowed to engage in soulful dialogue, magic happens."(Wheatley, 1999) Third, physicians should be given the chance to participate in the dialogue regarding which data are most effective at measuring flow. As we said before, if they are not with you on the takeoff, they won't be with you on the landing. However, it must be clear that *not* measuring data is not an option.

Finally, measurements should be tied as directly as possible to the work processes and systems themselves. Indirect measures are far less effective than focused, direct measures of those areas under the team's span of control. Physician leaders should meet with their respective team members and review the results frequently. Face-to-face meetings should be held no less than quarterly, and monthly or weekly updates can be used as necessary to communicate either progress or the lack thereof. In particular, seeking out those physicians who have improved their metrics is an excellent way of rewarding them, which will be discussed in more detail in Stage 9. It is also difficult to overstate the importance of regular review of the balanced dashboard by the physician leader as a means of assuring accountability.

Stage 7: Implementing Physician Behavioral Standards

"We are what we repeatedly do. Excellence is not a virtue,
but a habit."

—Aristotle

Written physician behavioral standards have always been a part of the most high-performing organizations in healthcare. However, beginning in 2009, the Joint Commission on Accreditation of Healthcare Organizations (JCAHO), requires a written code of standards to attain accreditation. Several important factors are critical with regard to physician behavior standards. First, they must be tied to the vision, mission, strategies, and goals of the organization, articulating a clear role for physicians in organizational change efforts, including flow. Second, the most effective performance standards are created by the physicians themselves. Our experience is that choosing physicians who will most resist the concept of standards and placing them on the committee to develop the standards is critical, according to the wisdom expressed by former President Lyndon Baines Johnson, who said:

I'd rather have that SOB on the inside of the tent urinating
out than on the outside of the tent urinating in.
(LBJ, quoted in Caro, 1990)

(As you might guess, LBJ's language was somewhat more colorful, but you get the point.) Having physicians participate in the genesis of the physician behavior standards helps assure that they will help champion their development. We often hear such physicians say of the final product, which they have had a hand in writing, "I didn't believe in this process at first, but the end result is something I can not only live with, but advocate for."

Written effectively, physician behavior standards say "who we are" and "what we expect of each other." Once they are developed, they should be utilized in training; many organizations have physicians sign them in the process of credentialing and re-credentialing to demonstrate their assent to the standards. Physicians should commit to the purposes identified in the physician behavior standards, including language regarding how deviation from such standards will be handled. These standards should clearly delineate both what expected behaviors are and what unacceptable behaviors are, including examples where appropriate. They should, whenever possible, be succinct and terse, speaking directly to the point. Physicians universally appreciate direct and straightforward statements.

In rolling out the physician behavior standards, it's very important to utilize the physicians who are A-Team high performers and physician champions. Utilizing physicians who are respected and who show courage and social skills in articulating the principles of the physician behavior standards is critical to success. Figure 6.3 gives an example of physician behavior standards we have utilized in our facilities.

**Figure 6.3: Physician Behavior Standards—BestPractices—
Inova Fairfax Hospital,
Department of Emergency Medicine**

1. Respect our Patients:

    a. Introduce yourself, make eye contact, sit if possible—
       "We want to offer you excellent care."

    b. Acknowledge the wait, good or bad.

    c. Verbalize need for privacy, pain relief, etc.

    d. Update care plan and time expectations.

    e. Use active listening.

2. Respect our Colleagues:

    a. On time every time.

    b. Positive influence, limit core negativity.

    c. Work output.

    d. Sign-outs at bedside.

    e. Interaction with nursing team is positive and proactive.

---

3. Respect the Hospital:

    a. Acknowledge and support hospital goals.

    b. Productive criticism.

    c. Treat contract as your personal contract.

    d. Learn and accept customer service standards and questions.

    e. Support and innovate flow initiatives.

4. Respect Ourselves:

    a. Life-long learning.

    b. Acknowledge individual weaknesses and knowledge gaps and target these for improvement.

    c. Compassionate scheduling.

    d. *Leave a legacy*—every patient, every day.

Stage 8: Dealing with Disruptive/B-Team/ Low Performing Physicians

The most powerful single thing that can be done to say to the team "We are serious about this" is to deal effectively with those disruptive physicians who are quintessential B-Team members and low performers. The fact of the matter is our fellow physicians, nurses, and other team members have put up with these disruptive behaviors for far too long. In fact, tolerating these kinds of behaviors seriously erodes the confidence that others may have in us as leaders of the healthcare enterprise. We can simply no longer promote or tolerate disruptive attitudes and actions if we are serious about change of any kind, but particularly flow.

Dealing with such physicians must be handled in a way that ties the behavior to objective measures that have been established, including not only the physician code of conduct, but the goals and objectives as delineated by the team in the vision and mission statements. Whenever possible, stress prevention in order to assure that those who are approaching out-of-bounds behaviors do not continue them. Or, as your kids will tell you, "Just don't go there." Thus leadership interventions on B-Team behaviors of low performers should be implemented early as opposed to late. The goal is improvement and remediation, not termination. However, if unacceptable behaviors continue, the principles of hardwiring and EBL demand that action be taken for those who cannot or will not respond to effective coaching and mentoring. As our colleague Dr. Robert Cates says, "There are some people you don't want to get even with, you want to get away from." (Cates, 2006) And as Quint Studer notes, "It's often better to work short than to work with low performers on an ongoing basis."(Studer, 2008)

It is extremely important in the course of dealing with B-Team members that we state clearly and concisely what the problem is and what its effects are. Far too often, counseling and mentoring are handled in an indistinct, non-confrontational manner that does not produce results.

> Dealing with low performers who exhibit B-Team behaviors can be among the most challenging aspects of healthcare management and leadership. For more detailed information on dealing constructively with low performers, go to www.studergroup.com/hardwiringflow and download the pdf labeled "Dealing with B-Team Behaviors."

Physicians may not initially react well when they are told that their behavior is disruptive or distracting. Disconfirming data comes hard to physicians who have always taken pride in being "best in class." We have found that the wisdom of Elizabeth Kubler-Ross, originally from her landmark research on death and dying, is also applicable to the grieving process of being confronted with the realization that you are perceived as a B-Team member or low performer. (Kubler-Ross, 1970) Those stages are:

1. Denial—"The data must be wrong!"
2. Anger—"Who accused me of this? I demand to confront them!"
3. Bargaining—"All right, this is an aberration. It won't happen again."
4. Acceptance—"I hate to say it, but I acknowledge I have important issues to deal with."

5. Peace—"It was painful to realize, but I can see how this is a better path for me—and for those with whom I work."

Stage 9: Recognizing Physicians—Reward Your Champions!

The power of praise is one of the most important tools we have at our discretion to help reinforce the fact that we appreciate our A-Team high performers. Physicians, far from being immune to this sort of recognition, generally respond extremely positively to it. In our travels through healthcare, we have repeatedly heard physicians say that, despite the fact that they have practiced for 10, 15, or 20 years in a given healthcare system, they have never received praise or recognition from the system. This makes the institution of efforts to reward our physician champions even more powerful, as it often seems in stark contrast to their previous experience. Physician recognition has consistently been shown to improve physician satisfaction, loyalty, perception of leaders, and even performance itself. It is also a distinctive means of "branding" your organization as physician-friendly and physician-centric.

If your efforts to recognize physicians are to be effective, you must focus on several aspects of such efforts. First, rewarding your champions must be hardwired into the system. In other words, team leaders at all levels of the institution need to adopt the practice. Hardwiring helps demonstrate that a dramatic change has occurred in the organization and that the institution is truly pursuing partnership with its physicians around the vision, goals, and strategies delineated. Second, the praise should be in an appropriately public setting. While private praise is certainly appropriate in some circumstances, assuring that others know your appreciation for the work of the physician champion is extremely important. Third, rewarding your champions needs to be consistent and persistent, meaning it needs to be continued over time, so that it becomes a part of the culture of the organization. There are a number of means of rewarding your champions, including managing up, thank-you notes, e-mails, formal physician-recognition rewards, and even recognition at both the medical staff and board levels. One of the most powerful ways of managing up physicians is through the nursing staff. Nurses are widely considered to be among the most trusted of all professions. Training nurses in managing up with key words at key times can be extremely helpful:

> Mrs. Smith, Dr. Sanchez will be the gastroenterologist
> performing your procedure. He's one of our best, he is extremely
> experienced, and he has taken care of many of my patients. I
> know he'll do a good job and I'm quite sure you'll like him.

To be sure, nurses should not be encouraged to say anything they don't believe, but the fact is most of our nurses and support staff do have positive feelings about the medical staff with whom they work, or they wouldn't remain long at those institutions. One of the central keys in rewarding our champions is to transition the effort from an occasional occurrence to a consistently executed behavior. Physicians can also be helpful in this regard, particularly as they utilize consultants.

> Mr. Jamison, I've asked Dr. Lamberti and his team to come
> by and see you. Dr. Lamberti is a pulmonologist for whom
> I have great respect and admiration. He will examine you and
> his recommendations will be very helpful to us in
> coordinating your care.

In our experience, this aspect of culture is contagious. The more nurses and physicians begin to manage up and recognize each other, the more rapidly progress is accelerated. But perhaps most importantly, we have found that medical staff and employee satisfaction both improve, usually dramatically, once this culture of regarding your champions takes hold. One comment we heard recently from a medical staff member illustrates this:

> You know, we all do a difficult but rewarding job. However,
> lately, when I get in my car to head home at night from the
> hospital, I always seem to have a smile on my face, because I
> know the people I work with appreciate what I do.

Working with physicians as partners and establishing a new paradigm in which to practice are among the most challenging issues we have to face in improving flow, since they constitute a truly rate-limiting step toward progress. However, once this new partnership is created and embraced, particularly by the innovators and early adopters, our experience—and that of countless others—is that a catalytic reaction occurs and the pace of positive change accelerates dramatically.

CHAPTER 7

EMERGENCY DEPARTMENT FLOW: THE HOSPITAL'S FRONT DOOR

Several critical observations lead to the assumption that the Emergency Department (ED) is perhaps the most important place to put both the flow toolkit and the principles of evidence-based leadership to work:

1. Emergency Departments are busier than ever, due to general population increases *and* fewer EDs.

2. Patients are older, sicker, and more complex than they have ever been.

3. Shortages of emergency physicians and experienced ED nurses are a widespread reality.

4. For many EDs, the boarding of patients awaiting hospital beds effectively "cuts EDs down in size" by one-third to one-half, using beds and nurses intended for incoming ED patients.

5. Patient safety (Litvak, et al. 2002) and patient satisfaction (Figure 7.1) decline as ED delays increase. Staff satisfaction declines as well, leading to burnout in ED staff members.

All of these facts, which are well known to your ED staff, make the application of the principles of hardwiring patient flow and implementation of the Flow Toolkit essential, since the Emergency Department is the hospital's front door to the community.

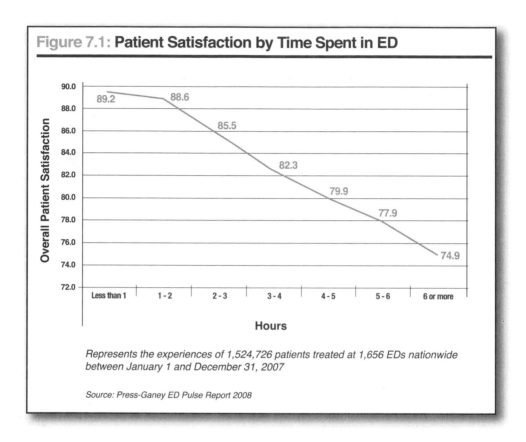

Figure 7.1: **Patient Satisfaction by Time Spent in ED**

Represents the experiences of 1,524,726 patients treated at 1,656 EDs nationwide between January 1 and December 31, 2007

Source: Press-Ganey ED Pulse Report 2008

We have observed that patient satisfaction decreases in inverse proportion to the amount of time patients spend in the ED (see Figure 7.1). We have observed that staff satisfaction decreases and staff burnout increases as waiting times and ED crowding increase. There is another, darker observation: A crowded waiting room may be the most dangerous place in the hospital, filled with ill or potentially seriously ill patients who are in too many cases unattended and poorly monitored.

Are waits and delays inevitable? The answer is "no." But making sure they don't happen in your ED and your healthcare system depends on implementing processes and improvements based on the principles outlined in Chapters 1 and 2 for improving flow. In this chapter, we will look specifically at strategies for improving flow in the Emergency Department.

WHERE TO BEGIN: THE FRONT DOOR DRIVES FLOW

As the point of entry for the largest number of patients—the hospital's front door—the ED is a critical part of the healthcare system and a logical place to begin working on improving flow. To achieve excellent performance, there must be a focused strategic vision for the Emergency Department and for the team. As we have observed repeatedly: The front door drives flow. For a typical ED, approximately 75 percent of patients are ambulatory and present to the triage area, with the remaining 25 percent coming by ambulance or helicopter. Those who present to the triage area are generally less acutely ill or injured than those who come by ambulance—and are, paradoxically, more challenging to please.

The "front door" not only drives flow, it drives the perception of flow. Stop and think. What images come to your mind about your department? What do your patients think about your ED? What do your healthcare team members think about your department? As a practical step, spend two to four hours in the department as a "flow detective" or "flow anthropologist" (as we noted in Chapter 3), simply observing processes and people as the ED goes about its work. You will undoubtedly note that some of the processes you observe are different in action than in design. Recall Chris Argyris's concept of the espoused theory versus the theory in action discussed in Chapter 2. Pay particular attention to the dissonance between what you thought was happening and what is actually happening. Understand how your system really works. When observing and analyzing recurrent process and performance problems, remember our lesson from Chapter 2: The system was (and is) perfectly designed to produce precisely the results it produces. What part of your system needs redesigning to avoid these problems? Leader rounding will help identify what works well—the what, the why, the how, and the who. During the first three to four weeks of redesigning your ED's systems and processes, focus groups from every section within the department should meet to discuss the department, analyzing what works as well as what doesn't. (We readily admit that it is far easier to focus on the shortcomings of a system than it is to appreciate the positives. Appreciative inquiry is seldom "hardwired" into our healthcare genes.) Your staff members have worthy ideas about how to improve processes, but they are seldom asked in an organized and productive way for their operational and performance insights. This is leader rounding at its best and most fundamental. Administrators should round with day, evening, and night nurses, lab personnel, X-ray personnel—in short, all of the key members of the patient-care team. After a short period (e.g., a month) of such information gathering, your team should have an abundance of useful information to begin making changes. As W. Edwards Deming observed long ago, the people who actually do the work often have the best ideas on how to make things better. An ED can frequently be turned around based on implementing and reliably executing what people already know.

The strategic vision you develop for your department requires a clear set of goals everyone can see, feel, understand, believe, and rally around. Whatever your vision for your Emergency Department is, team leaders need to articulate it clearly and motivate everyone to achieve it. If team members have conflicting visions of success, trouble lies ahead. Once you have defined the vision clearly, make sure your hospital and healthcare system as a whole sees the ED as a key component of your healthcare delivery system. Conveying this point should not be difficult: Typically the ED accounts for 50 percent of the inpatient admissions, 75 percent of the plain radiographs, and 50 percent of the CT scans and ultrasounds in the entire hospital. The ED is a major "supplier" of patients and a major "customer" of services and should be treated as such by every other department.

Once you have defined the goals for your Emergency Department and once these goals are recognized and validated within your healthcare system, hold people on your team accountable to the goals. Measure and monitor your results—how you are actually performing—and create improvement over time. By the way, *improvement* to many people means adding more staff, adding more space, or adding more information technology systems. To leaders, it should mean starting with the creation of better processes and making better use of your people.

DESIGNING THE PROCESS

Once you have done the analysis, defined the vision, and set the goals, what comes next? Start by marrying theory with concrete ideas, and then test changes to your processes—on a small scale at first. This will help determine whether a change, in fact, improves your ED's performance. A test involves a real change in operations or performance. Meeting with leaders, collecting data, and developing guidelines are important, but these are not tests of change. In devising a test, three questions should guide evaluation of potential actions: Are they easy or difficult to carry out? Are they high-impact or low-impact improvements? Do they increase value and decrease waste as our patients move through the service transitions and queues in our systems? Patient flow goals should always govern the planning and evaluation of actions. Each test should include a timeline, a team leader, and measures of effectiveness (performance measures) of the change.

Where do you start testing changes? If we look at patient flow as a system, we see that as in any system there are inputs, throughputs, and outputs. In the Emergency Department, the inputs are patients coming into the ED, either by ambulance or through triage. The outputs are discharged patients or those admitted to the hospital or transferred to another hospital. Focusing on throughputs might seem the natural place to leverage efforts to improve and optimize flow. For the ED, the biggest opportunities to affect patient flow are actually at the front end and the back end of the ED. If you are a member of the Emergency Department performance improvement (PI) team, the logical place to start is at the beginning, the front end—this is where the ED, as a department and as a team, has the most control and influence over patient flow, resources, and service. If your patient flow needs and opportunities are greater at the back end of your ED, you have to appreciate that you have less local control and influence over this part of your care delivery system. *Improvements in patient flow and admissions on the back end of the ED require a focused multidisciplinary approach and significant input and support from the inpatient team members. If boarded patients occupy a significant percentage of your ED beds and your staff's time and energy, then this is a serious situation that must be addressed.* We discuss opportunities to improve inpatient flow and admissions in Chapters 8 and 10. We will discuss improvements in both front end and back end operations and flow in the following sections.

IMPROVING FRONT END FLOW

The goal of improving patient flow is to maximize service capacity—how many patients you are able to care for—without sacrificing quality of care. Here are six vital action steps to begin improving flow on the front end so you can work toward achieving this goal:

1. Measure your <u>patient demand</u> by hour and design a system to handle it.
2. Make sure your <u>triage processes enhance flow</u>, not form a bottleneck. Use a system to <u>segment patient flow</u>.
3. <u>Design</u> and fully deploy a <u>"fast track" approach to your uncomplicated patients</u>.
4. Commit to the "right stuff"—<u>the right space</u>, <u>the right staffing mix</u>, *and* <u>the right staff</u>.
5. Establish a <u>results-waiting area</u>.
6. Devise and implement a reliable method to <u>track patients and results</u>.

These six indispensable actions provide a compelling approach to improving ED flow, safety, and service, particularly when paired with the critical patient flow concepts listed in Figure 7.2.

Figure 7.2: Critical ED Patient Flow Concepts

- The front door and your front end processes drive flow.
- Triage is a process, not a place.
- Get the patient and the doctor together as quickly and efficiently as possible.
- "Fast track" is a verb, not a noun.
- Keep your vertical patients vertical and in motion.

- Patients who need few or limited resources should not routinely wait behind those patients who need multiple resources— regardless of how heavy the ED patient volume is.

- For horizontal patients, real estate matters. For vertical patients, speed matters.

- We want to be fast at fast things and slow at slow things.

- Flow occurs when doctors do "doctor stuff" and nurses do "nurse stuff."

- Good IT won't fix bad processes—and mediocre IT makes things even worse.

- Making people unhappy and then sending them a bill is not a healthy business model.

- Satisfaction does matter—for you, your team, and your patients.

Let's take a more detailed look at these steps and concepts.

Measure Patient Demand

The key questions to ask in setting out to predict demand are those we mentioned in Chapter 2: How many patients are coming? What month, day, and time are they coming? What services are they going to need? Will our service capacity match patient demand? Recall from Figure 2.2 that the demand curve of patient arrivals in your ED will match that of any other ED in the country—and you should know what your demand is going to be. To get specific numbers for your predictions, track data; understand when the department is busy and when it is not. Break specific arrivals and times down by chief complaint, triage assessment, EMS arrivals, Emergency Severity Index level (ESI level) (which we'll explain later), and ancillary testing and services utilization. Track data for the past week, month, or year. Track the demand for space, ancillary services, and staff resources. Once you analyze the data and understand it, you will know what resources you need by day, by shift, and even by hour. Evaluate whether your department is prepared to deliver the necessary services to meet the expected or predicted demand. Match staffing to patient arrivals, and match lab and radiology services to the demand for these services. Figure 7.3 shows what happens when physician service capacity does not match patient demand, in an ED with about 25,000 annual visits.

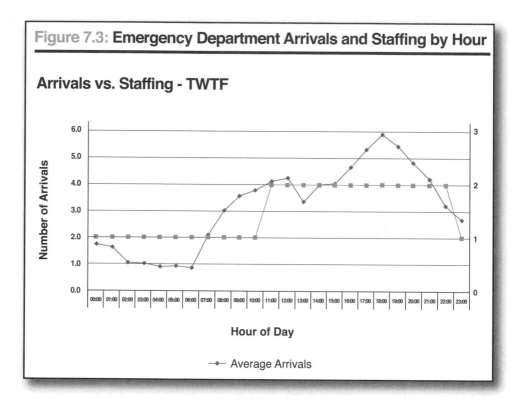

Figure 7.3: Emergency Department Arrivals and Staffing by Hour

Arrivals vs. Staffing - TWTF

In the very early morning hours there is sufficient physician capacity. There is a sharp and consistent rise in patient arrivals shortly before 7:00 a.m. to around noon, leaving the ED understaffed to meet demand during that morning period. Through early afternoon, staffing is about right, but then comes another jump in patient arrivals, presenting demand the physician staffing can't match—or handle. The patient demand and load is predictable. The hospital or the ED group has scheduled the mismatch.

When you have tracked data in detail over time and evaluated demand versus service capacity, you will have the tools you need to start improving flow on the front end. If there is a discrepancy between patient demand and service capacity, fix it. Do not forget to develop, in addition, a response plan for when demand unexpectedly spikes. *Hope is not a plan*.

Here's an example of what can happen when a hospital system predicts patient flow and adjusts accordingly:

Florida hospital developed a model for forecasting patient flow that proved to be highly accurate in predicting ED and admission volume. Using the results of this forecasting model, the hospital adjusted staffing patterns to follow the model's predictions, achieving a decrease of 1.8 FTEs in the new schedule. The patient volume required for the hospital to break even under the old process was 203 patients per day; staffing to meet the projected demand dropped the break-even point to 183 patients per day—which is closer to the actual volume.

Managing Triage Effectively: Triage is a process, not a place or a bottleneck

A critical point to realize about triage is that it should not be a bottleneck. It should collect only enough information to determine the severity of the patient's condition and which patient flow segmentation group the patient belongs to (see the next section). Triage should not be a substitute for insufficient staff, space, or services. *Triage is a process, not a place.* The prime function of triage should be to evaluate and expedite patient care, not to determine which patients can wait for care. Ideally triage should be a quick-look patient evaluation resulting in placement of the patient into the correct and available patient-care flow stream. *Ideally, triage should facilitate, and not delay patient care.*

Figure 7.4: The "Front End" Flow Cascade: A Portfolio of Programs to Increase Value and Eliminate Waste

1. Direct to room or "Pull 'till you're full"
2. Bedside registration
3. Advanced triage/advanced initiatives (AT/AI)
4. Team triage
5. "Supertrack"
6. A "Fast Track on Steroids"
7. A Level 3 "Fast Track" or "Lean Track"

Team triage is a concept first developed and implemented at Inova Fairfax Hospital's Department of Emergency Medicine under a Robert Wood Johnson Urgent Matters Grant. It is a part of the flow cascade (Figure 7.4), described previously in Chapter 4.

In team triage, several healthcare providers work together to promptly assess, treat, and discharge Level 4, 5, and even some Level 3 patients. ("Level" refers to ESI levels—we'll get to them.) The rest of the Level 3 patients go either to a core treatment area or a results-waiting area, a process that allows the ED to address any backlog of patients waiting for triage and care by efficiently sorting, evaluating, and treating them promptly and appropriately—matching resources and level of care to patient needs. Design and operate your systems to immediately assess, treat, and determine the bed and care needs of all of the patients who arrive at your front end, using ESI levels (or a similar triage system) as a tool or guide to effectively sort, segment, and distribute the patient load or flow.

Many EDs currently use a serial set of queuing processes: reception (followed by waiting), triage (followed by more waiting), assessment (followed by even more waiting), treatment (followed by yet more waiting), and finally discharge. Team triage adopts a simple one-queue process: reception, followed by a one-stage process of assessment, treatment, and discharge. This process can enhance effectiveness of the department significantly. With team triage immediately handling Level 5, 4, and many Level 3 patients, for example, EDs can segment, treat, and either discharge or distribute patients into a results-waiting room. This carves out 10 to 30 percent of patients who therefore never reach and never need the beds in the back of the department at all. Here is how one exceptional Emergency Department and healthcare system designed its triage process:

At Mary Washington Hospital, the first stop for patients entering the ED entails a combined quick registration and quick assessment.

Those considered Level 3 patients go on to team triage, which consists of an intake team of two providers (physicians or physician assistants [PAs]), two registered nurses (RNs), one paramedic, two scribes, and one patient-service representative/health-unit coordinator (PSR/HUC). There are five rooms for evaluation in team triage. From there, patients pass on to either a treatment area or a results-waiting area. From there, they are discharged.

In a team triage or patient intake process, the initial quick triage involves a nurse conducting a brief patient assessment: name, age, vital signs and a cursory history, focused questions about the clinical condition, and a decision on where the patient should go: Is this patient "really sick" and needing to go immediately to the high-acuity area in back? Is this patient really "not that sick" and able to be sent immediately to the fast track? Is this patient a Level 3 patient who might need treatment or testing and thus a likely candidate to pass on for a full team triage evaluation? Since the patient will receive a full evaluation after the quick triage, the triage nurse does not have to be absolutely sensitive or specific about the patient's actual diagnosis. You do need a seasoned professional who can quickly ascertain "sick" or "not sick" and act accordingly. *Triage is not a place for the inexperienced or indecisive.*

In the model team triage area, patients who reach the intake team receive a focused history, physical exam, lab or X-ray services, or intravenous fluids (IVs). The patients then proceed to the results-waiting area if they do not require further care or proceed to the fast track to receive further care from mid-level providers—e.g., continuous IVs, antibiotics, treatment of a laceration. Incidentally, one reason for using mid-level providers in the fast track is that (surprisingly...) one doctor handing a patient off to another doctor for active and concurrent management often just doesn't work well— the second physician wants a test the first didn't order, or vice versa. A physician handing off a patient to a mid-level provider, however, often seems to work well, though attention must be paid to protocols, roles, and responsibilities. After completing the care, the mid-level provider either discharges the patient or consults further with the physician. This model has produced excellent results at several institutions, including Anne Arundel Medical Center in Annapolis, MD (Gummerson, 2009).

Examine your current triage process and ask yourself a key question: Does triage add value for your ED? You can answer that general question by addressing these specific questions:

- Does triage improve throughput?
- Does triage increase safety for patients?
- Does triage improve quality of care?
- Does triage increase patient satisfaction?
- Does triage decrease costs or increase revenue?

Does triage add value to your ED processes—does it facilitate or improve safety, service, or quality? Answer these questions for your ED and its triage processes and make changes accordingly. One way to tell if triage is working well is whether it meets this key flow concept: **Get the patient and the doctor together as quickly and efficiently as possible.**

Getting People Together

Because flow depends so much on diagnostic and treatment decisions, a simple and effective way to improve flow is to get the doctor (or the mid-level practitioner [PA or NP]) and patient together as quickly as possible. The sooner they do meet, the faster and more effectively the patient will move through the department. "Introduce" the doctor and the patient as quickly and as efficiently as possible. Almost without exception, patients do not think their ED care has "really" begun until they see a doctor or mid-level provider. Look for and eliminate bottlenecks that get in the way of this process of "door to doc." By "introduce" we mean get them face-to-face and begin the evaluation and treatment of the patient. This illustrates why having a physician or PA in triage can work so well. From the patient's point of view, a perfect flow model would have a patient enter the department to find an available patient care room occupied by a waiting physician with open arms and a big smile. You may not achieve this model, but you do want to see how close you can come to it.

Improving flow is not the only benefit of getting patient and doctor together as soon as you can. You are not moving patients quickly just to drive flow; you are getting patient and physician together quickly for an appropriate evaluation. Doing so is the most effective way to handle patients, and it is also the safest and most satisfying. Patient satisfaction and safety both increase when patients see a clinician quickly.

Segmenting Patient Flow: Keep Your Vertical Patients Vertical and Moving

Levels and Streams

Let's discuss the ESI levels. The ESI (Emergency Severity Index) system is an approach to triage level assignment that includes an evaluation of clinical severity and resource needs. It is an effective, useful, and reproducible tool for dividing and sorting incoming ED patients into patient care groups.

The ESI system establishes five levels for assessing patients who enter the ED. This is one system we recommend for segmenting patient flow. Another is the Canadian Triage and Acuity System (CTAS). Whatever system you decide to use, basing your patient-intake processes on a good one helps smooth patient flow. Both ESI and CTAS distinguish five levels of severity. If you are currently using a system that has four triage levels, it should be sufficient. If you are currently using a three-level triage system, however, it is likely neither sensitive nor specific enough to improve front end flow, and you should consider adopting a four-level or five-level triage system.

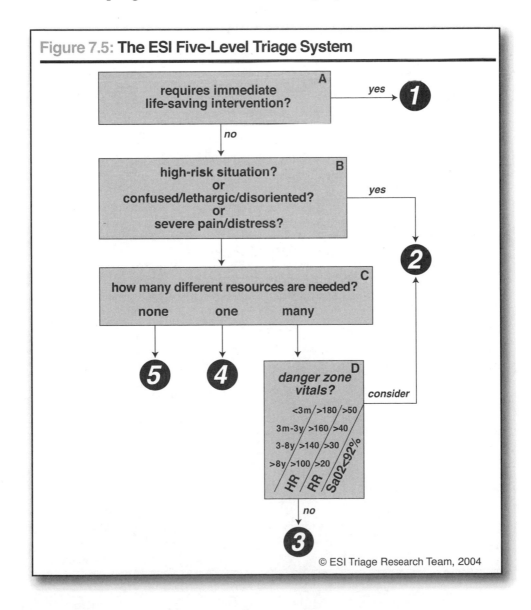

Figure 7.5: The ESI Five-Level Triage System

© ESI Triage Research Team, 2004

The ESI system runs the gamut from a patient who is literally going to die soon without an immediate intervention (Level 1) to a patient who doesn't need anything other than an evaluation or treatment by a physician or nurse (Level 5). Level 2 patients are severely ill and will require multiple resources; Level 4 patients need a simple X-ray, lab test, or injection. Level 3, as we implied earlier, covers a broad range of conditions, and so treatment needs can be more difficult to determine easily with a quick look. The great bulk of our patients fall into this in-betwen category: ESI Level 3s. A significant advance in emergency medicine service operations in recent years has been an increasing ability to "fast track" 20 to 30 percent or more of the Level 3 patients. These Level 3 patients, identified according to specified criteria, and Level 4 and 5 patients can usually be fast tracked *(remember that fast track is a verb and not a noun)*. Figure 7.5 shows the specific details of assessing patients coming into the ED with the ESI system. (Note the somewhat counter-intuitive nature of the process that the patients who require the most resources [Level 1] can be triaged very quickly, while it may take longer to triage Level 3, 4, and 5 patients. Despite this, the system does increase value for the provider and the patient by segmenting acuity and flow.)

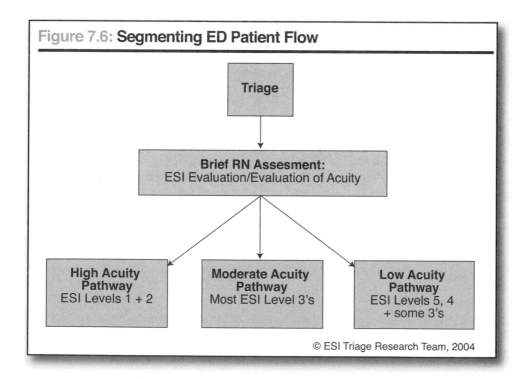

Figure 7.6: Segmenting ED Patient Flow

Triage

Brief RN Assesment:
ESI Evaluation/Evaluation of Acuity

High Acuity Pathway
ESI Levels 1 + 2

Moderate Acuity Pathway
Most ESI Level 3's

Low Acuity Pathway
ESI Levels 5, 4 + some 3's

© ESI Triage Research Team, 2004

Another way of thinking through the segmentation of incoming patient flows is to break patient flow into four incoming streams: patients needing minor urgent care (for example: sprained ankles, fractured wrists, simple lacerations), who can be fast tracked; patients coming for an urgent or perceived urgent medical or surgical problem who need a workup (X-rays, lab tests, treatment) but are identified at the start (90 percent of the time) as patients who will discharged after treatment in the ED; complicated medical and surgical patients who most likely will need to be admitted; and critical care and trauma patients. The second stream (workup and discharge) and third stream (workup and admit) present the biggest operational challenges to ED patient flow because they will require significant resources—staff, space, and supplies—and because some will be admitted and some will not. Patients in the second stream (workup and discharge) often do not require a bed, so front end improvements for this group involve triage, team triage, advanced triage/advanced initiatives (AT/AI), fast track, super-track, and results-waiting processes.

Whichever system of segmentation you use, examine the path for each segment and consider these questions:
- What are the essential steps?
  o How can they be compressed?
- What are the nonessential steps?
  o How can they be removed?

You do not have to make the process perfect for everyone. If you can improve the process for 30 to 40 percent of your patients, then you will improve flow significantly for everybody. For example, as we discuss in more detail in Chapter 10, team triage (TT) at Inova Fairfax Hospital reduced length of stay by 62 percent for TT patients but also reduced overall length of stay throughout the entire day by 15 percent.

Vertical versus Horizontal

An even simpler approach that can help you model and appreciate segmenting patient flow uses the notion of vertical and horizontal patients, as we discussed in Chapter 3. Vertical patients are—no surprise here—ambulatory, and typically they are well, younger, and arrive by triage. They are in the ED because they perceive an urgency or a need for urgent and accessible care. They could have gone a number of places—and they chose yours for their care. Those who can "vote with their feet" (meaning leave your ED and go elsewhere) often do—unless you make it easy and satisfying for them to stay. They value speed, convenience, and service—in other words, satisfying them mostly involves non-medical factors.

Vertical patients will not require beds for any length of time. If they need beds at all, they need them for evaluation, private consultation, treatment, or monitoring. All other time spent in beds for them is non-value-added time.

Horizontal patients, as the name implies, are going to need a bed. They arrive by ambulance and they typically are older and sicker. They perceive or actually have a serious or even life-threatening condition. They value speed, safety, accuracy, and preservation of life and limb. They are less concerned with convenience. Their chief concern is "Am I going to live?" or "Is this serious?"

Which patient group do you think is the hardest to please? The vertical patients are the least sick and the hardest to satisfy—and our patient satisfaction surveys reflect this truth. Which group do most of our patients fall into? The vertical group. Keeping these concepts in mind about vertical and horizontal patients can be useful in designing your system of patient segmentation and patient service.

A critical flow axiom in this regard is the concept from Figure 7.7: *Keep your vertical patients vertical and moving.* As we noted earlier, not all patients need beds; a patient should be in a bed only if it is medically necessary and only for as long as it is medically necessary—increasing the benefit-to-burden ratio for the patient and increasing bed turns. About 20 to 30 percent of Level 3 patients do not need a bed for long (and Level 4 and Level 5 patients rarely, if ever, need a bed for long). The difference between having a patient in a bed for a short time for a focused evaluation and putting a patient in a bed for the entire time they're in the department is a variable with a tremendous impact on flow in the department. A highly related concept from Figure 7.7 is that *patients who need few or limited resources should not routinely wait behind those patients who need multiple resources, regardless of how heavy the patient volume in the department is.*

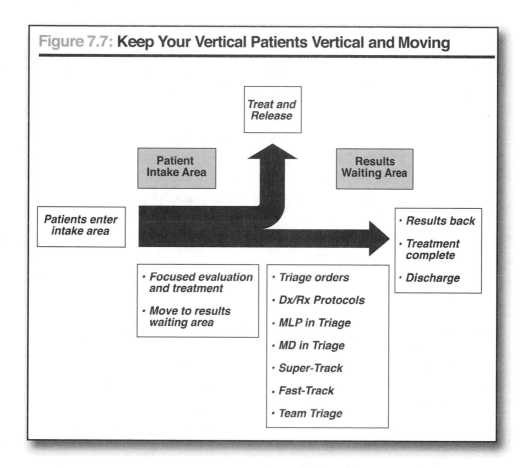

Figure 7.7: **Keep Your Vertical Patients Vertical and Moving**

Treat and Release

Patient Intake Area

Results Waiting Area

Patients enter intake area

• Results back

• Treatment complete

• Discharge

• Focused evaluation and treatment

• Move to results waiting area

• Triage orders

• Dx/Rx Protocols

• MLP in Triage

• MD in Triage

• Super-Track

• Fast-Track

• Team Triage

Bed Turns and Flow

Who is the most valuable member of your healthcare team in the ED? Physicians should shield their egos here, because they might not like the answer. Frequently the most valuable member of the team is the gurney or bed in which the patient is seen. The gurney may be the scarcest resource in the department and on the team. Bed turns are similar to table turns in restaurants, as discussed in the T.G.I. Friday's example in Chapter 2. T.G.I. Friday's goal is not to keep customers at their tables for as long as possible; it's to turn over the tables as fast as is feasible while still maintaining good service. Like a restaurant table, a hospital bed or an ER gurney is a rate-limiting server. As such, we consider it a vital component of patient care ("a critical server") and, in fact, a member of the healthcare team. It should not be a park bench for our patients.

Remember the concept from Figure 7.2: ***For horizontal patients, real estate matters. For vertical patients, speed matters.*** Consider: If the average length of stay in the department is four hours, then a bed can handle six patients per day. But if the average length of stay is six hours, then the same bed can handle only four patients per day. Part of the work and opportunity in segmenting patients is focusing on which patients really need beds and for how long. Optimizing bed turns involves asking these questions:

- Does your bed capacity match patient demand?
- Are patients in bed for the shortest time that is medically necessary?
- Are the patients who are in bed only those patients who actually need a bed?
- Are boarded patients or outpatients occupying ED beds?

If you increase the rate of your bed turns (and also engineer methods to increase the percentage of your patients who "don't need a bed at all"), then you significantly increase the capacity for patient volume—and improve patient flow. In building upon the strategy of segmenting patient flow, focus on whether a patient needs a bed at all and, if so, for what purpose and for how long. Keeping a vertical patient vertical or putting a patient in a bed for only five to ten minutes dramatically improves the metric of how many patients a bed can handle in a day.

Running the Fast Track

One of the most important of the key flow concepts
from Figure 7.2 is this one:
"Fast track" is a verb, not a noun.

Many Emergency Departments have chosen to create a pathway for patients with non-acute illnesses and injuries, typically known as a "fast track," although there are many other names used in an attempt to "brand" the area. But for those with a flow mentality, fast track is not an *area* where we see minor care; it is a *process*. It is something we *do* to move patients through the system more efficiently. Viewed through this lens, we can (and often do) "fast track" many patients, including patients with potentially serious problems, such as chest pain and trauma. It is the process, not the geography, that is critical. Nonetheless, this point does not detract from the fundamental value of creating both a process and an area where less acute illnesses and injuries can be evaluated and treated. The fast track primarily serves easy-to-treat patients, those who require few resources. Effective use of the fast track allows you to simplify and standardize the operational and clinical approach to patients who fall into this category. Your fast track is not a casual add-on or overflow unit; it is a critical component of your work to improve flow. A successful department can often treat 30 to 40 percent of its patients in its fast track (or in its front end processes as a whole—fast track, super track, and team triage). Devote sufficient space and resources, focusing particularly on the right mix of space, process, and people. Matching hours of operation, space, and staff to patient demand is critical: If the patient load is high from 10 a.m. to 11 p.m., then operating hours for the fast track should be 10 a.m. to 11 p.m. (or perhaps the fast track should open at 8:30 or 9 a.m.—you need to anticipate and catch the rising volume early, not try to catch up from behind). In designing your fast track, start with something fundamental: physical layout. Flow is affected not only by processes but also by how the physical space in your department is configured. The fast track should be in or near triage so that patients who need few resources can be quickly routed there and treated.

Your work in forecasting patient flow should have a specific component that addresses the fast track. You should know from effective forecasting the likely patient volume and acuity scenarios by hour of the day; this information will equip you to plan staffing patterns to match these scenarios. Often, mid-level providers can staff the fast track, with a physician consulting and technicians assisting.

We've talked about the fast track as one operation, but actually we can refine it and break it down further. One part of a fast track function can be a super track: a two-bed or three-bed unit, with a physician or mid-level provider and a technician, exclusively for ESI Level 4 and 5 patients. This unit often comprises two treatment rooms, a procedure chair, and a results-waiting area. The super track should be as close to the entrance as possible; cutting the distances patients and staff must walk for care and treatment reduces their length of stay in the department.

We can leverage the "fast track" mental model further by incorporating this design concept into processes for several of our other patient segments who do not match the usual characterization of fast track patients or who do not fit into the usual model of patients who are "easy to treat." For example, in the four streams of patients we identified, we noted that in the second stream (treat and release), 90 percent would likely be going home and so can often be routed through triage, fast track, team triage, and results-waiting. For the incoming stream of critical care and trauma patients arriving by ambulance, the ED usually has advance notice they are coming and what their diseases or injuries are—you have 5 to 45 minutes of advance notice, you know the patient will need a bed, and you know what resources the patient will require. You know (or could know) from your forecasting model how many of these patients are likely to arrive, what kinds of diagnoses they will present with, and how many beds they will need in any given 24-hour period. This foreknowledge allows you to proactively formulate a model and a plan for moving these patients efficiently and effectively through the department. There is a stream of patients, we noted, who have a high likelihood of being admitted after diagnostic and treatment administration in the ED. Three separate studies have found, in fact, that when an ED doctor or nurse first encounters and evaluates one of these patients, he or she can accurately predict whether the patient will need to be admitted 90 percent of the time. If your current process has such patients waiting four to six hours before getting a bed when you know fairly quickly who will need a bed and who won't, you could or should put them on a "fast track": Adjust your system and processes to move those horizontal patients through to a bed as quickly as possible.

Here is another way to go about "fast track" thinking: Four or five diagnoses probably account for 60 percent of the complicated medical patients in the ED. Examine each of those diagnoses and then determine how your system can more effectively move patients in that category through your diagnostic and treatment pathway. Doing so is "fast track as a verb" at work.

Here is an example:

A hospital's Emergency Department focused on the patterns
and processes for chest pain patients, identifying a key
rate-limiting step: obtaining cardiac enzymes. The ED
then changed its system to run bedside diagnostic enzymes.
Making that one change cut its typical evaluation

and treatment time for chest pain patients from
four hours to one hour.

Get the Staffing and the Team Right: Letting Doctors Do "Doctor Stuff" and Nurses Do "Nurse Stuff"

Improving the process design and eliminating non-value-adding steps are critical actions, but they are not going to be fully effective if you don't commit to dedicating physicians, nurses, PAs, and radiology and lab technicians to triage, fast track, and other front end operations and ensure that they function effectively as a team. You also need to commit to having the proper support services, tests, and supplies available in the front end. An ED team will typically have a triage nurse, a charge nurse or patient flow coordinator, and an emergency physician leading it. Working well together and communicating effectively are hallmarks of a high-performance team. Mid-level providers and technicians, as well as scribes or others in similar positions, complete the team, and you should ensure you have the right mix of staff, based on your forecasting and your analysis of your needs, to handle patient volume effectively at every hour.

Questions to Ask

In examining your current processes, ask these questions:

- Do a high number of patients wait in rooms for physician evaluations?
- Are numerous patients with test results back waiting for discharge?
- Is there a long wait from triage to bed assignment?
- Do too many people arrive in your department and then walk away?
- Does patient demand exceed physician service capacity?

If you answer many of these questions "yes," then you need to examine your staffing patterns and remodel accordingly. If physicians are a constraint, deploy the strategies we have we discussed in Chapters 2 and 5; substitute for physicians with PAs, technicians, and scribes. Streamline physician processes, eliminate non-value-added activities, or increase the number of physicians. If nurses are a constraint, follow the same thought process and execute accordingly.

- Recall from Chapter 2 our point about scarce resources. *Members of your healthcare team should be doing only the tasks that they are uniquely qualified to do; they should engage only in value-added activity.* Flow occurs when doctors do "doctor stuff" and nurses do "nurse stuff."

Clinicians should be making diagnostic and treatment decisions and managing the team and patient flow. They should not be entering data. They should not be searching for supplies. Flow occurs when doctors do "doctor stuff," nurses do "nurse stuff," and appropriate support staff does the "support stuff." Ensuring each core discipline focuses on their unique and leveraged contributions is at the heart of adding value and eliminating waste for the two most expensive resources ("critical servers") in your ED—the doctors and the nurses. So often in healthcare, when we don't know who should do the "paperwork" or transport patients around, we assign that task to a nurse. Why give a nurse a task that an aide or technician can do? Nurses should do the jobs that only they can do. So should lab technicians or any other members of the team. Look at job descriptions and think about unique and focused abilities. Refine each job accordingly.

Teamwork in the ED

An important part of managing the ED team is making sure your care delivery model emphasizes effective teamwork. An ED has many transitions and hand-offs; the better we can optimize them, the more smoothly patients flow through the system. The experience of one of us as medical director of an ED shows how much impact optimizing transitions and teamwork can have.

Under the original system, patients returned from X-ray to wait in their rooms. The X-rays were left on a shelf underneath the X-ray view box. Eventually I would notice that the patient was back from X-ray and would go review the X-rays. If our department wasn't too busy, this system worked reasonably well. But the busier we got, the worse this system worked—keeping track of patients' comings and goings was difficult, and I was often forced to ask patients if the X-ray was done or the labs drawn. For the patient, hearing this question from the person who was supposed to be directing their care did not inspire confidence in the team or in the system. So we adopted a new system. We asked, *Who is the first person to know an X-ray has been done?* Obviously, it was the X-ray technician. We trialed a new process—we had the technician bring the patient back from X-ray, as in the previous process, but now the technician would circle through the doctors' and nurses' station, take a bright pink, 4 x 6 laminated card labeled "X-ray done" in large letters, and stand that card and patient chart up in the physician's "to do" box. On average, we cut 45 minutes per visit for patients requiring X-rays. This means we cut 45 minutes from the visit of 40 percent of our ED patients. All it took to achieve that result was a clear hand-off signal.

See what that one move does for patient capacity: In a department with 50,000 annual visits, with 40 percent requiring X-rays, we cut close to an hour off 20,000 individual visits. We liberated almost 20,000 service hours for our department. You can likely gain significant results by similarly optimizing any significant transition with a hand-off delay.

Pushing versus Pulling

Emergency Department patient flow is like a rope: It works great when you pull, but pushing doesn't get you far.

One concept we use in regard to improving flow is pulling patients through the system. Effective, coordinated teamwork is a necessity for successfully "pulling patients through" rather than "pushing them through." Every person on the team should anticipate where the next patient (or "customer for their services") is coming from. In the context of bed turns, rather than have the triage nurse say, "I need a bed; do we have one available?" (pushing), the staff member coordinating bed use—and you do have a person coordinating bed use, don't you?—should look ahead and ask, "Where is my next patient going to go?" Lab technicians can go through the department, looking for the next draw. As with many efforts to improve flow, you do not have to achieve perfection. If you can improve your processes in this way by 20 or 30 percent, flow improves significantly for all patients in the ED.

Here is a practical example of the value added by using a "pull" versus a "push" concept.

> At Inova Fairfax Hospital, a flow team carefully examined the number of chest pain patients who did not have acute EKG changes but did need to be monitored and have sequential cardiac enzymes performed. A Chest Pain Short Stay Unit was created to care for these patients, according to clearly established, evidence-based protocols—an example of "fast tracking" them through the system. This change improved flow for these patients and created additional capacity for the ED, partly because it made it much easier to obtain beds for these patients. But one of the most powerful aspects of the program was the philosophy instilled in the nurses of the Chest Pain Short Stay Unit by their nursing director, who was passionate about pulling patients into the unit as opposed to having them pushed into the unit from the ED. As a result, the nurses routinely "patrolled" the ED, asking the nurses and physicians if there were any candidates for the Chest Pain Short Stay Unit and offering to get involved early in their care and expedite their transfer. The pull-versus-push concept created flow for the patients while also making the process much easier for the emergency physicians and nurses.

Waiting for the Results

You've probably guessed by now that the results-waiting area should be close to triage and the fast track. Its purpose is to handle long radiology and lab turnaround times without using ED beds for those patient waits. It should be visible, so patients are neither overlooked nor forgotten, and it should be designed with customer service as the first priority (see Maister 1985 and Jensen et al. 2007 for ideas on how to make waiting a better experience for patients). If a patient comes in with a simple ankle injury and needs an ankle X-ray, that patient does not need a bed. The results-waiting area accelerates flow by avoiding tying up a bed for such a patient. If the patient is quickly routed through triage to X-ray, and then to a results-waiting area, that patient's satisfaction is likely to be high even with a wait for the results. Making the waiting area a pleasant place to sit, with magazines or televisions to give the patient something to help occupy the time, will help keep patient and staff satisfaction high. And don't forget to keep patients informed about the probable length of their wait.

Tracking: Do You Know Where Your Patients Are?

The healthcare team needs to communicate among themselves, and to do so team members need the best information they can get. The more visible patient data and patients themselves are, the more likely your team is to succeed. A tracking system should make data available and visible. A "virtual patient care team" should follow a patient's progress through the system, with a technician or secretary monitoring results on a computer dashboard and guiding patients to "their next stop on the journey" when these results are available. The diagnostic, treatment, *and* operational data should be visible to everyone on the team, on their computer screens. Nurses, for example, should know when the department starts to back up.

By tracking various aspects of ED flow (cycle times for key processes and results) using a good patient flow dashboard, you can monitor patient care in "real-time" cycles as they occur, and everyone on the team can see when, where, and why ED operations and service become turbulent or backed up. Having the right information available in real-time allows you to avoid directionless chaos when the department starts backing up; you ought to be able to see precisely where the delays in the ED are building and you should be able to react accordingly by deploying the appropriate resources or improving the bottleneck process(es). A good tracking system should be able to serve as a real-time, early warning system that enables you to respond effectively to quality and performance issues. Continuous and transparent tracking of patient flow and key performance indicators helps with forecasting future needs as well.

Keeping patients visible also plays a role in improving flow, thus the importance of having the fast track and results-waiting area near triage so that team members can keep tabs on where the patients are. Simply being aware of where patients are and what stage in the process they're in is one reason a 25,000 visit ED often works better than a 60,000 ED—nurses know where the doctors are and vice versa, and the staff knows when patients come and go. If you do have a large department, you can split it into effective smaller units by having several teams rather than one large group. A team responsible for some but not all of the patients and clinical space, with well-thought-out "rules of engagement," a highly refined sense of "situation awareness," and using modern tracking methods can monitor and deliver patient flow effectively and be in a position to help out other patients and teams.

IMPROVING BACK END FLOW

Here is an enticing fantasy for an ED doctor or nurse: An inpatient admission is identified, a patient who doesn't need to be treated intensively in the department, someone who needs care that could be provided just as quickly and easily in a hospital room on an inpatient unit. An ED staff member makes a phone call, and someone comes by and cheerfully whisks the patient upstairs. In a perfect world, we would like to facilitate an admission as soon as we decide it's necessary. This scenario seldom happens in real life. But you *can* improve and shorten the process of admitting from ED to inpatient bed (and, if you are an ED physician or nurse, you can occasionally fantasize…). As we discuss in more detail in Chapter 10, at Inova Fairfax Hospital we addressed this issue by creating a system that proactively identifies beds for the next several admissions, known as Be-A-Bed-Ahead, which dramatically reduces time to bed for admitted patients.

Make no mistake—allowing the ED boarder problem to persist is a recipe for disaster. Two insights are important here: *If the boarding burden is a real but infrequent problem, a great deal can be accomplished with the critical flow concepts we have presented.* All the elements of the Flow Toolkit—reducing variation, forecasting, demand-capacity management, queuing, and so on—can play a part in helping the patients and the team "struggle through" those times when ED boarders are present. However, *if your boarding burden is overwhelming—you, your patients, and your team are in real trouble.* We have never seen an exception to this observation. If one-third to one-half of your ED beds are tied up with boarders on a regular basis, your flow efforts will, in our experience, be met with minimal and only temporary success. Simply stated, if your ED space and service capacity has been cut by one-third to one-half and you are still seeing the same number of patients with the same acuity, you and your team's efforts are best focused on attacking and solving the boarder issue. This is discussed both in this and in the following chapters. This is not to say that all ED flow efforts need to be abandoned, but simply that the maximum leverage for change is joining "The Boarder Patrol" in search of ways to eliminate or minimize this burden.

Initial Steps to Improve the Admissions Process

What can Emergency Department team members do to facilitate work on improving or solving the "Boarding Burden"? You should take three steps to kick-start improving the admission process:

1. Define the magnitude of your admission problem or opportunity for performance improvement.
2. Flow-chart the current ED admission process.
3. Collect data on the reasons for admission delays.

Defining the Magnitude of the Problem

Collect data on the length of stay in the ED for patients admitted from the ED to inpatient units. In obtaining data, try to record the time from the decision to admit a patient to the departure of that patient from the department. Also collect data on total ED boarding hours or other delays in the care of admitted patients.

Flow-chart the Admission Process

Gather four to eight people who are intimately familiar with the admission process from your department. These should include, for example, a physician, nurses, a ward clerk, and admission personnel. Flow-chart the admission process using markers on Post-its and paper (or computer software if it is handy) until those present all agree that the flowchart accurately reflects the current ED admission process ("the current state"). Then identify potential areas for improvement, including process simplification and reducing wasted steps or activities ("your future state").

Collecting Data on Delays

To obtain data on admission delays from the ED, monitor these delays for a month or two, or however long you need to obtain what you regard as a reasonably accurate and relevant sample data set. When you have gathered the data, identify the top three reasons for admission delays. Those reasons become the constraints that you should address first in the next stage of improving the process. Examining delays in detail can be revealing. The experience of one of us in an ED provides an example of what you can learn from taking the time to study delays in admissions.

We in the Emergency Department were convinced, absolutely certain, that admission delays occurred because nurses in the hospital's inpatient units refused to take admissions from the ED because they were busy and just didn't want to take new admissions ("more work"). In a rational moment, we committed to study our admission delays for one week. The results? Yes, 20 percent of the time nurses did not take an admission when they could have done so. However, 80 percent of the time, they did not take admissions because either they had not received admission orders or they did not have a clean bed. What a lesson…and what an opportunity to improve the process.

Having specific and accurate information of this sort provided an effective approach for improvements in the process, allowing ED staff to focus on the actual, and not perceived, causes of the great majority of delays. We even managed to develop a multidisciplinary approach to the delays with full participation by the inpatient units.

Once you have taken these initial steps, you will be ready to start taking concrete actions to improve the process. The next step will be no surprise to anyone who's equipped with a Flow Toolkit. Start predicting your admissions.

Forecasting Admissions from the Emergency Department

Here's another point that will not surprise those equipped with the Flow Toolkit: Admitted patient flow from the ED into the hospital is predictable.

Like many other aspects of hospital flow, it follows a mathematical model, a Poisson distribution. Analyzing your most recent admission flow history (start with the mean or median—a measure of central tendency—and then add an allowance for variation) is the simplest and easiest way to forecast flow in the near future. Here's how to go about this analysis:

- Gather a set of data.
- Stratify the data.
- Use the data to predict admissions.

In collecting the data, start with at least 30 days of data on your admissions by day of the week and ideally by shift as well. When stratifying admissions, do so by type of admission and number of admissions per shift and by day of the week. When you have completed these steps, use the results to predict admissions for the next day and week by type of admission and number of admissions per shift (or by whatever unit of time you find most helpful). Once you do start predicting ED admissions, follow up on the predictions by checking their accuracy. You can refine your predictions by working on how to make the admission predictions more precise and relevant by calculating the average and the variance. A further refinement is analyzing and predicting what units or services admitted patients will go to. Once you do have a forecast for ED admissions, communicate this forecast to the hospital's patient-placement staff. This forecast should be part of a general hospital effort to improve flow, augmenting a hospital-wide approach to forecasting admissions. It can be specific, concrete, and helpful as we'll see next.

Predicting as You Go

A general forecast of patient flow and admissions, based on an analysis of recent history, is valuable in preparing the ED for likely scenarios to be faced each day of the week and each clinical shift in the day. Each day, and each shift, the healthcare team should act and use the actual and predicted admissions forecast to prepare for and leverage flow of patients admitted from the ED. Figure 7.8 lists steps to take in this process.

Figure 7.8: Identifying and Communicating Potential Admissions from the Emergency Department

1. Have up-to-date information on ED patient status visible on a white board or electronic system.

2. Communicate with patient placement when the decision is made in the ED to admit a patient.

3. Establish ED board rounds to review patient status.

4. Based on board rounds, predict admissions for the next four hours.

5. Communicate those predictions to patient placement.

The communication to patient placement should take place within 15 minutes of the decision to admit and should trigger an established process for placing a patient in an inpatient bed. In setting up the "whiteboard" rounds (or board huddles) as part of your forecasting process, decide who should participate, how the team should conduct the rounds, and when they should occur. As we said in Chapter 3 about board rounds in the hospital in general, rounds or huddles should not take much time—2 to 10 minutes in the ED. The staff members present should cover key issues that will affect patient placement and factors that will expedite anticipated admissions, then assign and carry out tasks related to the decisions reached. Engaging in this process should enable the team to make a reasonable estimate of which patients will potentially be admitted over the next four to six hours and thus also how many patients are likely to be admitted to the hospital from the Emergency Department within that time. Having these predictions give both the ED and the hospital a head start on admitting patients throughout the day. Patient placement (and dare we say the inpatient units…) can begin to prepare bed assignments for patients coming from the ED.

Many hospitals have hospital-wide bed huddles in the morning; if so, an initial prediction of probable ED admissions should be given at the huddle. It should be based on assessments of the ED patient load at the time, as well as on the historical data you've collected, which should tell you average numbers of admissions from the department for the day and even by shift. The ED can and should contribute as well to contingency plans for projected admission demand-capacity mismatches. (An admission demand-capacity mismatch is when the actual plus predicted number of patient admissions exceeds the actual plus predicted number of available inpatient beds.) Examples of actions to increase flow in such situations are determining which patients meet what criteria for a specialty bed and considering what tests can be expedited to aid admission.

Making a Reservation

Some hospitals now are acting in advance on the admission predictions from historical data. In an act of pulling rather than pushing patients through the system, they are scheduling admission time slots throughout the day for ED admissions based upon historical averages and predictions. Doing so helps aid patient flow from the ED into hospital units, often preventing backlogs. The more information patient placement has from the ED, both from predictions based on historical volume and real-time reports and adjustments each day, the smoother this scheduling process will work.

Smoothing the Way for Admissions

In examining reasons for admission delays, we cited not having admission orders or available beds as bottlenecks. Here are some ways of easing such constraints, as well as smoothing admissions in general.

Admission Orders

Admission orders can be written. Admission orders can be verbal. Admission orders can be faxed or called to a dedicated voicemail line. The goal should be a refined and reliable process with minimal variation and delays. Faxed admission orders, for instance, can accelerate admissions from the ED. Department and hospital personnel should agree on the format of the faxed order in setting up the process; when ED staff make a decision to admit a patient, they should fax the admission order within 30 minutes, and once they have faxed the order, they should transition the patient to the appropriate unit within 30 minutes. "Bridging" or "Admit-hold" orders using a standardized template are another alternative. Again, the accepted format should be part of the process, and orders should be ready within 30 minutes of the decision to admit. An ED physician or nurse should be available to communicate with the attending physician. (The orders should suffice for the inpatient unit to care for the patient). We are not advocating any one technique or process. We are advocating a "no delay" (or "minimal delay") process. The goal here is timely, effective, and safe transmission of the orders and transportation of the patient to the floor.

Patient Flow Coordinator

An ED patient flow coordinator can play a significant role in smoothing the admissions process and improving flow. The coordinator should monitor flow in the ED and communicate predictions and admission decisions to hospital units. This person serves as the "air-traffic controller" and as the expediter of patient flow in the ED. At Inova Fairfax Hospital, this position is actually called "the FlowMaster." Teamwork plays an important part in setting up this position; the exact role, responsibilities, and authority should be established in advance and documented. ED nurses, particularly, must agree that the coordinator's tasks facilitate patient admissions to inpatient units for the position to be effective.

Ideally, the ED coordinator works in conjunction with a hospital patient flow coordinator or "bed czar." Here is where the real-time monitoring system discussed in Chapter 2 improves flow, with the hospital coordinator monitoring bed availability on the dashboard and anticipating patient needs for a bed—this information should be accurate and visible to all the key admission-process stakeholders.

A significant opportunity to improve flow exists with this position. The ED coordinator can monitor not just the flow of patients but also keep track of lab and imaging results and make sure they transition with the patient into inpatient units.

Other Admission Flow Tools

Other innovations can help make sure inpatient beds are available when patients are ready to transfer. Establishing a call center for patient intake and a bed hotline in which one telephone number (*1-800-ADMIT* or

1-800-One Call Does It All) and a limited number of calls enables the ED to accomplish all necessary tasks for transferring patients to hospital units is helpful. So is making sure admission and discharge criteria are clearly understood on the hospital units, with use of the admit/discharge criteria monitored and tracked and the units and attending physicians accountable for performance. Integrate discharge planning into the admission process: Plan discharges at the time of admission and schedule them, make earlier discharge rounds, and cooperate with housekeeping to coordinate how discharges and admissions flow together into a smooth process.

In executing transfers from the ED to hospital units, you can take several additional steps to smooth flow:

- Pull rather than push.
- Adopt common documentation.
- Centralize dispatch for transport and dedicate a team for peak times.
- Coordinate ancillary services.
- Use an express admission team.

Pulling means placing responsibility for admission on the receiving end. Once the ED has identified and notified the unit to which the patient will be admitted, that unit should take the initiative to move the patient into it. Having common documentation for transferring patients facilitates the transmission of relevant information and smoothes the hand-off. In coordinating ancillary services, make sure dietary and pharmacy requirements, for example, transfer automatically with the patient; standardize the hand-off.

Table 7.1 provides a chart to help you visualize the methods we've been discussing. In planning improvements to your systems, rank priority and projected starting date in the appropriate columns.

Table 7.1: Accelerating Admissions from the ED and Optimizing Patient Flow

Improvement	Priority	Start Date
Define the magnitude of your admission problem		
Flow-chart the ED admission process		
Collect data on reasons for admission delays		
Forecast admissions from the ED		
Identify and communicate potential admissions from the ED		
Facilitate admissions from the ED		

FLOW IN THE EMERGENCY DEPARTMENT: SOME OTHER CONSIDERATIONS

We have looked at specific methods for improving flow in this chapter. In working toward that goal, consider some general points as well. Remember our key principle that patients needing no or few resources should not wait behind patients requiring multiple resources? Team triage, a super track, and the fast track address that principle. With our patients requiring multiple resources, our goal is not to try to rush them through the ED on the grounds of patient flow. A 24-year-old man with a sprained ankle is a candidate for the fast track; we want to turn him around quickly. An 80-year-old woman with severe abdominal pain, however, may require four to six hours (or longer) to fully evaluate with serial physical exams, lab testing, CT scans, and perhaps a surgical consultation or two; the lengthy time and the services in the ED constitute value-added work in this case. *We want to be fast at fast things and slow at slow things.*

Who Owns the Process?

Nobody ever washes a rental car....

Teamwork in improving flow doesn't just mean an ED staff working together or various units coordinating their activities. Changing the system for the better depends on instilling the will to improve patient flow in both individuals and in the organization as a whole, and it depends on the wholehearted commitment of administrative leadership to the effort. You can gather ideas to propel the attempts to improve flow, but you need to persistently execute those ideas over time—often taking one to two years to fully optimize your key micro-systems. The will to keep working at the task separates the almost-improved departments from those that achieve dramatic improvements. Many EDs and hospitals will work on implementing new ideas for weeks, even months, partially completing the implementation, and then lose focus before hardwiring improved and reliable processes. The administrative leadership of the healthcare system must understand the necessity and benefit of improving flow and support the measures being implemented to achieve that goal, including commitment of adequate project manager time and resources and ensuring interdepartmental collaboration. Look at it this way: If you successfully address one issue each week, when you look back 52 weeks later, you will see a large difference in quality, safety, and service—with the added bonus of improved patient and staff satisfaction.

Anticipate the Big Disruptions

Naturally, no ED can plan ahead for every possible scenario that disrupts patient flow. That's unrealistic. (If life were completely predictable and manageable, we wouldn't need emergency rooms at all!) What we *can* do is identify the critical bottlenecks—the ones that we know set off a domino effect of disruptions and delays—and figure out how to anticipate and alleviate them. In other words, we don't have to fix every problem. We just have to zero in on the ones that will yield the biggest returns on our investment of time and effort.

A Canadian ED study, for instance, examined throughput time for chest pain patients in an ED and focused on what effect a major trauma case had on throughput for the chest pain patients (as a marker for global ED throughput time). (Schull et al. 2003) The researchers discovered that a typical trauma case disrupted or delayed ED flow for 90 minutes. If you're trying to improve flow and you know this statistic, you can log and analyze major trauma cases (or similar predictable time-consuming cases) and then plan how to handle them efficiently and effectively. For example, you can prepare a special team to deal with these cases and thus prevent system-wide delays. You can refine your patient intake and evaluation processes. You can arrange for limited and short-term help. (Please focus on the principles involved and not the illustrated specific actions we present here.) Preventing one problem (or significant delay) can help you avoid having to fix five to ten others.

A Few Final Thoughts on Flow

Several other concepts deserve consideration as we "pull all the arrows out of the quiver" in our attempts to improve ED flow. The first is a pair of related points from our critical flow concepts: ***Good information technology (IT) will not fix bad processes. And mediocre IT will make everything worse, not better.*** As we noted in another chapter, our friend and colleague Dr. James Adams has noted that, "IT is a false god in healthcare." By this he means that IT alone will not save us unless it is in fanatical service of continuously improving processes and flow. It is the use of IT, and not just its existence, that is critical in this regard. Mediocre IT, not just bad IT, does little except waste our time and distract us from getting to the real issue of improving services and processes, which will increase value and eliminate waste through increasing benefits and decreasing burdens.

Second: ***Satisfaction matters—for you, your team, and your patients.*** As we noted elsewhere, ***making people unhappy and then sending them a bill is not a healthy business model.*** Without question, the "science of clinical excellence" is the most important thing we do in the ED—and in healthcare overall. Nonetheless, the "art of customer service" is the most frequent thing we do in the ED and in healthcare everywhere. Furthermore, the art is upfront and obvious to the patient, while the science is much harder to discern. We must be dedicated to both, but we must never neglect the art with the excuse that we were "too busy" with the science.

These points about improving flow take us back to the situation we pointed out at the beginning of the chapter. Every hour you cut from throughput in an ED with unmet patient demand liberates the service capacity and potential to handle significant increases in ED patient volume. When you improve flow, you can serve more patients, with less effort, and you can serve them better. Quality, safety, and service are all improved. Improving flow is good for your patients and it's good for your healthcare team.

CHAPTER 8

INPATIENT FLOW: RETHINKING THE HOSPITAL EXPERIENCE

Hospitals and healthcare systems face increasingly complex challenges to smoothly running operations. Some of the challenges stem from conditions in the world at large: Across the country hospitals are experiencing demand for inpatient services growing at a rate not seen in well over a decade, a trend that will continue because of the aging of baby boomers and a steep increase in the general population.

TALKING POINTS: THE BABY BOOMERS ARE COMING

Here are a few facts to note about our population:

- Demographic growth is driven by the elderly.
- The 65-and-older age cohort will experience a 28 percent growth in the next decade.
- This cohort will constitute 15 percent of the total population by 2016.
- A higher proportion of patients in this cohort, in comparison to other age groups, are triaged with an emergent condition.

- One-quarter of Medicare beneficiaries have five or more chronic conditions, see an average of 13 physicians per year, and fill 50 prescriptions per year....

Meanwhile, hospital systems and communities have reacted to the excess capacity of a bygone era by closing hospitals and EDs and reducing the number of beds, leaving many hospitals struggling to squeeze patients into full houses. This straining against capacity limits has effects that ripple into further crowding in the ED and outpatient units. Furthermore, as more patients are managed as outpatients, the demand for ED and outpatient services and facilities grows. A further patient flow stressor on hospitals and EDs comes when physicians who can't admit patients directly into the hospital send them to the ED to gain admission. Another flow stressor for the ED is physicians sending patients to the ED to be admitted because they feel the patients get excellent care delivered by "an additional set of eyes, ears, and hands" (the ED physician and nursing team), including the expediting of initial laboratory and imaging studies as well as implementation of the care plan. Compounding rising admissions and high occupancy is the changing nature of inpatient demand: Medical admissions are growing much faster than surgical admissions, filling an increasing proportion of inpatient beds. And these medical patients are sicker and more complicated than ever.

Challenges also arise from recent conditions specific to hospital systems. Hospitals have achieved minimal reductions in length of stay across the last five years, in part because the "low-hanging fruit has been plucked" (the easy gains have been wrung out of the system), in part because managing disease(s) and clinical process is complex, and in part because attending physicians and other care providers often resist hospital efforts to further standardize care by maximizing or "hardwiring" the use of clinical pathways. While physicians do contribute in various ways to delays that build up, hospital processes themselves often slow patient care. Evidence also suggests that delays in patient care don't happen solely because of hospitals and physicians, but that a complex array of forces can slow the care of patients. And as we saw earlier, delays can cascade, creating bottlenecks further along the process of care. An additional reason is that some institutions simply lack the courage and leader accountability to execute the cultural changes in the physician, nursing, and administrative realm that are a prerequisite for improving flow. This is a key reason why, in our view, hardwiring must precede flow.

Smooth patient flow is a desirable but difficult objective. Complex medical and surgical illness(es), interdependent queuing networks, unscheduled demand, and multiple participants in the process all contribute to reduced patient flow and sub-optimized systems and processes. The symptoms of poor flow are not hard to spot. As we have pointed out in earlier chapters, problems on the front end *and* the back end affect throughput in ways that become noticeable. Barriers to entry can slow or stop flow. If an ED has trouble getting patients admitted into the hospital, a backlog develops that strains staff and creates long waits. This backlog can compromise the quality of care or cause diversions. Barriers to exit can slow or stop flow as well. If a patient is not discharged efficiently, a space or bed needed for someone else is unnecessarily unavailable; again, backups can develop throughout the system. Barriers in the middle of the patient's journey can slow or stop flow. If the ICU cannot transfer patients to the floors because beds are not available, other patients in turn must wait for ICU spaces, and patients often must be moved to less than ideal places because the system is not flowing smoothly—again possibly compromising the quality of care. As we have noted, patient safety and satisfaction and staff satisfaction suffer when flow is poor. Clearly, improving flow has become more important than ever.

YOU'LL KNOW IT WHEN YOU FEEL IT

We have described various components of flow and various strategies for increasing flow in previous chapters. But what does flow *feel* like? If we can see the effects of poor flow, we can surely feel the effects of good flow. An approach that may help is describing flow in psychological terms, an approach we described in more detail in Chapter 1. Some of the ways used to describe flow as a mental state are:

- Flow as optimal experience;
- Being "on the ball";
- Being "in the zone"; and
- Being "in the groove."

You are in the flow, as psychologist Mihaly Csikszentmihalyi has said, when the work is effortless. He describes flow as a mental state of operation in which a person is fully immersed in what he or she is doing and feels an energized focus, full involvement, and success in the process of the activity.

So if poor flow leads to patient and staff frustration, good flow brings satisfaction and the feeling of a good experience. Creating that feeling by capturing the operational performance required is our goal. If we succeed, our hospital is a more enjoyable and satisfying place in which to work and a more appealing place for patients to come. But we don't just feel good—we provide better and safer care, we treat more patients, and we bring financial rewards to our system.

OPTIMIZING THE SYSTEM

Many hospital systems that set out to improve flow establish a committee to identify suspected barriers to flow, then develop projects intended to remove those barriers and thereby improve flow. This approach often fails, for three reasons:

1. A project-based approach often fails to identify and optimize the true bottlenecks.
2. A project-based approach often fails to allocate sufficient resources—people, time, and money—and often can implement only a single project at a time.
3. A project-based approach seldom optimizes the whole system.

Often the committee chooses what it deems to be bottlenecks by looking at averages, reacting to a crisis, or adopting another hospital's flow project rather than measuring and monitoring real-time patient flow to determine what is actually a critical bottleneck affecting flow at a particular time and place in a particular facility. And as we saw in Chapter 2, working to improve activities that do not constitute a critical bottleneck does not add significant value to the process and therefore does not improve flow. Because hospital resources are limited, hospitals can work on only a few perceived bottlenecks at a time. Some may in fact be real bottlenecks, but working on minor bottlenecks when there are other, more critical ones tends to improve only part of the system and risks failing to act on the most significant bottlenecks—the bottlenecks or constraints that truly impede flow for the entire system. Optimizing just part of the system will usually not optimize overall hospital flow.

To improve flow in your hospital, you must differentiate three subsystems of the overall hospital system:

1. The administrative system;
2. The patient care system; and
3. The support system.

You must appreciate something about these three subsystems. The clinical care component is clearly the glamorous one. Healthcare shows are popular on television—but have you ever seen a television program titled *Discharge Planning?* Not likely. And you're not likely to see *Hospital Housekeeping* on the fall lineup, either. But these contributors to the hospital system are critical to patient flow. Where flow is concerned, all three subsystems are equally important. From an overall performance improvement standpoint, administration is particularly significant, because top administrators must fully agree on the need to improve flow, wholeheartedly support the efforts to do so, allocate resources, and forcefully ensure coordination among departments. The notion of coordination brings up an important point: Flow problems cannot be solved by any one department. The solution requires high levels of both cooperation and integration. A further point to consider is that you cannot simply install a solution. You can make use of principles, models, tactics, and strategies; we have discussed many of them in this book. But a perfect model that can be used in all systems does not exist. Success requires effective diagnosis of the problems and effective testing of the changes using multiple "plan-do-study-act" (PDSA) cycles (Jensen, Mayer, Welch, et al. 2007).

We will look in the rest of this chapter at some ways you can and should go about this process. Some of what we will discuss appears in earlier chapters but is worth looking at again from the perspective of the whole system. Some of the points elaborate on or look at different aspects of the principles of improving flow that we have discussed earlier. And some points apply to specific parts of the system in ways we have not discussed so far.

COMPONENTS OF THE ADMINISTRATIVE SYSTEM

An administrative model for optimizing flow has four parts (as illustrated in Figure 8.1):

1. A bed management process;
2. Real-time demand-capacity processes and measures;
3. An early warning and response system; and
4. Mid- to long-range forecasting.

Let's look at each of these concepts.

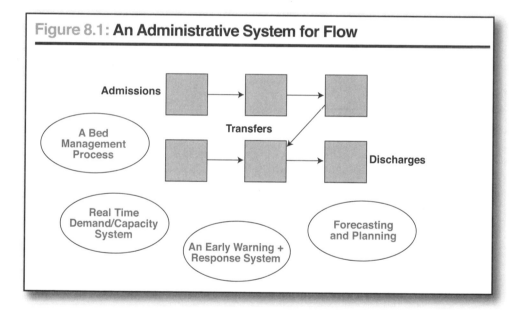

Figure 8.1: **An Administrative System for Flow**

A Bed Management Process

The goal of bed management is to efficiently transition patients throughout your system. A bed management process comprises the many activities that repeatedly come together to attain that goal. Examine the process you now have in place and determine what the critical path is to most effectively orchestrate and move patients through the system. What steps in the process add value and facilitate efficient progress along that critical path? What steps do not? Defining the critical path helps you see what steps are effective and which ones are not. Optimizing flow means eliminating unnecessary steps and inefficiencies.

Inpatient Flow: Rethinking the Hospital Experience

Increasingly hospitals are striving for more effective bed management through more precisely focused staff roles (a bed coordinator and perhaps a more general patient flow coordinator or expediter) and strategies such as bed huddles. The bed coordinator not only manages bed allocation but also the use of resources, in particular housekeeping, that affect bed management. Hospitals are also increasingly using technology in bed management—calls on cell phones, text messaging, and widespread computer networks, for example, can all make bed management flow more smoothly. Perhaps the most significant high-tech method, *when deployed and utilized effectively*, is an electronic board that visually displays bed status and patient flow information throughout the hospital so that real-time tracking can occur and is visible to everyone involved (Figure 8.2). An electronic tracking board offers the further benefit of a data warehouse that enables you to data mine and forecast demand based on ongoing bed management data.

In Chapter 10, we discuss examples of the successful implementation of bed management processes, including Inova Health Systems' programs Be-A-Bed-Ahead (BABA), which prospectively identifies and preassigns beds, and Adopt-A-Boarder (AAB), which decreases the boarder burden in the ED by having inpatient units take ED boarders and put them in their hallways instead of the ED hallways. What would be the reaction of the nurses in your inpatient units to a program like this? If your organization is typical, there would be substantial resistance—maybe even refusal—of the nurses to take such patients. This is a clear example of the necessity for leadership accountability. Clearly, our patients are best served by being in the right room and on the right team. If this best option is not available during peak times, is the patient better served by being in the uncarpeted, highly public hallway of the ED where she is cared for by ED nurses with no training or expertise in inpatient care and where there are multiple new patients arriving by the hour? Or is the patient better cared for in an environment where each of several units accepts one patient into its carpeted hallways where the patient can be cared for by nurses who have been trained and indeed have chosen to work in the inpatient setting—and whom they will eventually have sent to their unit anyway, once a discharge from the ED occurs? Without question, this level of change requires strong leadership accountability and team member engagement.

Figure 8.2: The InPatient Flow Dashboard

- Real-time demand/
    capacity monitoring
- Automates tracking information
- Forecasting
- Data mining

Real-Time Demand-Capacity Processes and Measures

If any one method is critical to making patient flow work hospital-wide, it is a real-time system for predicting, tracking, and optimizing demand and capacity. It aids both short-term flow, allowing each unit of the hospital to see exactly what is happening within it, and long-term flow, allowing you to plan to match capacity to demand. You must be able to predict at the unit and hospital level the capacity of the unit or hospital to accept admissions and the demand for beds in a particular unit and hospital, and you must be able to predict this demand and capacity in the beginning and in the middle of a particular day as well as reviewing your status at the end of the day—this process is so much more helpful and elegant than just looking at the midnight census. So you actually need to plan from three different points of view, availing yourself of the data you accumulate in your real-time tracking system:

1. Long-term planning—thinking months ahead, considering seasonal variations or individual day of the week variation;
2. Intermediate-term planning—adopting a length of stay perspective, thinking ahead over a three-to-seven-day time frame; and
3. Short-term planning—thinking and forecasting both admissions and discharges the day of or even the day before.

As you accumulate data and develop plans, you can take into account the current census, up-to-date predictions of admissions, discharges, transfers, available beds, the surgery schedule, historical averages, and so on.

Practically speaking, the most important component of hardwiring and optimizing hospital-wide patient flow is to implement a successful short-term—"day of and day before"—planning and execution process and a system-wide outlook on patient flow. ("We are all in this together, taking care of our patients and our people.") (Please see the IHI Flow Community and Seminar work for detailed information on the development and implementation of a Real-Time Demand Capacity [RTDC] process, with its attendant plans and adjustments at www.ihi.org.)

A caveat: We do understand and believe that if there is a gross mismatch between the need and demand for your beds and the available supply that sometimes the correct and necessary answer is more space and more beds. We understand that no matter how one tries to smooth operations, you cannot squeeze ten pounds of coffee into a five-pound bag. What we often see, however, are hospitals and EDs running at 95-120% of capacity, and hardwiring flow and optimizing operations can go a long way, if not all of the way, toward improving and solving the demand-capacity mismatches.

As you begin developing a successful short-term—"day of and day before"—planning process and capability, you want to work toward being able to assess at a given time during the day whether the demand for that unit can be met by the capacity of that unit. As you do work toward that goal, aim at being able to clearly articulate at some point, "Today I cannot meet my demand" or, "Today I can meet my demand." If in fact you cannot meet your demand with the capacity you have today ("Today I cannot meet my demand"), then you must develop a plan and successfully execute the plan in response. After you put the plan into effect, you can assess the results of the plan and, as necessary, implement a longer term improvement project to hardwire a fix or cure if this is a particular recurring problem or impediment to patient flow. In other words, you are taking steps in this order: predict capacity, predict demand, develop a plan for when demand exceeds capacity, and then evaluate the success or failure of predictions and plans. Figure 8.3 shows this process in the graphic form of a flow chart that simplifies these ideas.

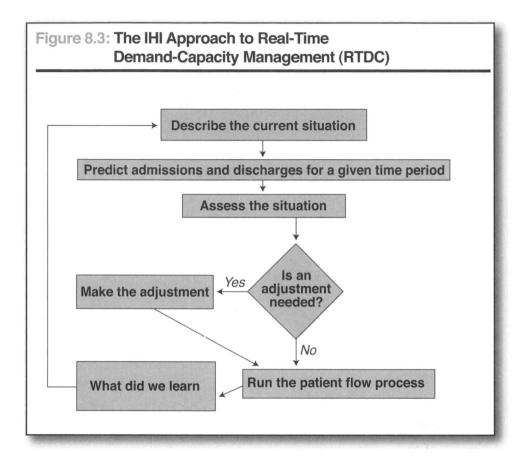

Figure 8.3: The IHI Approach to Real-Time Demand-Capacity Management (RTDC)

Remember from Chapter 7 the point that front-end improvements can affect flow dramatically? We can translate this concept into daily real-time demand-capacity management. To do so, match service capacity and patient demand in real-time for the first six hours of each workday. If you match capacity and demand in the beginning of the day, you can often eliminate or markedly reduce the subsequent buildup in demand over capacity; to put it another way, if we can smooth or optimize flow during the first part of the day, we can frequently avoid the overload that occurs later in the day. Smoothing (or load leveling), combined with the successful execution of proactive plans and adjustments, mitigates the "pig-in-the-python" effect and addresses the reality that you cannot store service time. Available service capacity at a particular time, if unused, is lost forever once the time and opportunity has passed. That service capacity cannot be deployed later during a backlog. Knowing when capacity will not meet demand (a demand-capacity mismatch) enables you to develop plans to successfully accommodate service demand, both for individual units and the hospital as a whole.

See Chapter 10 for a brief description of the successful implementation and desirable results of implementing a real-time demand capacity system.

Measuring real-time demand and capacity and matching the two may seem a discouragingly technical and arcane process, requiring specialized knowledge and trained personnel, but in truth it is straightforward, simple, and it happens all the time outside hospitals. Our colleague Roger Resar, MD, relates an example (personal communication) from his own life of how someone used trial and error to fine-tune a system of real-time demand-capacity matching using no sophisticated technology or techniques.

My small hometown in Wisconsin had an Applebee's restaurant that went out of business. In its place, a family who had emigrated from Eastern Europe opened a restaurant that catered to families with what residents of the area, many with Polish or German roots, considered comfort foods, such as spareribs and sauerkraut with dumplings, one of the most popular items on the menu. Now the restaurant business is highly competitive, and many restaurants close each year. This restaurant has succeeded; it is consistently filled with customers. They don't go there for hamburgers, and they are not going to be happy if they can't get the spareribs, sauerkraut, and dumplings. I (Roger) talked with the owner at length about how he manages the restaurant. He can predict how many people are going to order the spareribs and sauerkraut on a given day. Here's how: He started out with an estimate, and when he overshot on the amount he would need, then he cut back a little on his supplies—but if he cut back a little too much and he didn't have enough, then he raised his order a little, and he continued fiddling with this process until he knew that on Wednesday, based on the size of his restaurant and the hours that he was open, he would have to fill x orders for spareribs, sauerkraut, and dumplings. This owner did not have an advanced degree, but he's able to figure out exactly how

much he needs every day based upon the capacity and the
demand. Yet I can go into a sophisticated academic hospital—
and it cannot make a similar prediction.

Developing a successful real-time demand-capacity system allows you to
identify the true bottlenecks that you will need to address to have a critical
impact on flow. Equally important, like Dr. Resar, we have found abundant
examples of flow in many businesses in our own community, if only we can
open our eyes to them. Indeed, once you "catch the flow bug," you will be
amazed at how many instances you see daily where flow principles are—and
are not—at work.

An Early Warning and Response System

If you ensure effective bed management and implement real-time
measures to match demand and capacity, you will in large part have
optimized and perhaps even fixed hospital flow—your normal daily
operations will flow smoothly. No matter how good your flow process is,
however, large fluctuations in demand and capacity will occur. The goal
of having an early warning and response system is to manage these large
fluctuations on a real-time basis. To do so effectively, you need signals
that the system is getting out of control—preferably before it is too late.
(Remember that "trouble is much easier to prevent than to fix" and "hope
is not a plan.") Use the real-time dashboard we've discussed in earlier
chapters to monitor actual demand and capacity. Make signals highly
visible. WellSpan York Hospital, for example, developed a unit grading
system and a dashboard (as have others) to define three possible zones for
each unit—using objective criteria and measures and a green, yellow, and
red signal or classification system. Prominently displayed on the hospital
intranet for each unit to see, this process indicates current flow
conditions. Green means flow is smooth. Red means that a zone is in
trouble. Yellow functions as an early warning of trouble brewing. (See
Figure 8.4.)

Figure 8.4: WellSpan Hospital's Patient-Flow Zone System

"Day of" Early Warning: WellSpan York Hospital

Green Zone	Yellow Zone	Red Zone
Definition: Availability (Combination of the following): ICU, Telemetry, Med/Surg: Beds available to meet expected demand Patients in ED Waiting Room <10 Patients in ED Hallway: 0	**Definition:** Availability (Combination of the following): ICU: 4 beds Telemetry: Patients waiting >4 hours Med/Surg: Patients waiting >4 hours Patients in ED Waiting room: 10-15 or any patient with an ESI of 2 Patients in ED Hallway: 1-5	**Definition:** Availability (Combination of the following): ICU: 0 beds with Gridlock Telemetry: EAU/ED patients on hold >6 hours Med/Surg: EAU/ED patients on hold >6 hours Patients in ED Waiting room: >15 or more than 1 patient with an ESI of 2 Patients in ED Hallway: >5 Two or more patients who meet trauma team criteria in main ED or in shock
Notify: Hall monitors reflect "green zone"	**Notify:** Clinical director on call Administrator on call OOP Dept Chairman/ Service Line Leader Directors of Imaging, Housekeeping, Lab, and Transport YHLT via email Update hall monitors to reflect "yellow zone" status	**Notify:** Clinical director on call President of the Medical Staff All staff - FYI screen Put notice of "Red Zone" status on power chart Update hall monitors to reflect "red zone" status

Have contingency plans in place for actions based on those signals (see, e.g., a follow-up by WellSpan York based on their zone system in Figure 8.5). These are well-thought-out plans, developed in advance, *not solely developed as part of on-the-spot crisis management*. The relevant staff members should meet when they can think clearly, calmly, and unemotionally (i.e., a before-action review and planning process) and focus on specific conditions and the danger signals, and then agree on standard operating procedures to mitigate demand-capacity mismatches that would be emerging under those specified conditions. These plans should include guidelines for notifying others within the system. Problems *are* easier to prevent than to fix. Having a system to warn you of developing problems and then a plan already in place to resolve them enables you to avoid gridlock. Build in hardwired responses to soften or solve the problems associated with fluctuations in demand and capacity. (There is an important caveat in regard to this process: These should be plans that the hospital and staff fully intend to implement and carry out. Well-designed plans [perhaps we should call these "good-looking" plans] that are seldom or never implemented, or well-designed plans that have no chance or hope of being implemented or that rely on unreasonable expectations for help, resources, or behavioral changes simply breed employee and patient cynicism and foster learned helplessness on the part of the frontline staff.)

Figure 8.5: WellSpan York Hospital's Bed Capacity Guidelines

Green Zone	Yellow Zone	Red Zone
Actions: Conduct Bed Huddle Meeting at least every morning Care Management to work with Nurse Managers and Physicians to expedite discharges Prioritize Imaging and Lab tests for patients being admitted and discharged Administrative Coordinator (AC) has ultimate authority related to bed placement including all transfers/Direct Admissions must be approved by the Administrative Coordinator "One hour rule" for physicians seeing patients in the ED is enforced Floor nurses must take call/fax report as soon as the bed is ready. Patient is sent immediately AC and Housekeeping Supervisor prioritize rooms to be cleaned	**Actions:** Provide bed status update at least every two hours in the ED and huddle if needed Staffing expectations are increased to reflect 100% occupancy Send additional RN/LRN staff to ED to care for admissions/holds Initiate Team Triage in ED Deploy additional transport staff to ED Deploy additional housekeeping to ED and/or inpatients units based on priority discharge beds Open overflow areas Relocate non-urgent ED patients back to the waiting room while awaiting results of diagnostic tests (to free up bed) Consider admit to LTAC Contact VNA to bring in additional resources to support early patient discharge/admission avoidance Care Managers initiate rapid discharge review process YH provide transportation for discharged patients who need it	**Actions:** Continue actions initiated during the Yellow Zone Consider the need to go on Divert Open additional overflow units/beds. Urgent Care Center extends hours of operation Set up and staff discharge holding area(s) Transfer ED patients who require admission to Gettysburg Hospital or Hanover Hospital if they are not on divert Physicians to conduct evening rounds as appropriate Notify NH/Rehab of need to discharge patients in the evening Evaluate the possibility of cancellation of scheduled, elective procedures and transfers. Assess elective volume of cases for next three days

Mid-Range to Long-Range Forecasting

When you are starting to forecast, refer to the Flow Toolbox in Chapter 2 and use queuing theory, moving averages, and statistical forecasting tools to help you predict demand a week ahead, a day ahead, and throughout each day. As with the early warning system, a chief goal of forecasting is to plan for and respond to large fluctuations in demand or capacity. The real-time demand-capacity measures you've implemented will provide you data over time that allow you to understand what variation in demand you're likely to experience tomorrow, or next week, next month, or next season (i.e., during the summer, or next winter). You then develop plans to match your capacity to that predicted and expected demand. Compiling and studying data over time gives you a way to predict particular variation that is likely to occur every year, but at a particular time of the year (i.e. seasonal), not just week in, week out variation. Similarly, it enables you to predict fluctuations likely to occur on a particular day of the week.

IMPROVING FLOW IN THE HOSPITAL: SOME SPECIFIC IDEAS

We have looked at general principles of flow management and theories to use in implementing those principles, as well as specific methods to use. Let's take a look now at some other specific ideas hospitals have put into practice in various units in recent years to enhance flow that have not fit into our discussion thus far.

Hospitalists—or Hospital Medicine

Hospitalists are physicians (often internists) who operate a medical practice solely in a hospital, managing hospitalized patients, an innovation from the late 1990s. By virtue of being based in the hospital, they are often in a position to expedite patient care and shorten the length of stay. As the number of inpatients grows and the proportion of medical inpatients compared with surgical inpatients also rises, hospitalists are likely to become an increasingly valuable resource in managing patient flow. They are present 'round the clock, and their clinical expertise aligns closely with patient needs in a hospital. Administrators should not neglect another important implication of the presence of hospitalists: They are uniquely positioned to advocate and help implement projects to improve processes and increase throughput, an advantage facilitated by optimizing their workflow and aligning incentives. Intimately familiar with patient care processes and the complex relationships between nurses, other clinical staff, and other hospital-based physicians, hospitalists are, in fact, one of the best sources of leaders in flow improvements for the next generation.

They can also be extremely helpful in managing timely discharge of patients, which can be a huge advantage in increasing bed turns. As our colleague Dr. Robert Cates points out (personal communication), "Sometimes we don't need a 'hospitalist.' We need a 'dischargist.'"

Smoothing Discharges

Many hospitals have a policy of discharging patients in the morning. Yet in many of those same hospitals, most discharged patients do not leave the hospital until late afternoon. The discharge process is complex, takes time, and often requires actions by multiple members of the hospital team—nursing, dietary, pharmacy, and respiratory therapy departments, for example. Setting a policy to discharge patients by a fixed point in time is setting up a potential bottleneck. Multiple processes and discharges go on in the hospital at the same time, and the ensuing bottleneck creates delays and overloads throughout the system, from the ED to the ICU to the rehabilitation unit. Departments acting independently of the others and failing to communicate with them can compound the problem.

Here is an obvious example pointing to the need to coordinate the hospital's activities on a system-wide basis. Smoothing discharges involves some of the same tools we've discussed in connection with other activities in the hospital:

- Creating a pull through the system by planning for discharge at admission.
- Scheduling discharges so that they're staggered.
- Orchestrating discharges between the various departments involved.
- Making earlier discharge rounds.
- Arranging post–acute care services prior to discharge.
- Establishing partnerships with long-term care facilities and outpatient clinics to coordinate transfers.

Adopt a Boarder

"This is the captain. We're 23rd in line for take-off. Sit back, relax, and we'll get you to your destination—eventually." You may have become resigned to hearing this statement when you fly, but in the Emergency Department, while it may be common, it is unacceptable. If patients who are being admitted to your hospital but have nowhere to go are lining the hallways of your ED and occupy significant amounts of time and staff, then the problem of boarded patients is the single biggest problem your healthcare system must solve for your Emergency Department staff and for your patients. The problem is usually caused by flow and capacity problems in the system as a whole. But whatever the causes, a patient who is sick enough to be admitted does not need to be lying on a hard stretcher in the hallway of a noisy, brightly lit, crowded ED where privacy, sleep, and bathroom facilities are limited.

The cost of boarding patients in ED hallways isn't simply a crowded Emergency Department. If you have a 20-bed ED, every bed that is occupied with a boarded inpatient admission reduces your ED's productive capacity by 5 percent. Holding 10 boarded patients means that your productive capacity has been cut in half—you are effectively operating out of an ER that is half the size of the one you think you have. Effective capacity *may* be reduced even further, because these patients are often complex clinical cases and require a fair amount of nursing time and attention.

Here is an example of how the boarder burden can be made more "real" simply by using creative language to describe the situation.

Boarders have been a major issue for us for a very long time. In fact, we are seeing highly experienced ED nurses leaving because, as they say, "I didn't go into ED nursing to take care of inpatients." So we are also seeing problems with recruiting and retaining enough A-Team, high-performing, experienced nurses. On the latter front, we often hear the charge nurse say at the start of the shift, "We're working short today—we're down a fourth of our nurses." One day I arrived in the ED in the morning to find half of the ED beds occupied by boarders and was told there was little or no hope of finding them inpatient beds in the near future. As luck would have it, the hospital CEO

came by on leader rounds and I told him, "Bad news, Boss.
We're working short—half of the ED beds didn't show up
today!" He got it and a major boarder initiative was
launched soon after.

You get the point. When leaders are rounding, they are "closer to the action." This ED medical director found a clever way to illustrate a common point. Imagine if you closed half of your operating rooms and told the surgeons and the nurses they would still have to perform the same number of surgeries with the same quality and service standards in the same amount of time—with half the space! We doubt this would go over well.

Dr. Peter Viccellio has reported that patients who are boarded in the ED average one day longer LOS than patients who are admitted to inpatient beds. This difference can result in significant financial costs. In addition, patient satisfaction takes a nosedive. Placing patients in a hospital gown in a narrow hospital gurney in an ED hallway is not a recommended method for pleasing them. Evidence indicates as well that quality, service, and patient safety decline when inordinate numbers of patients are boarded in the ED. Data from the Joint Commission on Accreditation of Healthcare Organizations (2002) indicate that nursing errors increase dramatically when staff capacity is exceeded because of such conditions.

One solution is to house these patients temporarily in the hallways of inpatient units. Dr. Viccellio at Stony Brook and Dr. Thom Mayer at Inova Fairfax Hospital have pioneered the concept of in-house hall bed placement and developed the ED Full Capacity Protocol (Stony Brook University Medical Center 2001) and the Adopt-A-Boarder program, respectively. Placing patients in upstairs hallways can be an acceptable temporary solution. When Dr. Viccellio first implemented the concept at the medical center at the State University of New York at Stony Brook, he found that actually placing patients in hallway beds of inpatient units proved difficult. The vision of a patient lying in an inpatient hallway was such a powerful stimulus to the inpatient staff that they acted to expedite patient transitions so that a bed became available.

Hospitals that have implemented plans for placing such patients in the hallways of inpatient units have found diversion hours go down and revenues go up, processes improve, and hospital and ED staff start to feel like "we are all in this together—taking care of our patients and our people."

A Microcosm of the Hospital: The ICU

The Intensive Care Unit is an operational model of the entire hospital, and it is critical to patient flow. You can apply all the principles for improving patient flow and use all the tools in the Flow Toolkit in the ICU as you would anywhere else. Just for starters, here are some flow-specific points about the ICU:

- Use multidisciplinary rounds led by an intensivist, incorporating a daily goals sheet.
- Establish protocols for high-volume physician-nurse interactions (e.g., vent weaning, sedation).
- Involve the ICU manager in the morning bed huddle.
- Develop medical emergency teams to provide a higher level of care outside the ICU.
- Coordinate with institutions and organizations for end-of-life care.

Gaining Capacity without Building

One way to approach the issue of demand and capacity is to think in terms of working on your system's processes, so that as flow improves, your system can serve more patients and thus increase capacity without actually adding staff or building new facilities. The tools of improving flow all help in this regard, but a key one is to decrease the length of stay, through such actions as multidisciplinary rounds, coordinating admissions, transfers, and discharges, and optimizing teamwork of the staff. Increasing throughput often results in hours, not days, gained; in a time of capacity constraint, however, hours of delay can make the difference between manageable and unmanageable capacity.

Another way to look at demand and capacity within existing constraints of facilities and resources is the notion of shaping patient demand. Any steps you can take to control patient demand help in this regard. If you can preempt ED visits, for example, you can smooth flow to that unit. Here are some ways you might accomplish that goal:

- Providing adequate treatment and control of asthma in a community setting;
- Increasing the percentage of the local population who get flu shots;
- Improving outpatient services for CHF, hypertension, or COPD;
- Improving outpatient mental health services.

Smoothing elective surgical admissions, as we'll discuss in Chapter 9, helps in the surgical suites and units. Developing, implementing, and holding to optimal admission and discharge criteria and decreasing readmissions fall into this category as well.

LAST BUT NOT LEAST

We have discussed several specific principles from the Hardwiring Flow Toolkit in this chapter. Take a look at your hospital and its microsystems and think through how you can hardwire flow in your hospital. Don't forget and don't ignore the other tools in your toolkit that are available—managing waits, for example, and managing variation. The general strategies from Chapter 2 and the ideas applied within specific units, as discussed in Chapters 7, 8, and 9, can and will work in many situations. Remember, too, that in working to improve flow you cannot and do not simply install a solution. You observe and analyze, adjust and test, seeing what works and why within your system. Figure 8.6, based on the IHI Flow Community work, shows a workable and probably desirable systems approach to improving hospital-wide patient flow.

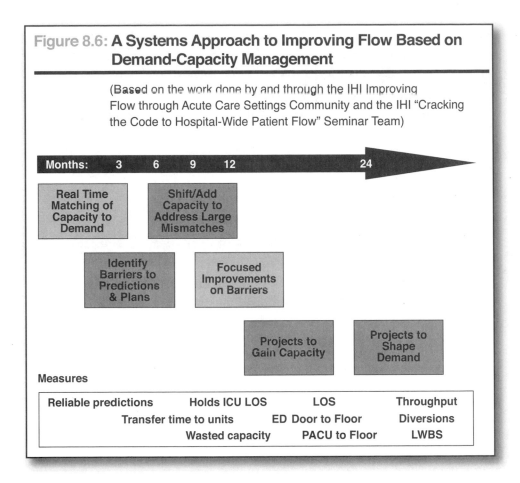

Figure 8.6: **A Systems Approach to Improving Flow Based on Demand-Capacity Management**

Finally, as you work toward smooth flow throughout the healthcare system, in all units, don't forget the lesson from Chapter 7 about improvements in the front end leading to improvements throughout the Emergency Department. In terms of the hospital as a whole, focused efforts on optimizing flow in critical microsystems of the larger hospital system will pay dividends throughout the entire system. So concentrate especially on patient flow in the ED, the ICU, telemetry, surgery, PACU, as well as the attendant hand-offs and transitions.

And never forget the overriding reasons for your work to improve flow: The most important reason is that it's good for the patients, and it's good for the people who take care of those patients. Your guiding phrase should be "the right patient, in the right bed (place), with the right team, getting the right care, at the right time—every time." Improving flow may involve dealing with current conditions that cause patient dissatisfaction and low staff morale, but you should approach improving these conditions from a positive perspective, not a negative one. As Peter Drucker has noted in *The Effective Executive*, focus on the opportunities rather than on the problems. And always remember the importance of teamwork. We want commitment and not just compliance. As Harry Truman observed, "It is amazing what you can accomplish if you do not care who gets the credit."

CHAPTER 9

SURGICAL FLOW

Flow—You stop "thinking" and just do. "Go with the flow." "In the zone." We know what that feels like, and we strive for or hope to achieve it on a daily basis. What happens when flow in a surgical unit is not achieved? What happens when flow in a surgical unit is not well managed? If a unit is characterized by variations in processes, a lack of reliable forecasting, an absence of planning, and inefficient processes, the result is unreliable matching of patient demand and service capacity and thus unreliable predictions of staffing needs, including probable overtime. The operating room experiences peaks and valleys. The unit swings from unused ORs and beds to overcapacity and patient diversions. Patients experience delays in care. Surgeries get postponed. Competition springs up for staffing, beds, and equipment. Accordingly, satisfaction declines for staff and patients, and eventually surgical throughput and hospital throughput decrease, as does revenue, while boarded patients overflow the postanesthesia care unit (PACU), and deferred surgeries and perhaps surgical errors increase.

Consider a couple of observations in connection with the scenarios just described. For the most part, our surgical patients are scheduled in advance, and they arrive on time. We have them come in early, after all, just in case. Physicians, nurses, and support staff all know the schedule. The surgeries are scheduled, we know when the patients will arrive, and they do—and we can't get started on time. We hear various reasons why we can't: "The surgeons don't get here on time." "Well, our OR start times are posted on our schedule, but everyone knows they aren't that accurate—they're more suggestions than a schedule."

If the scenario we've described applies to your hospital's surgical unit, the good news is you can take steps to improve. You can address issues within your processes, refine those processes, and optimize them, using your Flow Toolkit. You can identify inconsistencies in your scheduling process, recognize and plan for variation in surgical case length, and zero-in on inefficiencies in coordination of placement and scheduling for patients who need to be admitted. In this chapter, we'll look at some of the tools you can use to improve flow in your surgical unit.

KEY PRINCIPLES FOR SURGICAL FLOW

Here's a crucial point: Patient flow is predictable. Sound familiar? We keep coming back to it, because it underlies improvement to patient flow in any unit of the hospital. As we said earlier in a mathematical moment, elective surgeries are planned for and scheduled, and emergency surgery follows a Poisson distribution. And we return again to the same questions, which you should ask yourself in the surgical unit: How many patients are coming? When are they coming—by time of day, day of week, month of year? What services are they going to need? Is our service capacity going to match patient demand? Go back to the demand-capacity management principles discussed in Chapter 3: Match service capacity to patient demand; implement a real-time dashboard; measure real-time demand and capacity and once you've measured them continue to monitor them; establish predetermined triggers for effective back-up plans; predict demand based on historical data.

With your Flow Toolkit ready, focus on these key principles for surgical flow redesign:

- The goal is to optimize surgical throughput for all patients, not just for one surgical patient segment or for one surgeon, group, or specialty.
- Start time should not be a bottleneck.
- Patients who need few resources (simple cases) should not routinely wait behind patients who need many resources (complex or difficult cases).

- Improving your processes on the front end of the OR will help identify significant throughput bottlenecks.
- Focus on improving processes at the front end of the OR and throughput bottlenecks under your control or influence, and there is much you can accomplish to hardwire surgical patient flow.

You should focus on both OR processes and perioperative processes to optimize flow in the surgical unit. Figure 9.1 lists the primary methods to achieve this goal; the following sections discuss them in detail, and then we consider several other issues as well.

Figure 9.1: Tactics for Optimizing Surgical Flow

1. Prepare a complete and timely preoperative work-up

2. Clearly define the start time

3. Start on time

4. Plan for and accommodate variances
    in surgical case length

5. Install "air-traffic control": Use an RN
    perioperative facilitator

6. Ensure reliable and effective scheduling of and
    communication with surgeons

7. Plan for and manage surgical cases with
    unpredictable lengths

8. Refine postoperative patient placement

A Complete and Timely Preoperative Work-up

Starting on time is key to the entire effort, and one of the first steps to make sure you do start on time is to fully complete the preoperative work-up well before that start time. Not only should the work-up itself be completed well in advance, your processes should ensure that results are available and communicated to critical members of the surgical team comfortably in advance as well. Tests and work-ups need to be scheduled and performed, and the resulting information needs to be distributed to and acted upon by key members of the team. You have to pay attention and coordinate the flow of tasks and information to ensure optimized and reliable perioperative and postoperative processes. Incomplete work-ups are a significant and common reason for delayed surgical starts. Delayed starts, in turn, adversely affect not only the OR schedule as a whole but other processes of the surgical unit as well.

Achieving the goal of complete and timely work-ups requires team coordination. Surgeons and anesthesiologists need to agree on preoperative testing and service protocols at the outset. Surgeons should order tests as soon as the decision is made for surgery and follow established and agreed-upon protocols—and only the necessary tests should be ordered. Surgeons should have available pre-printed preoperative order forms; those forms should direct the test site to forward results immediately. Once results are in, the surgical team should review them immediately and take any necessary follow-up actions at least two to four days before scheduled surgery.

Make sure you assign anesthesia staff to the OR to help plan start times, and build anesthesia preparation time into your preoperative processes. Again, teamwork is essential; coordinate the exchange of information between anesthesiologists and surgeons.

A Clearly Defined Start Time

If starting on time is key, then one preliminary step is essential. Everyone involved in the surgery must agree on a point in time that they can all recognize clearly. That point is defined not by an arbitrary setting of hour and minute but by an action: the incision. The start time should be the moment when the incision is planned. It is a definitive point that everyone can recognize and work around, and everyone should understand clearly that no surgical instrument touches the patient until all preoperative work has been completed and surgery is ready to begin. Not only does using the incision time ensure smoother flow, it helps ensure patient safety. When you're confident your team has completed all processes, you can be confident the patient is properly anesthetized and ready for surgery—and it can proceed safely.

In setting the incision time, you should take into account process variation—which can and should be predicted by your analysis of historical operative and surgical flow data. Once you set the time, communicate it to everyone involved. Post the time in the OR as the scheduled start time.

An On-Time Start

What is the number one issue in placing to-be-admitted surgical patients? Delayed start times in the OR. They affect not only the OR schedule but every part of surgical flow. Pick a typical case and ask the staff in your OR what the start time is and see what answers you get. What's posted on the schedule may not be what everyone is thinking.

If you've taken the steps outlined already in this section, you'll be ready to work on ensuring the start times. Coordinate the team to work backward from the incision time—the real start time—in the various processes that need to happen before the surgery can begin. Synchronize all perioperative processes to end before that start time; account, for example, for preoperative preparation of the patient and the room, preparation of equipment, and briefings. Standardize room setup and prepare commonly used drugs, equipment, and supplies in advance. By standardizing advance preparation, you'll avoid last-minute discovery of missing supplies. OR staff members should work together to determine the best processes for room setup for different kinds of cases. You should periodically review the procedures at staff meetings to make sure they remain current and remain the best way to proceed.

Say you want to make your incision at 10:30 a.m. Figure 9.2 outlines a timeline encompassing some of the primary stages before the surgery can begin.

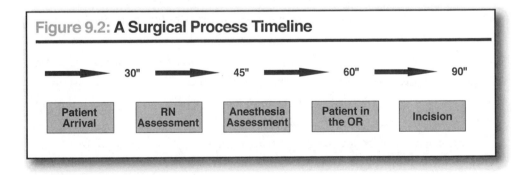

Figure 9.2: A Surgical Process Timeline

The time intervals in the figure show in each case the time from the patient's arrival before that action needs to be completed or when the action will happen. The patient arrives 90 minutes before the incision time, at 9:00. If your flow processes are well established, every member of the surgical team and those involved in the perioperative processes know what they need to do and when. Thus, the preoperative RN has 30 minutes from arrival to assess the patient. The anesthesiologist has 45 minutes; the anesthesia staff can come whenever they want, but they know that their assessment needs to be completed by the end of that 45-minute span. The patient is in the OR 60 minutes after arriving. Everyone on the team is in the OR before the 10:30 start time and the surgeon makes the incision right at 10:30. Goals and timelines are established, expectations are clear, results are tracked, and trended—what could be simpler or more helpful?

Variances in Surgical Case Length

We know from experience that all cases are not equally complex or acute, and different types of cases take different amounts of time to treat in the surgical unit, as they do elsewhere in the hospital system. This variance in types of cases and case length can throw off scheduling and disrupt flow if not planned for and managed. But variance can be managed effectively. Doing so contributes significantly to maintaining smooth patient flow; managing variance in case length presents an opportunity to maximize the probability of correctly scheduling cases and to minimize the potential to incorrectly schedule cases.

You will not be surprised to learn that effective management of variance begins with gathering your historical data and then analyzing the data in order to forecast future case-length variance. Your data gathering and analyzing will allow you to forecast variance in case length specifically for individual surgeons and for types of procedures. Once you are equipped to predict case length, you can schedule appropriately, including preparation time and transition time after surgery. As you begin to forecast, you should check that your information is accurate in two ways: First, ask your staff to assess it; generally, staff members can accurately gauge case length for individual procedures and surgeons. Second, continue to collect data and review the data periodically to assure that projected case lengths are the most current. This process is not about rushing patients and surgeons through their cases. It is about planning for and consistently allocating and optimizing the right amount of time for your surgical cases based upon your planning and studying your surgeons and case mix. Take one final step: Post the appropriate case lengths on the OR schedule.

One method to use in managing case-length variance is to stagger start times for first cases in the morning. Figure 9.3, for example, shows a typical schedule to start the day.

Figure 9.3: Staggered Start Times

Case	Starts	Room
1	7:30	A
2	7:45	B
3	8:00	C

Starting cases at different times in different rooms takes into account varying complexity and thus allows for appropriate preparatory time and staff availability. The surgical team should work with schedulers to effectively schedule cases in staggered time slots. As an ongoing task, collect data to monitor whether cases are being appropriately scheduled and starting on time.

Air-Traffic Control

The analogy to air-traffic control helps us visualize the role of a significant person in the surgical unit, the perioperative facilitator. A registered nurse should fill this position. Having one person coordinate the processes of patient transitions and communication among various people enhances optimal perioperative flow in the OR and preoperative and postoperative areas. The facilitator monitors flow, adjusts schedules, and coordinates patient placement after surgery. That person communicates directly with staff leaders of daily operations in the preoperative and postoperative areas and the OR; the facilitator circulates through all areas and carries a cell phone to allow access at any time.

Scheduling Surgeons

As critical drivers of surgical flow, the surgeons must be taken into consideration if you are to maintain effective scheduling. Surgeons are key participants in ensuring the reliability of your processes, as well as patient and staff satisfaction. Part of coordinating scheduling in general is scheduling individual surgeons in particular, incorporating the time and preferences on their part needed to satisfy the requirements and goals of your processes and using their personal historical data on case length. You should develop consistent scheduling procedures in conjunction with the surgical committee and assure that the authority to enforce those procedures rests with the day-to-day leaders of operations in the unit. Review any problems that arise in scheduling procedures in a predetermined format.

As part of flow, maintain communication with your surgeons; make sure you have processes to assure that pertinent updates on scheduling are transmitted in both directions. Ongoing communication among all members of the surgical unit, but especially with surgeons, is essential to effective schedule management. Schedulers should confirm surgeon availability for scheduled case times. Design the process so that surgeons provide necessary information to allow effective scheduling. Use simple tools such as forms, checklists, and preference cards to gather that information.

Cases with Unpredictable Length

You've carefully gathered and analyzed data, developed forecasts, and prepared schedules based on those forecasts. But what about cases whose length is uncertain? Won't this unpredictability throw your schedule off? It certainly can. Unknown case length—long cases, in other words—can significantly disrupt the OR schedule. If that disruption happens, throughput slows. The effect spreads beyond the immediate OR schedule to the admission of surgical patients. Flow is impeded.

You can, however, minimize this potential disruption. In addressing this issue, you have two choices:

1. Place cases with unpredictable length in a separate room; or
2. Schedule them for the end of the OR day.

The surgical committee should determine what procedure you will use to identify and schedule such cases, and the procedure should be in place to make your handling of those cases routine.

Dedicating a separate room for cases with unpredictable length allows your unit to maintain its schedule for the other cases with more certain length without disruption. Scheduling the cases with uncertain length at the end of the day allows you to manage your predictable schedule smoothly.

Refined Postoperative Placement

One of the implications of using principles from the Flow Toolkit—forecasting, demand-capacity management, real-time monitoring, managing variation—is that links fall into place in a chain after earlier links have started the chain. Realizing this implication lies behind our emphasis on front end improvements in the ED and OR. Your nonrandom scheduled volume should be highly and reliably predictable. You should be able to predict accurately when patients will be ready for transfer from the PACU to an inpatient bed. In light of these assumptions, you should proactively plan for transfer of postoperative patients to the most appropriate beds. One approach is to designate a PACU coordinator—this person could be the charge nurse—to facilitate use of the PACU and transitions of patients out of it into inpatient beds. A representative from PACU should participate in daily bed huddles and real-time forecasting to help identify needed beds for postoperative patient placement.

Another method for aiding postoperative placement is using admission and discharge criteria. Having criteria in place enables you to place patients in the most appropriate, safest, and most efficient way. Clinicians should determine the criteria for placement procedures; day to-day leaders of operations should have the authority to implement them. And again, you should establish a predetermined format to review any problems arising from the procedures.

SMOOTHING SURGICAL PATIENT FLOW

We discussed natural and artificial variation in Chapter 2. Emergency or urgent surgery is an example of natural variation; it is going to occur, and you cannot avoid it. Significant variation in your elective, scheduled surgery is artificial variation.

Hospitals must manage the natural variation, but they must reduce any high variability in artificial variation and smooth the flow of scheduled cases so that flow is predictable and steady. Actions addressing the two different kinds of variation can be interrelated. If you set aside a room for cases of uncertain length (managing natural variation), for example, you smooth the flow of elective, scheduled surgeries and enhance their predictability (eliminating artificial variation).

Emergency or urgent cases are examples of natural variation, but they don't have to disrupt flow. The schedules you have developed from your analysis of your historical data should have anticipated the volume and types of emergency cases. There is still another refinement you can make to your process to manage natural variation, similar to the one in our previous example. Set aside a room for unscheduled surgeries. Fully staff this room for prime-time hours. In placing unscheduled cases in this room, determine priority of patient need and availability of surgical staff. Managing natural variation in this way helps smooth the flow of elective surgery and make it predictable.

Artificial variation often creeps in to the flow of elective surgery through surgeons' preference for midweek schedules. The *Wall Street Journal* has called this widespread practice "one of the biggest impediments to a smooth-running hospital" (Landro 2005). If you can distribute elective surgery more evenly throughout the week (an example of load-leveling and smoothing surgical flow), you can reduce artificial variation and smooth flow through the OR and throughout the hospital. Achieving this goal takes administrative leadership, because surgeons must agree to any changes for them to be effective and to last. Leaders must work with individual surgical practices to alter scheduling practices to match predicted capacity.

The Flow Toolkit provides help. If you've analyzed your data, you will have evidence to demonstrate how surgical volumes and practice patterns relate to demand-capacity management. Projections of the effects of improving patient flow show how smoother flow can increase surgical volume and decrease overtime, thus increasing revenue, patient safety, and patient and staff satisfaction.

OTHER SURGICAL FLOW CONSIDERATIONS

Several points we've made in earlier chapters apply as well to surgical flow. So keep in mind all the principles of improving flow, because they'll apply in this specific setting as well. For example, the idea of segmenting patient flow, which we discussed in Chapter 7 in regard to the ED, works in the surgical unit as well.

Here you start by distinguishing between inpatients and outpatients in designing your processes. Then go deeper—segment surgical flow by particular specialty or case mix; each will have its own optimized processes. And as we implied earlier in the chapter, you will need a dashboard to track patients and results.

A simple method like the one in Figure 9.4 (for use in smoothing elective surgery) will help analyze and optimize surgical patient flow. It will also help prepare forecasts.

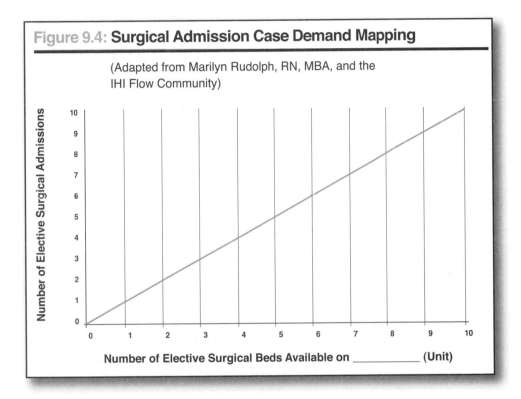

Figure 9.4: Surgical Admission Case Demand Mapping

(Adapted from Marilyn Rudolph, RN, MBA, and the IHI Flow Community)

To track the flow of elective surgery, put a dot at the intersection of number of beds available and number of elective surgery admissions at the time of the morning bed huddle. Label dots by date and day of week. A dot above the line represents more patients than beds available; a dot below the line means you have excess beds. Connect the dots, and you have actual demand versus capacity over time, with data on the overall pattern and on relative activity for each day of the week. Constructing such a graph can help you place patients in the short-term, in real-time, and gives you a better grasp of how demand and capacity relate in the long-term.

Don't Overlook the Obvious

Let's say you've adopted all the ideas presented earlier in this chapter. You are ready to go, with all surgeries designed to start on time and processes in place to keep throughput smooth. What may seem like simple routine tasks can still disrupt your entire operation. So examine *all* aspects of flow through your unit (recall our advice to walk around, observe, and listen before you start designing new and improved processes). For example, have you taken OR cleaning and turnaround into account? Having an established set of procedures enables your unit to operate more efficiently, increases throughput, and thus optimizes flow. OR staff members together should determine the best turnaround procedures for individual specialties and various kinds of cases. As with other processes, review them at staff meetings to make sure they are current and are the most effective ones.

And your surgical team may be ready to go—but is the patient? The transport of patients affects all parts of the unit, and without timely and efficient transport, your surgeries are unlikely to start on time. Your postoperative placement of patients is unlikely to happen effectively. Make sure you have processes in place for the different types of transport need that will occur in your unit, to and from various other units. You are probably going to need several options to cover a variety of needs. You're also going to need to carefully coordinate the multiple transports going on in real-time.

What's In It for Me?

Remember what you told the surgeons in talking them into spreading out elective surgeries throughout the week? Improving flow in your surgical unit leads to increased patient volume, better patient care, increased patient safety, and increased revenue. Specifically, implementing an effective flow improvement process leads to reliable real-time demand-capacity predictions and thus improved predicting of staffing needs, better toleration of census peaks, fewer bed holds, and less internal diversion. The number of postponed surgeries should decline steeply. So should the number of boarded patients and surgical errors. When the process is done well, quality, efficiency, staff satisfaction, and revenue all go up. And your people get to go home on time. As we stressed in earlier chapters, reducing throughput time by what may seem like modest amounts can lead to significant gains in flow—leading to gains in safety, service, and satisfaction.

CHAPTER 10

CASE STUDIES IN FLOW

"Well done is better than well said."

—*Benjamin Franklin*

We've laid out steps you can take and methods you can use to improve flow in your hospital system—but real examples of hospitals that have put these principles and techniques into practice can both illuminate the possibilities and inspire us. In this chapter, we will look at healthcare systems that have done so, how they did it, and what was learned. We've singled out selected aspects of each experience to focus on, though the studies may contain multiple components of the flow improvement processes. Some of the studies are snapshots of improvement; others are a more in-depth look at procedures. At the end of each, we have highlighted which of the elements of the Flow Toolkit (from Chapter 2) are best represented in the case study. Note that because of the level of detail in some studies, we've occasionally changed the name of a hospital. With those points in mind, let's get started on our tour of actual experiences with flow.

BEFORE THE BEGINNING: FORECASTING

In Chapter 7, we discussed the results when the staff of the Emergency Department at Florida Hospital in Orlando began proactively forecasting patient flow. Here's how the ED team went about developing their process.

Realizing the need to better match patient demand and the desire for new standards in performance, the ED team realized they did not have in place processes to achieve their goals. They were already engaged in improving ED patient flow for the "easy to treat" patients using the Lean system (the management system Toyota uses) as a method for improvement; they then worked on improving flow of the more complex patients and processes. They studied various models for predicting demand and settled on an analysis of recent demand combined with weighted averages. They tracked the data from their ED. Several important patterns were uncovered:

o Mondays have the highest volume of patients.
o Tuesdays, Wednesdays, Saturdays, and Sundays have the lowest volume.
o The day after a holiday always "acts like" a Monday.

Meanwhile, leaders of the team held bed huddles to discuss possible actions to meet patient demand, centering on staffing needs and coverage in the department. Based on their observations and discussions, the team developed a pilot project and tested it. The pilot project involved creating a new track using a secondary triage room and a deployment of an optimized "lean track," staffed with a nurse, a physician, and a mid-level practitioner for treatment during the peak demand hours on Mondays, 11 a.m. to 6 p.m. On Tuesdays, Wednesdays, Saturdays, and Sundays, on the other hand, the team reduced staffing coverage because of the lower volume. Total coverage hours for the week remained the same.

In addition to the results we discussed in Chapter 7, during the pilot project, Florida Hospital's ED documented a 12-minute improvement in the average time from a patient's arrival in the ED and that patient's encounter with a doctor. Florida Hospital was also able to predict, on average, hospital admissions from the ED and the need for inpatient beds by shift and by day of the week.

This information, relayed in the morning hospital bed-control huddle, allowed the hospital to start proactively planning for admissions from the ED.

This case study illustrates the utility of forecasting patient flow. Note how rapidly forecasting can be studied, analyzed, and deployed. Also note how one department, in this case the ED, can impact change throughout the entire hospital with the timely and thoughtful application of the Flow Toolbox. Demand-capacity management, forecasting service demand, and managing variation all played roles in this effort.

URGENT SPACE RELIEF—WITHOUT BUILDING NEW FACILITIES
(What to do when you didn't build it and they came anyway...)

The winter flu season of 2001 exacerbated the pre-existing crowding at a private hospital in North Carolina. Older, sicker patients were arriving at the ED in large numbers, requiring detailed medical work-ups and leading to increased admissions to the hospital. In fact, so many patients were boarded in the ED hallways, no one could make their way through the hallways without navigating the cluster of beds and patients. Even though the ED had a 6-bed fast track in addition to the 17 main ED beds, patients who required few resources ("fast track patients") waited for hours due to the service backlog. This log-jam would start early and last late into the night. It frustrated the staff and discouraged patients, leading to "dismal" patient satisfaction numbers on surveys and increased risk, hospital staff knew, of compromising patient safety.

The department had 60,000 annual patient visits. Hospital administration realized quick action was needed to match treatment capacity to the rising demand. The president of the hospital proposed that the ED staff find an alternative site to treat patients with less urgent needs—and finalize this option within three days. The ED staff began considering options. The hospital did not have any vacant space near the ED. An off-site preoperative work-up area, however, was in use only during the day shift on weekdays. A 10-bed unit, it had once been the Intensive Care Unit. The ED team realized this area was well configured for a fast track and might be used in the evening to take the pressure off the ED during peak volume hours.

That Friday afternoon, a quickly formed task force, including leaders from a number of the hospital's departments, gathered. With the location established, *over the next three days,* those leaders considered every possible issue in connection with turning the preoperative area into a fast track during the evenings. Figure 10.1 shows obstacles they knew they faced.

Figure 10.1: Challenges to Implementing a Proposed New and Off-site Fast Track

- Find nursing staff to cover eight more hours a day despite current vacancies
- Find medical providers to cover eight more hours a day, not included in a recently arranged schedule
- Arrange for appropriate linens and supplies
- Ensure access to medications and their security
- Assure the area would be clean and ready for surgical patients arriving at 5:30 a.m.
- Provide signage and assistance to guide patients 250 feet from the ED to the new area
- Adjust the computerized real-time tracking system to include these patients
- Ensure triage guidelines for patients sent to new unit go with the patients
- Provide registration capability in new unit

On Monday, the task force convened to review the active issues. The group set the opening of the new unit for seven days later. Exactly one week later, the new adjunct 10-bed fast track opened, and the first patients arrived at the unit for treatment. Ten days after the administration had decided to act to resolve the issue of crowding in the ED, the hospital had established a new fast track to handle increasing demand. In it, a nurse, a PA, and a secretary saw an average of 36 patients during each eight-hour shift over the first two weeks. From the hospital's perspective, costs of adding the additional fast track were modest—staffing and supplies—and financial, medico-legal, and public relations benefits were significant. Data confirmed the substantial advantage the new unit provided, including:

- Before it opened, an average of 20 patients a day were leaving the ED without being seen. If the average fee for each of those patients was $250–500, the hospital was losing $5,000–$10,000 each day just from patients leaving without being seen. After it opened, during those first two weeks, only one patient left without being seen.

- Waiting time before entering a treatment room was 64 minutes on average for fast track patients in the evening. After it opened, that waiting time averaged 29 minutes.

- After the new unit's first month of operation, patient satisfaction surveys for those treated in the new fast track showed a raw score 10.2 percent higher than other ED patients. That score equated to an increase from the 50th percentile to the 88th percentile in satisfaction.

- After the new unit opened, the electronic tracking board showed 8 to 10 patients waiting to be seen in the main unit on average during peak evening hours compared to 28 to 35 in previous weeks.

Administration's analysis of opening the new fast track concluded that patients now waited for shorter amounts of time and fewer patients waited at all. Patients were not the only ones more satisfied; so was the staff. In the view of hospital administrators, the care the ED provided was both safer and more profitable.

> This case study illustrates effective and timely demand-capacity management. It illustrates that sometimes, with enlightened, engaged, and creative administrative leadership and teamwork, you can increase your capacity to meet your demand. This is also an effective example of

segmenting patient flow (Lean Thinking) and eliminating bottlenecks (think TOC or the Theory of Constraints). This example also shows how solving one flow issue can affect flow for the whole hospital. And lastly, never forget the importance of a committed rather than a compliant healthcare team.

THE FLOW CASCADE; THE FRONT DOOR DRIVES FLOW

Inova Fairfax Hospital's Emergency Department had long been highly respected for clinical excellence. But it was also, for a long time, highly capacity-constrained, seeing nearly twice the number of patients for which the space was designed. Construction was a planned-for and potential long-term fix, but the hospital needed a more immediate solution. A team comprised of ED personnel (nursing director, chairman, medical director, lab coordinator, radiology supervisor, physicians, and nurses) and the registration director began work. The guiding mantra of the Emergency Department Improvement Team (EDIT) was this:

Why? Why not?

In other words, the team looked at each process both from the patients' perspective and that of the providers with a view toward, *Why do we do it this way?* Whenever someone raised an idea concerning improvement, the question was, *Why not? Why couldn't we do it this way?*

The latter question was critical in identifying obstacles and steps or policies that impeded progress. The team found that the composition of the interdisciplinary committee was a critical aspect of success, since so many of the processes cut across multiple areas of the hospital, which were traditionally functionally siloed.

One of the first areas the *Why? Why not?* concept targeted was the triage area, where multiple patients arrived at a time, even though there were available beds, nurses, and doctors available to treat them. The EDIT team developed the model of "Direct-to-Room," in which patients were sent from triage directly to the treatment rooms. Another *Why not?* dealt with patient registration into the hospital's computer system, from which labs, radiographs, and other studies were ordered. Understandably, one obstacle was, *We can't do that—we have to register them first. We have to register them before they go to their rooms.* However, the director of ED registration herself pointed out, "Actually, we *do* register patients in the room already, since that's how we handle ambulance patients. We would just have to figure out how to do that for the Direct-to-Room patients." This led to the concept of "in-room registration," now widely used in hospitals throughout the country. It was an intriguing example of taking a process already in place (registering ambulance patients in the room) and choosing to extend that process to patients who presented at triage.

The EDIT team members wanted to extend progress to patients who presented to triage after all the rooms had been filled. The team identified a subset of patients with illnesses or injuries the diagnostic or therapeutic interventions for which were amenable to an evidence-based approach. This decision allowed for a consensus-generated set of tests and therapies that could be initiated at the triage area. The first *Why not?* raised was the need for physician orders for the tests and medications. Advance Treatment and Advanced Initiative (AT/AI) orders-standing, written physician orders, approved by the entire group of emergency physicians, addressed this issue. The need for some form of registration in order to obtain laboratory or imaging studies was another obstacle. Again, the registration members of the team came up with the creative solution of an abbreviated registration, known as "Quick-Reg," allowing a fast, baseline set of information to be obtained at triage. The EDIT team designed a program called Advanced Triage-Advanced Initiatives to care for patients with extremity trauma, abdominal pain with normal vital signs, mild vaginal bleeding, and kidney stones. Described as "getting the ball up in the air as soon as they hit the door," the EDIT team acknowledged that these studies would be ordered once the patient was in the room, so why not begin the studies at the triage area?

Mild resistance came from some emergency physicians who wondered if nurses were actually capable of ordering extremity radiographs. Using the *Why not?* approach, the team used two lines of approach. First, it posed the question: *Let me see if I have this right. If you had a chest pain patient and you went into the room and the ED nurse hadn't started a line, begun to treat the pain, put the patient on a monitor, obtained an EKG, and preliminarily interpreted it and ordered a chest radiograph, you would have them "up on charges." These same nurses can't be taught how to order extremity films?* Second, once the team addressed this resistance, it devised a two-hour course to teach the triage nurses the principles of extremity trauma radiographs and understanding ED physician orders. Over time, the team extended the AT/AI list to include other chief complaints and diagnostic categories.

> "Quality exists to the extent that value is added to a product or service." This case study illustrates the benefits of going on a bounty hunt to eliminate things that do not add value and a treasure hunt to find those things that do. Applying the principles of Lean Thinking, adapting Toyota's 5 Why's to the ED, and engaging the team lead to new and innovative ways of delivering care.

REMEDYING LONG DELAYS

Patient waits and delays were also the impetus behind changes in the ED at Rockford Health Care System. A team of physicians, nurses, and other staff members implemented a flow improvement initiative to resolve the problem of delays caused by the lack of a dedicated physician in their "express-care" area of the ED. The team identified from the outset what the problem was and set about addressing it by applying the principles of queuing theory, demand-capacity matching, and eliminating waste. After forming a plan of action, they conducted a trial test using a dedicated team in the express-care unit.

The trial resulted in the best performance their express-care unit had ever achieved. The average length of stay was 54 minutes compared to the 2007 average LOS of 143 minutes—a 62 percent reduction. An added benefit was that no patients left the ED without being seen (LWBS) on the trial's last day. The system placed its dedicated team in the express-care unit during the most severe winter flu season in years, when the hospital was busier than usual, enhancing the significance of the trial's results.

> Understanding the implications of queuing theory and patient arrivals, forecasting demand and then matching capacity, eliminating waste in front-end processes—all of this enabled a 62 percent improvement in performance and as a by-product created a significant increase in capacity that could be effectively deployed in the winter flu season.

EXTENDING THE TRIAGE FLOW CASCADE— THE ORIGINS OF TEAM TRIAGE AT INOVA FAIRFAX HOSPITAL

As we indicated in the example above, the EDIT team at Inova Fairfax Hospital had addressed part of the triage flow cascade by designing and implementing Direct-to-Room, which was used when rooms were available "in the back," and AT/AI, which used standing orders to begin the evaluation and treatment of patients with defined chief complaints at times when there were no rooms available. However, due to the significant capacity constraints and the increasing ED volumes, there were still times when there were no rooms available (particularly when ED boarders were present). Using data, the team found that there were predictable times on predictable days when rooms would not be available for 8 to 10 hours at a time, raising concerns with regard to quality of care, patient safety, patient and staff satisfaction, and turnaround times. In addition, the community reputation of the ED and financial concerns regarding lost patient revenues were also drivers of innovative change.

In the spirit of the *Why? Why not?* nature of inquiry, the team asked, *Why not?* with regard to this concept:

If we can predict when we will be "outgunned, outmanned, and outrun" with regard to having more patients than we have ED

> treatment rooms in which to see them, why not deploy a team of
> people at the triage area to begin these patients' treatment?

The EDIT team began with a series of trial days where an ED physician was placed at triage in order to determine how many and what type of patients might benefit from having a physician or mid-level provider (nurse practitioner or physician assistant) at triage. Almost immediately it became apparent that a physician or mid-level alone was insufficient, as the work created by the orders generated by triage evaluation could not be handled easily, either by the physician or the existing triage nurse, who had work of her own to do. For that reason, the "team triage" concept was born. Team triage was initially proposed to comprise an ED physician, nurse, and technician, but was quickly expanded to include a registrar and a scribe, in order to provide maximum efficiency and utility. Another key concept is illustrated here: By broadening the team to include all ED team members in the planning phase, the horizons of creativity to include all aspects of care expand.

The team successfully applied for a Robert Woods Johnson Foundation Urgent Matters grant to initially fund team triage. The project began with 10-hour shifts evaluating and treating patients at the triage area, and then moving them into rooms when available and transferring their care to the physicians and nurses in that area. Detailed data were collected on all of these patients, as well as control patients. Data included patient satisfaction, staff satisfaction, length of stay or turnaround time (TAT), patients left without being seen (LWBS), patient safety, and patient velocity, as well as financial analysis, including costs and revenues collected. The results were impressive in each of these areas. Total TAT during the team triage trial decreased by 15 percent or 46 minutes, from 330 minutes to 284 minutes.

This 15 percent reduction in TAT is for *all patients seen during the 24-hour period team triage was in effect*. For the patients actually seen through the team triage process, TAT fell 64 percent, from 330 to 118 minutes, a very dramatic reduction. Thirty-four percent of patients were "treated and streeted," meaning they were evaluated, diagnosed, treated, and either sent home or admitted without ever getting into an ED treatment room. A subset of patients with abdominal pain showed a time to treatment of pain reduction of 94 minutes. Twenty-seven percent of abdominal pain patients had either CT scans or ultrasounds done, with a reduction in time to completion of the imaging study of over 2.5 hours (157 minutes). Not surprisingly, patient satisfaction rose dramatically, both for team triage patients and for those who were not evaluated through this process. ED staff satisfaction also increased significantly due to the program. LWBS dropped from 4.45 percent of patients to 0.81 percent during team triage hours and from 4.45 percent to 1.72 percent for the entire day. This decrease meant that they were "capturing" an additional 6 patients per day who were not leaving, of which 1.5 patients, on average, were admitted to the hospital, with inpatient charges averaging around $8,000 for these patients.

Patient safety issues declined 80 percent in team triage and 20 percent overall. Patient velocity for the ED physicians rose from 1.9 new patients per hour to a peak of 4.7 and a median of 3.7. Cost per shift of staffing team triage was $1,750, which was dramatically offset by increased ED revenues of $3,650.

The team triage concept was a success on many fronts and has since been implemented, in various forms, at EDs across the country. One of the most powerful insights is that team triage had demonstrable and measurable benefits not only for those patients seen through the new process but also for patients seen throughout the day.

Team engagement and creativity, idea generation, rapid cycle testing, and process redesign all led to the development of team triage. Note that patient safety improved. Note that while team triage was deployed for 10 hours a day, flow actually improved throughout the entire 24-hour cycle. Demand-capacity management, forecasting, queuing, and eliminating bottlenecks, far from being sterile academic concepts without utility or relevance to those of us delivering care at the bedside, are practical tools and high-leverage strategies for successful improvements in flow.

FIXING LOW PATIENT SATISFACTION WITH TEAMWORK

Patient satisfaction at the ED at Camden-Clark Memorial Hospital in Parkersburg, West Virginia, in 2005 was about as low as it could get: Scores from surveys were at the 1st percentile nationally, and patients who left without being seen exceeded 10 percent of patients entering the department. In the judgment of administrators, morale was at an all-time low among ED staff.

The immediate focus became hiring the right staff and developing a culture of teamwork. The first step was to recruit and train a medical director and then a team of emergency physicians and mid-level providers. BestPractices trained the entire ED staff in its Survival Skills course and provided them all the tools and coaching necessary to improve customer service (Mayer and Cates 2004). Subsequent steps to improve flow included:

- Adding mid-level service providers (nurse practitioners and physician assistants) to the clinical mix to augment coverage;
- Implementing a scribe program;
- Arranging hours to optimize capacity and demand; and
- Addressing volume surges while they were under way, not afterward.

Within a year, the satisfaction scores shot from the 1st percentile to the 77th percentile, the largest one-year rise in the history of the Gallup scores. As a result, the Camden-Clark ED won the 2006 National Gallup Award for Healthcare Excellence. Even as service and customer satisfaction improved, ED volume increased as well as the hospital's market share. The number of patients leaving without being treated dropped below 3 percent.

> Fielding the right team *and* fielding a full team, establishing leadership, fostering genuine teamwork, and effective training in the "soft science" of service delivery allowed Camden-Clark to improve patient flow *and* patient satisfaction.

BURSTING AT THE SEAMS

Early in 1997, Nash General Hospital needed to act. Its Emergency Care Center had experienced almost 11 percent growth from the first half to the second half of the previous year. Over the previous four years, annual growth had averaged 3 to 5 percent. The ED had reached maximum capacity, and patients were experiencing very long delays in treatment. The number of patients leaving without being seen was increasing rapidly. Patient complaints were at an all-time high and staff morale was "dismal."

Compounding the problem, 11 full-time registered nurses had resigned in 1996. By early 1997, vacant positions included eight full-time nurses, a manager, and two assistant managers. Almost every day, patient volume overwhelmed the facility, and almost every day, it lacked a full staff of nurses. "There was a general feeling of panic among the staff," recalled one observer. To make matters worse, the only other emergency facility in the area was about to close, burdening Nash General with an additional 12,000 visits a year. The feeling of panic was warranted.

The hospital's administration knew it had no choice but to act. The hospital was limited in how much it could expand its physical plant. The Emergency Care Center saw more than 53,000 patient visits during a year, representing more than 50 percent of the hospital's patients annually. Administrators approached change positively. "We felt that the opportunity to effect change in the hospital experience of nearly 54,000 patients as the result of one quality improvement project was too great an opportunity to miss," said one staff member. "Our historically positive community reputation needed to be guarded and enhanced, not compromised by this sudden boom in volume and turnover in staff."

The Process of Improvement

The administration formed a team to improve patient flow with the goal of streamlining the processes of triage, treatment, and discharge. The team first compiled dependable baseline statistics for total cycle time for emergency patients: entry to triage, entry to being placed in a room, placement in a room to being seen by a physician, and preparation of discharge order to actual discharge. Meanwhile, the team conducted similar measurements in turnaround times for X-rays and lab studies.

As it gathered data, the team consulted with emergency staff, which saw clearly the need to redesign processes and eagerly volunteered suggestions. The care center manager and hospital's medical director met with staff members of each department involved in the collaborative effort. Those staff members were uniformly forthcoming with suggestions that the care center tried. Emergency nurses particularly helped resolve problems, as did X-ray and lab staff members. Nursing assistants cross-trained as secretaries so they could help input orders and charges during times of peak volume. Housekeepers helped create a system for communicating when beds needed cleaning immediately. Security officers proposed a change in the process of treating police-escorted patients to reduce waiting time.

At this point, the team began testing proposed changes. For example, three hours each morning for four days, every other patient who entered the center went straight to treatment rooms when beds were available for triage and registration. When the team compared the time that process took to the baseline time, it discovered the tested process saved 9 to 14 minutes per patient. By the end of that week, bedside triage and registration became center policy. "Nine minutes may not seem like much," said a staff member, "but multiply those nine minutes by the 200 patients we see some days, and you have just eliminated nearly 30 hours of waiting time for our patients."

In another test, the triage nurse helped discharge patients when no other patients needed triage. This step proved impractical, because new patients would have to wait for triage while the nurse was away. So the test changed to having the triage nurse help only with discharges from the fast track, which was next to the triage area. The nurse was alerted to new patients entering triage by the sound of the chart printer and so could reach them quickly, and the average stay in the fast track dropped by more than 15 minutes. Within 10 days, this arrangement became center policy.

Computerized tracking revealed significant facts about operations within the center. When patient volume was highest, X-ray times were longest; the center added an extra technician to the radiology staff for peak-volume times like Saturday, Sunday, and Monday. Patient-volume data showed that 58 percent of patients entered between 11:00 a.m. and 11:00 p.m., the hours the fast track operated. Of those patients, the fast track saw 27 percent. Average LOS for these patients was nearly half of other patients. Furthermore, 83 percent of patients entered between 9:00 a.m. one day and 1:00 a.m. the next day. The center extended the hours of the fast track from 12 to 16, matching capacity to demand, at a modest cost (half of an FTE). After the change, the center treated 43 percent of its patients in the fast track, and throughput time for those patients was more than an hour shorter than other patients.

Two nurses trained as forensic nurse examiners to treat victims of sexual assault, and the use of these nurses reduced throughput time for those patients by more than 60 percent, from an average 4 hours and 15 minutes to 1 hour and 45 minutes.

Figure 10.2: **Reducing Waiting Times in the ECC**

Nash Health Care Systems

Reducing Waiting Times in the ECC

Aim:	To reduce throughput time in the Emergency Care Center for all types of patients (Fast Track, Emergency and Admissions) by 25%.
Key Outcome Measures:	The duration of time from registration in the ECC to the discharge or admission time from in the ECC.
Sampling Plan:	5 charts selected at 4 times per day (1000, 1900, 2200, and 0200 for 3 types of patients: Emergency, Fast Track and Admission

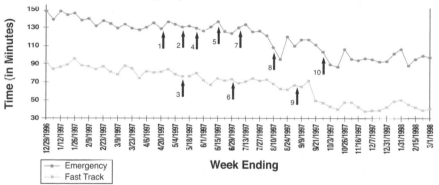

Emergency Care Center Turnaround Times

Some Details on the Changes:

Fast Track
- Expanded hours of Fast Track from 12-16 hours/day (3)
- Reduced handoffs in Fast Track (3)
- Cross trained NAII's to do computer/ secretarial duties (7)
- Rearranged NA coverage to cover the expanded hours in Fast Track (9)

Traige
- Changed triage nurse role, assisted with Fast Track when not busy (1)
- Triage/registration done in room if empty (1)
- Used protocol for extremity x-rays (6)

Other
- Developed system of cards to let physician know when x-rays, EKG's, etc., were complete (7)
- Respiratory therapy in Emergency Saturday, Sunday and Monday 0900-2100, cross trained to do EKG's, draw blood (5)
- In house admitting physician to do workup upstairs (2)
- Additional Radiology tech added for weekend coverage (4)
- Contest held among the 4 teams of caregivers to determine the best ideas for decreasing delays (8)
- Contest held among the 4 teams to determine best efficiency (10)

Results
- Decreased wait time in Fast Track by more than 50%
- Decreased wait time in main Emergency by 40%
- Chartered inpatient admission process team to facilitate admission of ECC patients
- These improvements made in spite of 20 increase in patient volume since January 1997

Results

Nash General, through its tracking process, now had a number of concrete statistics on results. It also had general observations from the staff: Each patient spent less time in the care center than previously, so treatment rooms were available to more patients each day. The patients waited less time for assessment and treatment, and the extension of fast track hours enabled staff to more appropriately match the acuity of each patient's illness to the level of practitioners who treated them. A significant change from the project was the "vast improvement" in staff morale and a "noticeably positive" attitude in the center. "Patient and family complaints about rudeness from nurses have practically disappeared," said one person involved in the project. Though patient volume was at an all-time high, the post-project workload did not seem as heavy to staff as before.

The following are statistical confirmations of the findings:

- In the year after the project began, the hospital treated about 21 percent more patients using less than 1 percent more staff.
- For emergency patients in general, process time for the complete cycle decreased by more than 40 percent.
- For fast track patients, that process time decreased by more than 60 percent.
- No nurses resigned from the hospital, compared with 11 the year before—and the hospital rehired 6 who had resigned that prior year.
- Patient complaints averaged 11 per week when the project started; in the two-week period at the end of the first year, the center received one complaint. In seven weeks during the last quarter of the year, the center received no complaints.

An engaged and committed leadership team, empowered by administration, harnesses the observations and ideas of all the various people and disciplines working in and around the ED. The team members and participants may not have been able to define the concepts of queuing theory (and perhaps with queuing theory, maybe not even spell it…), forecasting demand, matching capacity, eliminating waste, and applying the principles of Lean Thinking, but engaging the team led to refined, improved, and even innovative ways of delivering care. At the risk of being repetitious, never underestimate the importance of a committed rather than a compliant healthcare team.

FROM DOOR TO DOCTOR

Providence Health System's experience illustrates how targeting one aspect of flow can pay dividends. Providence decided to use a physician in triage during times of peak volume. The doctor would rapidly assess Canadian Triage Assessment System Level 2 and 3 patients, starting complete examinations and treatments earlier in the ED's process. The physician would also help the triage nurse determine which Level 2 and 3 patients the staff could safely treat in the waiting room or rapid assessment zone. This process helped avoid the use of stretchers requiring nurse staffing for acute patients. Depending on variation in patient flow during high-volume times, the triage physician would see more acute or less acute patients. The goals were to:

- Reduce delays in the time from entry until patients saw a physician for treatment;
- Reduce time of processes in the ED; and
- Reduce LOS for patients in the ED.

More specifically, Providence wanted to reduce the waiting time for Level 2 and 3 patients to less than 30 minutes for 90 percent of those patients, achieve average four-hour LOS for Level 1-3 patients discharged from the ED, and achieve average two-hour LOS for Level 4 and 5 patients discharged from the ED.

The hospital calculated that meeting these goals would generate an additional $1,000 to $1,200 per shift. It would reduce workload for other ED physicians, leading to shorter throughput times for an estimated five additional patients per shift beyond those affected by the physician in triage.

Achieving these goals would lead to an estimated total financial benefit of $1,500 per shift, offsetting the $750 additional cost of funding the position.

Providence ran a test of the idea for 42 shifts with a physician in triage, comparing data to 42 control shifts without the physician.

These results showed that having a physician in triage reduced waiting time for Level 1-3 patients by 27 percent and for Level 4 and 5 patients by 25 percent, and reduced LOS for Level 4 and 5 patients by 17 percent, though LOS for Level 1-3 patients did not improve.

> Segmenting patient flow, appreciating the concepts and implications of incoming patient streams, front-loading resources and care, the intelligent management of staff, beds, and space, and making the business case—all came into play in this case study from Providence Hospital.

UNLOCKING THE BACK DOOR OF THE EMERGENCY DEPARTMENT—BE-A-BED-AHEAD AND ADOPT-A-BOARDER AT INOVA FAIRFAX HOSPITAL

With any improvement project, it would be difficult to sustain progress if the patients and staff continued to be plagued with the problem of ED boarders. Created at Inova Fairfax Hospital, the "Boarder Patrol Team" was comprised of both ED and inpatient leaders, whose mission was to eliminate or massively decrease the boarder burden in the ED. The idea in part was: If we can unlock the back door of the ED by eliminating the boarder burden, we can open the front door of the ED—which is the front door of the hospital—to the community.

One of the first *Whys* was this:

Why can't we create a process wherein the bed board proactively identifies which bed(s) will be the one next assigned to patients, whether those patients come from the ED, OR, or transfer in?

Why can't we always "be a bed ahead" instead of a bed (or more than a bed) behind?

Very quickly, the elements of the Be-A-Bed-Ahead (BABA) program came into being. However, it became apparent that the cooperation and input of the inpatient units and the nursing supervisor were equally critical, particularly when "beds were tight" and forecasting discharges was a priority. The concept of twice-daily bed rounds was born, comprising the charge nurses of all inpatient units, the ED charge nurse, the nursing supervisor, and the administrator on call. Real-time monitoring for effective demand-capacity management was a key to the success of BABA. It was a daily occurrence for charge nurses on the inpatient units to tell the ED charge nurse, "Let us take that patient for you. I'll expedite them to the unit ASAP." This team spirit and communication breeds progress and progress breeds further progress, particularly innovative progress.

Adopt-A-Boarder (AAB) was another innovative solution born of this process. AAB arose from the simple observation that ED boarders were residing for seemingly countless hours in the uncarpeted, public hallways with no semblance of privacy (or, in some cases, decency). The AAB program was designed to be a threshold-activated process (greater than four ED boarders waiting more than four hours for an inpatient bed) guided by the nursing supervisor and the administrator on call, which assured that there was sufficient authority from hospital leadership to drive the change. As you might suspect, there were many concerns, including all of these, followed by the key words we used to deflect the resistance:

Table 10.1

No way—it's not safe.	If it's not safe on the inpatient units, it's even more so in the ED.
We can't use our hallways.	But it's OK if the ED uses theirs?
It's against fire code.	The ED is a part of the hospital-if it's against fire code here, it's against fire code there as well. Besides, we checked and the fire marshal says it is OK.
I'm not working under these conditions.	The ED nurses do every day with multiple patients.

The intriguing part is that, once the AAB plan was in place, very rarely did they have to enact it. Most of the time a bed was found before the patients were taken to the hallways on the inpatient units. At Stony Brook Medical Center, as we have noted, Dr. Peter Viccellio and his colleagues devised a similar program known as the Full Capacity Protocol, which has had similarly successful results.

"We are all in this together." More often well said than well done. Not in this case, however. The ED and the inpatient units realized, with hospital administration fully behind them, that they truly were all in this together when it came to managing admitted and boarded patients. Smoothing the load (load-leveling), matching capacity to demand, forecasting the need, real teamwork, and process redesign all led to both a new (and actually a "brand new" process) and improved patient care process. Inova utilized demand-capacity management, queuing, eliminating bottlenecks, and system appreciation in devising these programs.

REDUCING VARIATION IN SURGICAL FLOW

With high patient volume, the surgical unit at St. John's Regional Health Center in Springfield, Missouri, was often thrown off schedule when urgent or emergency surgeries occurred, pushing surgeries late into the evening. St. John's is an 866-bed acute care facility with 22 operating rooms that are usually in use. Surgeons and patients were both frustrated with the late hours, but the process in use was "the way things had always been done." The hospital decided to test the idea of segmenting emergency and planned surgical cases as a method of smoothing surgical flow. St. John's reserved one operating room solely for unscheduled surgeries. The change would mean surgeons could no longer fully schedule elective surgeries in all operating rooms. Under block scheduling, surgeons received blocks of time in the ORs; those blocks were about 80 percent full, and every OR had elective surgery scheduled until mid- to late afternoon. Urgent unscheduled cases were added afterward; emergency cases were taken immediately. An average 10 to 15 unscheduled surgeries a day meant that surgeries at 10 p.m. were not uncommon.

Try It Out

Surgeons resisted the change: "We are already too busy and they want to take something away from us. This is crazy." Staff was concerned that a dedicated room would sit idle. "Everyone assumed that because the flow of unscheduled surgeries can't be predicted, setting aside an OR just for 'add-ons' would be a very inefficient use of the space," one staff member said. But data from tracking showed that elective surgery was actually more variable than emergency surgery. The hospital extended the block schedule by two hours, leaving the same amount of time for elective surgery.

Results

After the project began, the hospital discovered the dedicated OR in fact did not sit idle but was used about 60 percent of the scheduled day. The number of late-night surgeries dropped drastically. The block schedule itself worked more effectively. After 30 days, the hospital decided to keep the new system. Here were some of the results:

- 5 percent increase in surgical case volume;
- 45 percent decrease in surgeries performed after 3 p.m.;
- All-time low in OR overtime;
- 4.6 percent increase in revenue; and
- Improved staff and patient satisfaction.

"At three and six months, we saw an increase in revenues simply because we were more efficient, and were scheduling our blocks more fully," observed one surgeon.

> "A problem well stated is half-solved." —John Dewey
>
> Define the problem, look at the data, trial solutions, find a champion, define the benefits (What's in it for me? What's in it for you?)...and you too can smooth surgical flow and at the same time please your OR staff and your surgeons. Demand-capacity management, forecasting service demand, eliminating bottlenecks, smoothing variability, and system appreciation were all key to St. John's success.

ELIMINATING A BOTTLENECK

Triage constituted a bottleneck at Wenatchee Valley Medical Center. The relatively new facility opened in December 2008 with nine ED beds and five fast track beds; 50,000 annual visits were projected. From the start, the front-end processes caused patient dissatisfaction; therefore, the center implemented an improvement project. Here's how the process of entering the ED worked when the project began:

- o The patient checked in at a front desk and filled out a brief information form—name, date of birth, and chief complaint.
- o The patient then waited for the triage nurse to arrive.
- o The triage nurse took the patient to an exam room to do a triage of needs, lasting five to six minutes.
- o The patient then returned to the waiting room to wait for treatment.

The average time from entry into the facility to triage was 17 minutes. Within 31 minutes, 90 percent of patients had reached triage. Those times may not seem unreasonable, but the staff realized they were causing a large bottleneck that delayed the overall process. The triage nurse had little visual contact with patients entering the waiting area, and the hospital did little to manage patients waiting in the reception area.

The project entailed moving the triage nurse into the reception area, giving the nurse the ability to visually assess arriving patients and turning triage into a proactive part of the ED process. Wenatchee Valley adopted an "on versus off" approach. "On" means capacity allows the triage nurse to assess patients in an exam room quickly for acuity level and best method of treatment. In-depth nursing evaluation and registration take place in the exam room. "Off" means capacity is limited or full. In that case, the triage nurse does a quick assessment—less than a minute—in the reception area, determining the safest and fastest method of care and sorting the patients by level of acuity. The nurse monitors patients in the reception area by taking vital signs every 30 minutes and keeping track of lab status and similar needs. Figure 10.3 shows the results of the project.

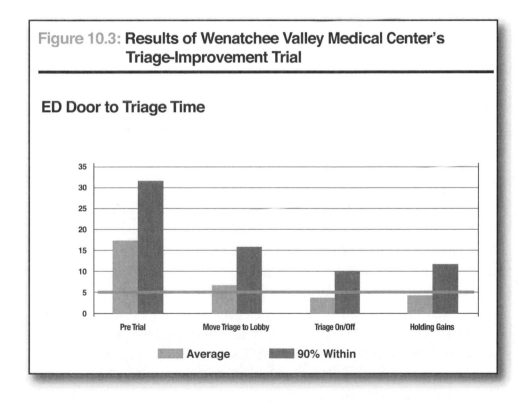

Figure 10.3: Results of Wenatchee Valley Medical Center's Triage-Improvement Trial

ED Door to Triage Time

The time reduction resulting from the process was dramatic. Following up on this initial project, Wenatchee Valley created a work group to streamline the triage process further, including implementing use of ESI levels for assessing patients' conditions. The work group also developed a competency checklist for triage to use in evaluating current staff and in hiring new staff. An overriding goal was to begin care of the patient in an exam room as soon as possible.

> Process flow-mapping, visual cues, making work visible, front-loading care, simplifying queues, managing variation, standardized work, and standardized processes all factored into the Wenatchee team success story.

ACTING TO AVOID INCREASING FLOW PROBLEMS

Northwest Community Hospital knew it had some flow problems and might be headed for more (Weintraub, Hashemi, and Kucewicz 2006). An audit by an outside consultant revealed that 25 percent of ED patients were treated in ED hallway beds rather than treatment rooms. In addition, the leadership team projected 68,000 patient visits in 2006 in a department built to handle 50,000. The multiunit team had already instituted multiple flow improvement measures (e.g., triage standing orders, point-of-care testing, adding mid-level providers to staffing, bedside registration, a patient-flow coordinator); therefore, options for implementing further improvement measures were limited. The audit confirmed that the only factor within the team's control that had not been addressed in flow improvement measures was time from triage to bed placement. The analysis also showed that the longest wait times were for Level 4 and 5 patients—those who were the least ill. The Northwest ED already had a fast track, but because of general overcrowding in the department, it was being used for general ED treatment of all but Level 1 patients. This change in usage meant delays of several hours for the least sick patients.

With these facts in mind, team leaders reasoned that the best approach to improve flow was to establish an advanced care triage area to assess and treat the lowest acuity patients. Space was a problem. The team examined the overcrowded facility and discovered that a storage area next to the ED registration area was not fully used. The team converted the storage area into the advanced care triage area with three beds, in separate areas divided by new walls and curtains. The new super fast track operated from 10 a.m. to 10 p.m., with a mid-level provider and patient-care technician.

As a result, Northwest's ED kept LOS for patients the same as it had been despite an increase in volume of 4,000 patients. Patient satisfaction scores rose from the 60th percentile to the 90th, and staff morale improved. Times for treatment phases have also improved; for example, time from entry to EKG has been cut from 15 to 20 minutes to 7 minutes.

Rising demand driving innovation, a search for space, understanding and segmenting patient flow, volume, and arrivals, and implementing a unique and optimized process (an anti-pooling measure but in this case a highly leveraged and beneficial one) all led Northwest Community Hospital to success with improved patient flow and improved patient satisfaction. Demand-capacity management, the elimination of bottlenecks, and astutely managing variation were the key tools at Northwest Community.

Little Things Mean a Lot

When you take a drive on the highway and traffic flows smoothly, you can roll down the windows, turn up the music on the radio, and enjoy the ride. But any minute you can come around a bend and end up stalled in a traffic bottleneck. The windows may still be down and the music playing, but you are no longer enjoying the ride.

The same experience happens in our hospitals. One day everything goes smoothly. The next day, lab tests take forever, patient turnaround times drag, and life is not as enjoyable and satisfying as it was the day before. Working to improve flow is working to make more days like the first one.

To continue the highway analogy, cars have come out recently with adaptive cruise control, which keeps the distance between one car and the car ahead constant. When cars ahead speed up, so do the cars behind; when those ahead slow down, so do the cruise-control cars. This feature is possible because of computers—we humans have too much lag time in our thought processes and reactions to achieve this state unassisted. How many cars do you think need to be equipped with this adaptive cruise control to solve traffic problems? Researchers have investigated this question, and the answer might surprise you: 20 percent. If 20 percent of all the cars on the road had adaptive cruise control, almost all traffic jams could be avoided.

The lesson for patient flow is that you don't have to fix every problem and every process. If your key processes frequently bog down, making a significant improvement in flow through the department for 20 to 30 percent of your patients may clear up the critical bottlenecks and make flow smooth. Realizing this point can effectively motivate your people, because reaching that goal is achievable. The goal is excellence, not perfection.

The traffic analogy holds in another sense as well. Delays in patient flow develop in a nonlinear way, just as highway congestion does, and they resolve in a nonlinear way as well: Once a traffic jam caused by an accident has developed, for example, removing the wreck that caused it will not immediately clear the jam. Every investment you make in preventing disruptions carries a large return. Trouble is easier to prevent than to fix.

YOU CAN DO THIS

We're sure you have your own case studies exemplifying the practical solutions that improve flow by increasing value and decreasing waste through the benefit-to-burden ratio as your patients move through the service transitions and queues that comprise our modern system of healthcare. We know that you will discover, as we have, that finding solutions to flow is like exercise—the more you do it, the easier it gets. Then we can feel, as Ben Franklin observed, that "well done is better than well said."

REFERENCES AND RECOMMENDED READINGS

CHAPTER 1

References

Axelrod, A. 2006. *Patton: A Biography.* New York: Palgrave Macmillan.

Bachmann, L. M., E. Kolb, M. T. Koller, J. Steurer, and G. ter Riet. 2003. "Accuracy of Ottawa Ankle Rules to Exclude Fractures of the Ankle and Mid-Foot: Systematic Review." *British Medical Journal* 326: 417.

Berry, L. L. 1995. *On Great Service: A Framework for Action.* New York: Free Press.

———. 1999. *Discovering the Soul of Service: The Nine Drivers of Sustainable Business Success.* New York: Free Press.

Berry, L. L., and K. Seltman. 2008. *Management Lessons from the Mayo Clinic: Inside One of the World's Most Admired Service Organizations.* New York: McGraw-Hill.

Berwick, D. 1996. "A Primer on Leading the Improvement of Systems." *British Medical Journal* 312: 619–22.

Black, J. R., and D. Miller. 2008. *The Toyota Way to Healthcare Excellence: Increase Efficiency and Improve Quality with Lean.* Chicago: Health Administration Press.

Block, P. 2002. *The Answer to How is Yes: Acting on What Matters.* San Francisco: Berrett-Koehler.

Covey, S. R. 2004. *The Eighth Habit: From Effectiveness to Greatness.* New York: Free Press.

Csikszentmihalyi, Mihaly. 1990. *Flow: The Psychology of Optimal Experience.* New York: Harper and Row.

———. 1993. *The Evolving Self: A Psychology for the Third Millennium.* New York: Harper.

———. 1996. *Creativity: Flow and the Psychology of Discovery and Invention.* New York: Harper Collins.

———. 1997. *Finding Flow: The Psychology of Engagement with Everyday Life.* New York: Perseus.

Deming, W. E. 1986. *Out of the Crisis.* Cambridge, MA: MIT Press.

Institute for Healthcare Improvement. 2003. *Optimizing Patient Flow: Moving Patients Smoothly through Acute Care Settings.* IHI Innovation Series white paper. Boston: Institute for Healthcare Improvement.

Jensen, K., and J. Crane. 2008. "Improving Patient Flow in the Emergency Department." *Healthcare Financial Management* 62: 104–6.

Jensen, K., T. A. Mayer, S. J. Welch, and C. Haraden. 2007. *Leadership for Smooth Patient Flow.* Chicago: Health Administration Press.

Juran, J. 1989. *Juran on Leadership for Quality.* New York: Free Press.

Kotter, J. 1996. *Leading Change.* Boston: Harvard Business School Press.

Lee, Q., and B. Snyder. 2006. *Value Stream and Process Mapping: Genesis of Manufacturing Strategy.* Bellingham, WA: Enna Products.

Meade, C. M., J. Kennedy, and J. Kaplan. 2008, October 7. "The Effects of Emergency Department Staff Rounding on Patient Safety and Satisfaction." *Journal of Emergency Medicine.* In Press. Abstract available at <www.sciencedirect.com/doi:10.1016/jemermed2008.03.042>.

Nash, M., and S. R. Poling. 2008. *Value Stream Mapping: A Complete Guide to Production and Transactional Mapping.* New York: Productivity Press.

Ohno, T. 1988. *Toyota Production System: Beyond Large-Scale Production.* New York: Productivity Press.

Peters, T. 2003. *Re-Imagine! Business Excellence in a Disruptive Age.* London: Dorling, Kindersley.

Senge, P. 2006. *The Fifth Discipline: The Art and Practice of the Learning Organization.* New York: Doubleday.

Shewhart, W. 1939. *Statistical Method from the Viewpoint of Quality Control.* New York: Dover.

Spear, S. J. 2004. "Learning to Lead at Toyota." *Harvard Business Review* 82: 78–86.

Stewart, P. *Jacobellis v. Ohio,* 378 US, 184. Washington, DC: US Government Printing Office.

Studer, Q. 2008. *Results That Last.* Hoboken, NJ: John Wiley and Sons.

Weick, K. E., and K. M. Sutcliffe. 2007. *Managing the Unexpected: Resilient Performance in an Age of Uncertainty.* New York: Wiley.

CHAPTER 2

References

Argyris, C. 1993. *Knowledge for Action.* San Francisco: Jossey-Bass.

Berwick, D. 1996. "A Primer on Leading the Improvement of Systems." *British Medical Journal* 312: 619-22.

Goldratt, E., and J. Cox. 1992. *The Goal.* Great Barrington, MD: North River Press.

Deming, W. E. 1986. *Out of the Crisis.* Cambridge, MA: MIT Press.

Edwards, N., M. J. Kornacki, and J. Silversin. 2002. "Unhappy Doctors: What Are the Causes and What Can Be Done?" *British Medical Journal* 324: 835-38.

Fatovich, D. M., Y. Nagree, and P. Sprivulis. 2005. "Access Block Causes Emergency Department Overcrowding and Ambulance Diversion in Perth, Western Australia." *Emergency Medicine Journal* 22 (5): 351-54.

Jensen, K., T. A. Mayer, S. J. Welch, and C. Haraden. 2007. *Leadership for Smooth Patient Flow.* Chicago: Health Administration Press.

Kaplan, J. 2009. Personal communication with the authors.

Maister, D. H. 1985. "The Psychology of Waiting Lines." In *The Service Encounter: Managing Employee/Customer Interaction in Service Business,* edited by J. A. Czepiel et al., 113-23. Lexington, MA: Lexington Books.

Silversin, J., and M. J. Kornacki. 2000. *Leading Physicians Through Change: How to Achieve and Sustain Results.* Tampa: American College of Physician Executives.

Further Recommended Readings

Argyris, C. 1992. *On Organizational Learning.* Cambridge, MA: Blackwell Business.

Berwick, D. M., and A. B. Godfrey. 1990. *Curing Healthcare: New Strategies for Quality Improvement.* San Francisco: Jossey-Bass.

Chakrapani, C. 1998. *How to Measure Service Quality and Customer Satisfaction.* Chicago: American Marketing Association, American College of Emergency Physicians.

Drucker, P. F. 1994. *The Practice of Management.* New York: Harper Collins.

Edmonds, M. I., and H. M. O'Connor. 1999. "The Use of Computer Simulations as A Strategic Decision-Making Tool: A Case Study of an Emergency Department Application." *Health Management Forum* 12 (3): 32–38.

Fitzsimmons, J., and M. Fitzsimmons. 2006. *Service Management: Operations, Strategy, Information Technology.* 5th ed. Boston: McGraw-Hill.

Gordon, J., A. J. Billings, B. R. Asplin, and K. V. Rhodes. 2001. "Safety Net Research in Emergency Medicine: Proceedings of the Academic Emergency Medicine Consensus Conference on 'The Unraveling Safety Net.'" *Academic Emergency Medicine* 8 (11): 1024–29.

Horton, S. S. 2004. "Increasing Capacity While Improving the Bottom Line." *Frontiers of Health Services Management* 20 (4): 17–23.

Institute for Healthcare Improvement. 2003. *Optimizing Patient Flow: Moving Patients Smoothly through Acute Care Settings.* IHI Innovation Series white paper. <www.gwhealthpolicy.org.> (17 September, 2005).

Institute of Medicine. 2006. "The Future of Emergency Care in the United States Health System." *Academy of Emergency Medicine* 13 (10): 1081–85.

Kaplan, R. S., and D. P. Norton. 1996. *The Balanced Scorecard: Translating Strategy into Action.* Boston: Harvard Business School Press.

Koenig, K. L., and G. Kelen. 2006. "Executive Summary: The Science of Surge Conference." *Academy of Emergency Medicine* 13 (10): 1087–88.

Langley, G. J., K. Nolan, T. Nolan, C. Norman, and L. Provost. 2009. *The Improvement Guide: A Practical Approach to Enhancing Organizational Performance.* San Francisco: Jossey-Bass.

McManus, M., M. Long, A. Cooper, and E. Litvak. 2004. "Queuing Theory Accurately Models the Need for Critical Care Resources." *Anesthesiology* 100 (5): 1271-76.

Nolan, T., M. Schall, D. Berwick, and J. Roessner. 1996. *Breakthrough Series Guide: Reducing Delays and Waiting Times Throughout the Healthcare System.* Boston: Institute for Healthcare Improvement.

Schafermeyer, R. W., and B. R. Asplin. 2003. "Hospital and Emergency Department Crowding in the United States." *Emergency Medicine* 15: 22–27.

Schein, E. H. 1992. *Organizational Culture and Leadership.* San Francisco: Jossey-Bass.

Hospital Emergency Departments: Crowded Conditions Vary Among Hospitals and Communities. Washington, DC: U.S. General Accounting Office.

CHAPTER 3

References

Black, J. R., and D. Miller. 2008. *The Toyota Way to Healthcare Excellence: Increase Efficiency and Improve Quality with Lean.* Chicago: Health Administration Press.

Carlzon, J. 1987. *Moments of Truth: New Strategies for Today's Customer-Driven Economy.* New York: HarperCollins.

Chalice, R. 2007. *Improving Healthcare Using Toyota Lean Production Methods.* 2nd ed. Milwaukee: ASQ Quality Press.

De Feo, J. A., W. Barnard, and J. Juran, eds. 2003. *Juran Institute's Six Sigma Breakthrough and Beyond.* New York: McGraw-Hill.

Dickson, E. W., Z. Anguelov, P. Bott, A. Nugent, D. Walz, and S. Singh. 2008. "The Sustainable Improvement of Patient Flow in an Emergency Treatment Centre Using Lean." *International Journal of Six Sigma and Competitive Advantage* 4: 289–304.

Gelrud, J., H. Burroughs, and J. Koterwas. 2008. "Emergency Care Center Turnaround Time—An Improvement Story." *Journal for Healthcare Quality* 30: 31–37.

Graban, M. 2008. *Lean Hospitals: Improving Quality, Patient Safety, and Employee Satisfaction.* New York: Productivity Press.

Inova Fairfax Hospital. "Inova's Red Rules for Safety." *Inova Health System.* <http://www.inova.org/clinical-education-and-research/education/residency-and-fellowship-programs/pdf/safety_error_prevention_red_rules.pdf>.

Institute for Healthcare Improvement. 2005. *Going Lean in Healthcare.* Innovation Series white paper. <www.ihi.org/IHI/Results/whitepapers/GoingLeaninHealthcare.htm>.

———. 2006. *Leadership Guide to Patient Safety.* Innovation Series white paper. <http://www.ihi.org/WhitePapers/LeadershipGuidetoPatientSafety/WhitePaper.htm>.

Jensen, K., T. A. Mayer, S. J. Welch, and C. Haraden. 2007. *Leadership for Smooth Patient Flow.* Chicago: Health Administration Press.

Kohn, L. T., J. M. Corrigan, and M. S. Donaldson, eds. 1999. *To Err is Human: Building a Safer Health System.* Washington, DC: National Academies Press.

A Leader's Guide to After-Action Reviews. 1993. U.S. Army. Training Circular 25–20. <http://www.au.af.mil/au/awc/awcgate/army/tc_25-20/table.htm>.

Leape, L., and D. Berwick. 2005. "Five Years after To Err Is Human: What Have We Learned." *Journal of the American Medical Association* 293: 2384–90.

Lee, F. 2004. *If Disney Ran Your Hospital: 9 ½ Things You Would Do Differently.* Bozeman, MT: Second River Press.

Mach, E. 1898. *Popular Scientific Lectures.* Chicago: Open Court.

Mayer, T. A., and R. J. Cates. 2004. *Leadership for Great Customer Service: Satisfied Patients, Satisfied Employees.* Chicago: Health Administration Press.

Mayer, T., and K. Jensen. 2008. "Flow and Return on Investment in Healthcare." *International Journal of Six Sigma and Competitive Advantage* 4: 192–95.

Studer Group. 2008. "Never Events Powerpoint." <www.studergroup.com/never/studer_group_never_events_slides.ppt >.

Reinertsen, J., M. Pugh, and M. Bisognano. 2008. *Seven Leadership Leverage Points for Organization-Level Improvement in Health Care.* **Innovation Series white paper.** <http://www.ihi.org/IHI/Results/WhitePapers/ SevenLeadershipLeveragePointsWhitePaper.htm >.

Russell, B., and A. Steinberg. 2009. *Red and Me: My Coach, My Lifelong Friend.* New York: HarperCollins.

Smith, B. 2003. "Lean and Six Sigma: A One-Two Punch." *Quality Progress* 36 (4): 37–41.

Spear, S. J. 2004. "Learning to Lead at Toyota." *Harvard Business Review* 82: 78–86.

———. 2009. *Chasing the Rabbit: How Market Leaders Outdistance the Competition.* New York: McGraw-Hill.

Studer, Q. 2008. *Results that Last: Hardwiring Behaviors That Will Take Your Company to the Top.* New York: Wiley.

Wears, R. L. 2004. "Six Sigma Is Really Only 4.5 Sigma." *British Medical Journal* 328. <http://bmjjournals.com/cgi/eletters/328/7432/162#50383>.

Wears, R. L., and C. A. Vincent. 2009. "The History of Safety in Healthcare." In P. Croskerry et al., eds., *Patient Safety in Emergency Medicine.* Philadelphia: Lippincott.

Weick, K. E., and K. H. Roberts. 1993. "Collective Mind in Organizations: Heedful Interrelating on Flight Decks." *Administrative Science Quarterly* 38: 357–81.

Weick, K. E., and K. M. Sutcliffe. 2007. *Managing the Unexpected: Resilient Performance in an Age of Uncertainty.* New York: Wiley.

Welch, S. 2009. *Quality Matters: Solutions for a Safe and Efficient Emergency Department.* Oakbrook Terrace, IL: Joint Commission Resources.

Womack, J., D. T. Jones, and D. Roos. 1990. *The Machine That Changed the World: The Story of Lean Production.* New York: Free Press.

CHAPTER 4

References

Argyris, C. 1993. *Knowledge for Action.* San Francisco: Jossey-Bass.

Bennis, W. 1989. *On Becoming a Leader: The Leadership Classic.* New York: Knopf.

Churchill, W. 1951. *The Second World War.* New York: Houghton Mifflin.

———. 1939. BBC Radio. 1 October.

Collins, J., and J. Porras. 1997. *Built to Last: Successful Habits of Visionary Companies.* New York: HarperCollins.

Collins, J. 2001. *Good to Great: Why Some Companies Make the Leap.* New York: HarperCollins.

———. 2009. *How the Mighty Fall: And Why Some Companies Never Give In.* New York: HarperCollins.

Covey, S. 1992. *Principle-Centered Leadership.* New York: Fireside.

Dinesen, I. 1957. "Review." *New York Times,* 3 November.

Kotter, J. 1999. *What Leaders Really Do.* Boston: Harvard Business School Press.

Krzyzewski, M. 2000. *Leading with the Heart.* New York: Warner.

Lewin, K. 1948. *Resolving Social Conflicts: Selected Papers on Group Dynamics.* New York: Harper & Row.

Maslow, A. 1999. *Toward a Psychology of Being.* 3rd Ed. New York: Wiley.

Studer, Q. 2008. *Results That Last.* Hoboken, NJ: John Wiley and Sons.

Twain, M. 2007. *The Wit and Wisdom of Mark Twain: A Book of Quotations.* Dover, DE: Dover.

Wooden, J., and S. Jamison. 2007. *The Essential Wooden: A Lifetime of Lessons on Leaders and Leadership.* New York: McGraw Hill.

Yeats, W. B. 1997. *Treasury of Irish Myth, Legend, and Folklore.* New York: Scribner.

Further Recommended Readings

Prochaska J., J. Norcross, and C. DiClemente. 1992. "In Search of How People Change: Appllictions to Addictive Behaviors." *American Psychologist* 9: 1102-14.

Reinertsen, J., M. Pugh, and M. Bisognano. 2008. *Seven Leadership Leverage Points for Organization-Level Improvement in Health Care.* Innovation Series white paper. <http://www.ihi.org/IHI/Results/WhitePapers/ SevenLeadershipLeveragePointsWhitePaper.htm>.

Heifetz, R. A. 1994. *Leadership without Easy Answers.* Cambridge, MA: Harvard University Press.

Kotter, J. 1996. *Leading Change.* Boston: Harvard Business School Press.

CHAPTER 5

References

Jensen, K., T. A. Mayer, S. J. Welch, and C. Haraden. 2007. *Leadership for Smooth Patient Flow.* Chicago: Health Administration Press.

Further Recommended Readings

Beckwith, H. 1997. *Selling the Invisible: A Field Guide to Modern Marketing.* New York: Warner Books, Inc.

Berwick, D. M., A. B. Godfrey, and J. Roessner. 1990. *Curing Health Care: New Strategies for Quality Improvement.* San Francisco: Jossey-Bass.

Chakrapani, C. 1998. *How to Measure Service Quality and Customer Satisfaction.* Chicago: American Marketing Association.

Cleverley, W. O., and A. E. Cameron. 2003. *Essentials of Health Care Finance.* Sudbury, MA: Jones and Bartlett.

Dempsey, C., and K. Larson. 2004. "Can't We All Just Get Along? Know Your Role in Fostering Hospital-Provider Collaboration." *Nursing Management* 35 (11): 32–35.

Evans, C. J. 2000. *Financial Feasibility Studies for Healthcare.* New York: McGraw-Hill.

Fitzsimmons, J., and M. Fitzsimmons. 2006. *Service Management: Operations, Strategy, Information Technology.* 5th ed. Boston: McGraw-Hill.

Henry J. Kaiser Family Foundation. 2007. *Health Care Costs: A Primer.* <http://www.kff.org/insurance/upload/7670.pdf>.

Institute of Medicine. 2001. *Crossing the Quality Chasm: A New Health System for the Twenty-first Century.* Washington, DC: National Academies Press.

Leatherman, S., D. Berwick, D. Iles, L.S. Lewin, F. Davidoff, T. Nolan, and M. Bisognano. 2009. "The Business Case for Quality: Case Studies and an Analysis." *Health Affairs (Millwood)* 22 (2): 17–30.

Martin, L. A., C. W. Neumann, J. Mountford, M. Bisognano, and T. W. Nolan. 2009. *Increasing Efficiency and Enhancing Value in Health Care: Ways to Achieve Savings in Operating Costs per Year.* Innovation Series white paper. <http://www.ihi.org/IHI/Results/WhitePapers/ IncreasingEfficiencyEnhancingValueinHealthCareWhitePaper.htm>.

Nolan, T., and M. Bisognano. 2006. "Finding the Balance between Quality and Cost." *Healthcare Financial Management* 60 (4): 66–72.

Stahl, M. J., and P. J. Dean. 1999. *The Physician's Essential MBA: What Every Physician Leader Needs to Know.* Gaithersburg, MD: Aspen.

Zelman, W. N., M. J. McCue, and A.R. Millikan. 1999. *Financial Management of Healthcare Organizations: An Introduction to Fundametal Tools, Concepts, and Applications.* Malden, MA: Blackwell.

CHAPTER 6

References

Archimedes, quoted in P. M. Senge. 2006. *The Fifth Discipline: The Art and Practice of the Learning Organization.* New York: Doubleday.

Beeson, S. 2009. *Engaging Physicians.* Gulf Breeze, FL: Fire Starter.

Bujak, J. S. 2008. *Inside the Physician Mind: Finding Common Ground with Doctors.* Chicago: Health Administration Press.

Cates, R. 2006. Personal conversation with Thom Mayer.

Covey, S. R. 2004. *The 7 Habits of Highly Effective People.* New York: Free Press.

References and Recommended Readings

Eddy, D. 1996. *Clinical Decision Making: From Theory to Practice: A Collection of Essays from the Journal of the American Medical Association.* Chicago: AMA Press.

Frederick the Great. 1998. *Frederick the Great on the Art of War.* Translated by J. Luvaas. New York: Da Capo Press.

Gardner, J. W. 1990. *On Leadership.* New York: The Free Press.

Hickson, G. B., C. F. Federspiel, J. W. Pichert, et al. 2002. "Patient Complaints and Malpractice Risk." *JAMA* 387: 2951-57.

Johnson, L. B., quoted in R. A. Caro. 1990. *The Path to Power: The Years of Lyndon Johnson.* New York: Alfred A. Knopf.

Kübler-Ross, E. 1970. *On Death and Dying.* New York: Simon and Schuster.

Lewin, K. 1997. *Resolving Social Conflicts.* Washington, D.C.: American Psychological Association.

Nietzsche, F. 2000 *Basic Writings of Nietzsche.* Translated by W. Kaufmann. New York: The Modern Library.

Reinertsen, J., M. Pugh, and M. Bisognano. 2008. *Seven Leadership Leverage Points for Organization-Level Improvement in Health Care.* Innovation Series white paper. <http://www.ihi.org/IHI/Results/WhitePapers/SevenLeadershipLeveragePointsWhitePaper.htm >.

Reinertsen J., A. G. Gosfield, W. Rupp, and J. W. Whittington. 2007. Engaging Physicians in a Shared Quality Agenda. Innovation Series white paper. < http://dodpatientsafety.usuhs.mil/index.php?name=Downloads&req=getit&lid=723>.

Rogers, E. M. 1995. *Diffusion of Innovations.* New York: Free Press.

Seneca. 1996. *Letters from a Stoic.* Translated by R. Campbell. London: Penguin Books.

Shaw, G. B. 2003. *Man and Superman.* Chicago: Barnes and Noble Classics.

Smith, L. 2009. Personal conversation with the authors.

Stengel, C. 2006. Quoted in *The Yale Book of Quotations.* Edited by F. R. Shapiro and J. Epstein. Yale, CT: Yale Press.

Studer, Q. 2008. *Results That Last.* Hoboken, NJ: Wiley and Sons.

Wheatley, M. J. 1999. *Leadership and the New Science: Discovering Order in a Chaotic World.* San Francisco: Berritt-Koehler.

CHAPTER 7

References

Gummerson, K. 2009. Phone conversation with Thom Mayer.

Jensen, K., T. A. Mayer, S. J. Welch, and C. Haraden. 2007. *Leadership for Smooth Patient Flow.* Chicago: Health Administration Press.

Litvak, E., M. L. McManus, and A. Cooper. 2002. "Root Cause Analysis of Emergency Department Crowding and Ambulance Diversion in Massachusetts." *Boston University Program for Management Variability in Health Care Delivery.* Report to the Massachusetts Department of Public Health.

Maister, D. H. 1985. "The Psychology of Waiting Lines." In *The Service Encounter: Managing Employee/Customer Interaction in Service Business.* Edited by J. A. Czepiel et al. Lexington, MA: Lexington Books. 113-23.

Schull, M. J., L. J. Morrison, M. Vermeulen, and D. A. Redelmeier. 2003. "Emergency Department Overcrowding and Ambulance Transport Delays for Patients with Chest Pain." *Canadian Medical Association Journal* 168 (3): 277–83.

Further Recommended Readings

Andrulis, D. P., A. Kellerman, E. A. Hintz, B. B. Hackman, and V. B. Weslowski. 1991. "Emergency Departments and Crowding in United States Teaching Hospitals." *Annals of Emergency Medicine* 20 (9): 980–86.

Asplin, B. R., D. J. Magid, K. V. Rhodes, L. I. Solberg, N. Lurie, and C. A. Camargo. 2003. "A Conceptual Model of Emergency Department Crowding." *Annals of Emergency Medicine* 42 (2): 173–80.

Bazarian, J. J., S. M. Schneider, V. J. Newman, and J. Chodosh. 1996. "Do Admitted Patients Held in the Emergency Department Impair Throughput of Treat-and-Release Patients?" *Academy of Emergency Medicine* 3 (12): 1113–18.

Building the Clockwork ED: Best Practices for Eliminating Bottlenecks and Delays in the ED. 2000. Washington DC: HWorks.

Pitts, Stephen R. 6 August, 2008. "National Hospital Ambulatory Medical Care Survey: 2006 Emergency Department Summary." National Health Statistics Reports, No 7. <www.cdc.gov/nchs/data/nhsr/nhsr007.pdf>.

References and Recommended Readings

"National Hospital Ambulatory Medical Care Survey: 2001 Emergency Department Summary." 2003. *Centers for Disease Control and Prevention, National Center for Health Statistics.* Advance Data No. 335. PHS 2003–1250. <http://www.cdc.gov/nchs/data/ad/ad335.pdf>.

Fan, J. 2005. "Cost-Effectiveness of an Emergency Department Fast-Track System for Low Acuity Patients." *Annals of Emergency Medicine* 46: S109.

Hoffenberg, S., M. B. Hill, and D. Houry. 2001. "Does Sharing Process Differences Reduce Patient Length of Stay in the Emergency Department?" *Annals of Emergency Medicine* 38 (5): 533–40.

Holland, L., L. Smith, and K. E. Blick. 2005. "Reducing Laboratory Turnaround Time Outliers Can Reduce Emergency Department Patient Length of Stay." *American Journal of Clinical Pathology* 125 (5): 672–74.

Hoot, N. R., and D. Aronsky. 2008. "Systematic Review of Emergency Department Crowding: Causes, Effects, and Solutions." *Annals of Emergency Medicine* 52 (2): 126–36.

Husk, G., and D. Waxman. 2004. "Using Data from Hospital Information Systems to Improve Emergency Department Care." *SAEM* 11 (11): 1237–44.

Jensen, K., and J. Crane. November 2008. "Improving Patient Flow in the Emergency Department." *Healthcare Financial Management.* 104–108.

Jones, S. J., T. A. Allen, T. J. Flottemesch, and S. J. Welch. 2006. "An Independent Evaluation of Four Quantitative Emergency Department Crowding Scales." *Academy of Emergency Medicine* 13: 1204–11.

Kyriacou, D. N., V. Ricketts, P. L. Dyne, M. D. McCullough, and D. A. Talan. 1999. "A Five-Year Time Study Analysis of Emergency Department Patient Care Efficiency." *Annals of Emergency Medicine* 34: 326–35.

McGuire, F. 1997. "Using Simulations to Reduce Length of Stay in Emergency Departments." *Journal of Social Health Systems* 5 (3): 81–90.

Olshaker, J. S., and N. K. Rathlev. 2006. "Emergency Department Overcrowding and Ambulance Diversion: The Impact and Potential Solutions of Extended Boarding of Admitted Patients in the Emergency Department." *Journal of Emergency Medicine* 30: 351–56.

Patel, P. B., and D. R. Vinson. 2005. "Team Assignment System: Expediting Emergency Department Care." *Annals of Emergency Medicine* 46 (6): 499–506.

Pines, J. M. 2006. "Profiles in Patient Safety: Antibiotic Timing in Pneumonia and Pay-for-Performance." *Academy of Emergency Medicine* 13 (7): 787–90.

Pines, J. M., J. E. Hollander, A. R. Localio, et al. 2006. "The Association between Emergency Department Crowding and Hospital Performance on Antibiotic Timing for Pneumonia and Percutaneous Intervention for Myocardial Infarction." *Academy of Emergency Medicine* 13 (8): 873–78.

Salluzzo, R. F., T. A. Mayer, R. W. Strauss, and P. Kidd, eds., 1997. *Emergency Department Management Principles and Applications.* New York: Mosby.

Schull, M. J., K. Lazier, M. Vermeulen, S. Mawhinney, and L. J. Morrison. 2003. "Emergency Department Contributors of Ambulance Diversion: A Quantitative Analysis." *Annals of Emergency Medicine* 41 (4): 467–76.

Schull, M. J., M. Vermeulen, G. Slaughter, et al. 2004. "Emergency Department Crowding and Thrombolysis Delays in Acute Myocardial Infarction." *Annals of Emergency Medicine* 44 (6): 577–85.

Solberg, L. I., B. R. Asplin, R. M. Weinick, et al. 2003. "Emergency Department Crowding: Consensus Development of Potential Measures." *Annals of Emergency Medicine* 42 (6): 824–34.

Special Investigations Division, Committee on Government Reform, U. S House of Representatives. October 16, 2001. "National Preparedness: Ambulance Diversions Impede Access to Emergency Rooms." Report prepared for Rep. Henry A. Waxman.

Tarnow-Mordi, W. O., C. Hau, A. Warden, and A. J. Shearer. 2000. "Hospital Mortality in Relation to Staff Workload: A Four-Year Study in an Adult Intensive Care Unit." *Lancet* 356 (9225): 185–89.

Vieth, T. L., and K. V. Rhodes. 2006. "The Effect of Crowding on Access and Quality in an Academic ED." *American Journal of Emergency Medicine* 24 (7): 787–94.

Weiss, S. J., A. A. Ernst, R. Derlet, R. King, A. Bair, and T. G. Nick. 2005. "Relationship Between the National ED Overcrowding Scale and the Number of Patients Who Leave Without Being Seen in an Academic ED." *American Journal of Emergency Medicine* 23 (3): 288–94.

Wiler, J. L., C. Gentle, J. M. Halfpenny, A. Heins, A. Mehrotra, M. G. Mikhail, and D. Fite. 2009. "Optimizing Emergency Department Front-End Operations." *Annals of Emergency Medicine* 20 (10): 1–20.

CHAPTER 8

References

Csikszentmihalyi, M. 1990. *Flow: The Psychology of Optimal Experience.* New York: Harper and Row.

Drucker, P. 1967. *The Effective Executive.* New York: Harper and Row.

Institute for Healthcare Improvement. 2004.

Jensen, K., T. A. Mayer, S. J. Welch, and C. Haraden. 2007. *Leadership for Smooth Patient Flow.* Chicago: Health Administration Press.

"Sentinel Event Alert: Delays in Treatment." 2002. *Joint Commission on Accreditation of Healthcare Organizations.* <www.jointcommission.org/SentinelEvents/SentinelEventAlert/sea_2 6>.

"Full Capacity Protocol." 2001. *Stony Brook University Hospital and Medical Center.* <www.hospitalovercrowding.com>.

Further Recommended Readings

Aiken, L. H., S. P. Clarke, D. M. Sloane, J. Sochalski, and J. H. Silber. 2002. "Hospital Nurse Staffing and Patient Mortality, Nurse Burnout, and Job Dissatisfaction." *Journal of the American Medical Association* 288: 1087–1193.

Bagust, A., M. Place, and J. W. Posnett. 1999. "Dynamics of Bed Use in Accommodating Emergency Admissions: Stochastic Simulation Model." *British Medical Journal* 319 (7203): 155–58.

Bellomo, R., D. Goldsmith, S. Uchino, et al. 2004. "Prospective Controlled Trial of Effect of Medical Emergency Team on Postoperative Morbidity and Mortality Rates." *Critical Care Medicine* 32 (4): 916–21.

Cowan, R. M., and S. Trzeciak. 2005. "Clinical Review: Emergency Department Overcrowding and the Potential Impact on the Critically Ill." *Critical Care* 9 (3): 291–95.

DeLia, D. 2006. "Annual Bed Statistics Give a Misleading Picture of Hospital Surge Capacity." *Annals of Emergency Medicine* 48 (4): 384–88.

Derlet, R. W., and J. R. Richards. 2000. "Overcrowding in the Nation's Emergency Departments: Complex Causes and Disturbing Effects." *Annals of Emergency Medicine* 35 (1): 83–85.

Falvo, T., L. Grove, R. Stachura, et al. 2007. "The Opportunity Loss of Boarding Admitted Patients in the Emergency Department." *Academic Emergency Medicine* 14 (4): 332–37.

Fee, C., E. Weber, and C. Maak. 2006. "Impact of Emergency Department Crowding on Door to Antibiotic Timing in Admitted Patients with Community-Acquired Pneumonia." *Academic Emergency Medicine* 13 (5 S1): 59.

Forster, A. J., I. Stiell, G. Wells, A. J. Lee, and C. van Walraven. 2003. "The Effect of Hospital Occupancy on Emergency Department Length of Stay and Patient Disposition." *Academic Emergency Medicine* 10: 127–33.

Institute for Healthcare Improvement. 2004. <www.ihi.org>.

Kelley, M. A. 1999. "The Hospitalist: A New Medical Specialty." *Annals of Internal Medicine* 130: 373–75.

Litvak, E., and M. C. Long. 2000. "Cost and Quality Under Managed Care: Irreconcilable Differences?" *American Journal of Managed Care* 6 (3): 305–12.

Litvak, E., M. C. Long, A. Cooper, and M. McManus. 2001. "Emergency Department Diversion: Causes and Solutions." *Academic Emergency Medicine* 8 (11): 1108–10.

McManus, M., M. Long, A. Cooper, and E. Litvak. 2004. "Queuing Theory Accurately Models the Need for Critical Care Resources." *Anesthesiology* 100 (5): 1271–76.

McManus, M. L., M. C. Long, A. B. Cooper, et al. 2003. "Variability in Surgical Caseload and Access to Intensive Care Services." *Anesthesiology* 98: 1491–96.

Needleman, J., P. I. Buerhaus, S. Mattke, M. Stewart, and K. Zelevinsky. 2001. *Nurse Staffing and Patient Outcomes in Hospitals.* Health Resources Services Administration Report. Boston: Harvard School of Public Health.

Nolan, T., M. Schull, D. Berwick, and J. Roessner. 1996. *Try Scheduling Hospital Discharges.* Boston: Institute for Healthcare Improvement. <www.ihi.org>.

Richardson, D. B. 2002. "The Access-Block Effect: Relationship Between Delay to Reaching an Inpatient Bed and Inpatient Length of Stay." *Medical Journal of Australia* 177: 492.

Rogers, A. E., W.-T. Hwang, L. Scott, L. Aiken, and D. Dinges. 2004. "The Working Hours of Hospital Staff Nurses and Patient Safety." *Health Affairs* 23: 202–12.

Rozich, J. D., and R. K. Resar. 2003. "Using a Unit Assessment Tool to Optimize Patient Flow and Staffing in a Community Hospital." *Journal on Quality Improvement* 28 (1): 31–41.

Salodof MacNeil, J. May 2004. "ICU Transfer Delays May Be Deadly." *Medscape Medical News* <www.ihi.org>.

Schull, M. J., J. P. Szalai, B. Schwartz, and D. A. Redelmeier. 2001. "Emergency Department Overcrowding Following Systematic Hospital Restructuring: Trends in Twenty Hospitals over Ten Years." *Academic Emergency Medicine* 8 (11): 1037–43.

Simmons, F. M. 2005. "Hospital Overcrowding: An Opportunity for Case Managers." Case Manager 16 (4): 52–54.

Sprivulis, P. C., J. A. DaSilva, I. G. Jacobs, et al. 2006. "The Association Between Hospital Overcrowding and Mortality Among Patients Admitted Via Western Australian Emergency Departments." *Medical Journal of Australia* 184 (5): 208–12.

Tarnow-Mordi, W. O., C. Hau, A. Warden, and A. J. Shearer. 2000. "Hospital Mortality in Relation to Staff Workload: A Four-Year Study in an Adult Intensive Care Unit." *Lancet* 356 (9225): 185–89.

Weissman, J. S., J. M. Rothschild, E. Bendavid, et al. 2007. "Hospital Workload and Adverse Events." *Medical Care* 45 (5): 448–55.

CHAPTER 9

References

Landro, L. 10 August, 2005. "Unsnarling Traffic Jams in the O.R." *Wall Street Journal.* <online.wsj.com/article_print/SB112362701513709147.html>. (24 August, 2008).

Further Recommended Readings

"Case Study: Flow Management at St. John's Regional Health Center." 26 October, 2005. *The Commonwealth Fund.* <http://www.cmwf.org/tools/tools_show.htm?doc_id=311206>.

"Managing Patient Flow: Smoothing O.R. Schedule Can Ease Capacity Crunches, Researchers Say." *O.R. Manager* 19: 1, 9–10.

McManus, M. L., M. C. Long, A. B. Cooper, et al. 2003. "Variability in Surgical Caseload and Access to Intensive Care Services." *Anesthesiology* 98: 1491–96.

CHAPTER 10

References

Mayer, T. A., and R. J. Cates. 2004. *Leadership for Great Customer Service: Satisfied Patients, Satisfied Employees.* Chicago: Health Administration Press.

Weintraub, B., T. Hashemi, and R. Kucewicz. 2006. "Creating an Enhanced Triage Area Improves Emergency Department Throughput." *Journal of Emergency Nursing* 32 (6): 502–505.

Landro, L. 10 August, 2005. "Unsnarling Traffic Jams in the O.R." *Wall Street Journal.* <online.wsj.com/article_print/SB112362701513709147.html>. (24 August, 2008).

Further Recommended Readings

"Case Study: Flow Management at St. John's Regional Health Center.". 26 October, 2005. *The Commonwealth Fund.* <http://www.cmwf.org/tools/tools_show.htm?doc_id=311206>.

"Managing Patient Flow: Smoothing O.R. Schedule Can Ease Capacity Crunches, Researchers Say." 2003. *O.R. Manager* 19: 1, 9–10.

McManus, M. L., M. C. Long, A. B. Cooper, et al. 2003. "Variability in Surgical Caseload and Access to Intensive Care Services." *Anesthesiology* 98 (6): 1491–96.

Resources

Accelerate the momentum of your Healthcare Flywheel^{SM}.
Access additional resources at www.studergroup.com/hardwiringflow.

BOOKS:

Hardwiring Excellence—A *BusinessWeek* bestseller, this book is a road map to creating and sustaining a "Culture of Service and Operational Excellence" that drives bottom-line results.

Written by Quint Studer

Excellence in the Emergency Department: How to Get Results—Written to motivate senior leaders and staff, implement evidence-based tactics, drive accountability, and create a culture of "always."

Written by Studer Group® Coach Stephanie J. Baker, RN, CEN, MBA

Eat THAT Cookie! How Workplace Positivity Pays Off...for Individuals, Teams, and Organizations—Written by Liz Jazwiec, RN, is packed with realistic, down-to-earth tactics leaders can use right now to infuse positivity into their culture.

Engaging Physicians: A Manual to Physician Partnership—A new book by Dr. Stephen C. Beeson, is a tested, staged approach to create physician loyalty, improve physician partnership, and generate superior organizational performance.

Leadership for Smooth Patient Flow—A book written by Kirk Jensen, Thom A. Mayer, Shari Welch, and Carol Haraden that will improve outcomes, service, and your bottom line.

Leadership for Great Customer Service: Satisfied Patients, Satisfied Employees—Written by Thom Mayer and Robert J. Cates, provides a thorough blueprint for creating and sustaining a practical customer service program.

For more information about books and other resources, visit www.firestarterpublishing.com.

MAGAZINES:

Hardwired Results: Excellence in the Emergency Room, Issue 5, 2006

This issue focuses on excellence in the Emergency Department. Article topics include cutting turnaround time with fast track, improving patient safety with ED communication tools, reducing patients who leave without treatment, and more.

Hardwired Results: Improve Outcomes with Evidence-Based Tools, Issue 7, 2006

This issue focuses on excellence in the Emergency Department. Article topics include improving clinical outcomes with hourly rounding, driving results with individualized patient care, maximizing team talents, and more.

Healthcare Financial Management, November 2008, p. 104-108

This article focuses on the nine strategies hospitals can incorporate to more effectively manage patient flow in the Emergency Department without sacrificing patient care.

Visit www.studergroup.com to view additional *Hardwiring Results* magazines.

ARTICLES:

Keep Your Patients Coming Back
MGMA Connexion • August 2008
Quint Studer

Discharge Phone Calls Deliver Quality Care, Higher Patient Satisfaction
Hospital News
Quint Studer

Evidence-Based Leadership
Projects@Work
Quint Studer

How to Achieve and Sustain Excellence
Healthcare Financial Management

WEBINAR TRACKS:

Foundations of Healthcare Leadership Webinar Series—Five webinar tracks focused on Evidence-Based Leadership tools and techniques. For more information on Studer Group's Webinars, visit www.studergroup.com/webinars.

DVD TRAINING RESOURCES:

Must Haves^{SM} Video Series

By implementing the Must Haves, healthcare organizations around the country are seeing better bottom-line results, including increased volume and decreased length of stay, as well as improved clinical outcomes, staff retention, and recruitment. Studer Group developed the Must Haves video series to help organizations hardwire these breakthrough practices into their culture. The videos consist of live lectures by Studer Group founder Quint Studer, followed by role-plays to let the participants see each of the Must Haves in action.

Hourly Rounding: *Improving Nursing and Patient Care Excellence*

Studer Group Patient Care Model and video/DVD training that contains a key strategy called hourly rounding. Hourly rounding is not only a call light reduction strategy, but also a proven tactic to reduce patient falls by 50 percent, reduce skin breakdowns by 14 percent, and improve patient satisfaction scores an average of 12 mean points.

AIDET^{SM} Five Fundamentals of Patient Communication

AIDET—Acknowledge, Introduce, Duration, Explanation, and Thank You—is a powerful communication tool. When interacting with patients, gaining trust is essential for obtaining patient compliance and improving clinical outcomes. AIDET is a simple acronym that represents how we can gain trust and communicate with people who are nervous, anxious, and feeling vulnerable. Studer Group has created AIDET as a comprehensive training tool that will enhance communication within your organization.

HighMiddleLow™ Performer Conversations

It is crucial that any organization have a method to re-recruit high performers, continue to develop middle performers, and move low performers "up or out" of the organization. If not, organizations hit a wall where progress slows and they cannot achieve their full potential. Based on work with hundreds of healthcare organizations, Studer Group has developed a critical management approach for moving organizational performance called highmiddlelow.

For more information on Studer Group DVD training resources, visit www.firestarterpublishing.com.

SOFTWARE SOLUTIONS:

Leader Evaluation Manager™: Results Through Focus and Accountability

Studer Group's *Leader Evaluation Manager* is a web-based application that automates the goal setting and performance review process for all leaders, while ensuring that the performance metrics of individual leaders are aligned with the overall goals of the organization. By using Leader Evaluation Manager, both leaders and their supervisors will clearly understand from the beginning of the year what goals need to be accomplished to achieve a successful annual review, can plan quarterly tasks with completion targets under each goal, and view monthly report cards to manage progress.

To purchase or learn more, please visit www.firestarterpublishing.com.

INSTITUTES:

Taking You and Your Organization to the Next Level with Quint Studer

Learn the tools, tactics, and strategies that are needed to Take You and Your Organization to the Next Level at this two-day institute with Quint Studer and Studer Group's coach experts. You will walk away with your passion ignited and with Evidence-Based Leadership℠ strategies to create a sustainable culture of excellence.

Foundations of Healthcare Leadership

After working with hundreds of high performing organizations and tens of thousands of leaders, we have identified the practical skills that separate the best leaders in healthcare from all the rest: talent management, communicating like a leader, managing your time and energy, mastering your professional development, and aligning the behaviors of a team. Unfortunately, most leaders haven't had the time or opportunity for formal training on these essential skills, which is why we created this new institute.

Nuts and Bolts of Operational Excellence in the Emergency Department

Improve patient flow and build service and operational excellence in your Emergency Department as Jay Kaplan, MD, FACEP, and Stephanie Baker, RN, CEN, MBA, both with extensive and ongoing real-life ED experience, share proven tactics such as Provider in Triage, Rounding for Outcomes, Discharge Phone Calls, Key Words at Key Times and AIDET^{SM}.

What's Right in Health Care^{SM}

One of the largest healthcare peer-to-peer learning conferences in the nation, *What's Right in Health Care*^{SM} brings organizations together to share ideas that have been proven to make healthcare better.

To review a listing of Studer Group institutes or to register for an institute, visit www.studergroup.com/institutes.

For information on Continuing Education Credits, visit www.studergroup.com/cmecredits.

COACHING:

Studer Group coaches hospitals and healthcare systems providing a detailed framework and practical how-tos that create change. We work side-by-side establishing, accelerating, and hardwiring the necessary changes to create a culture of excellence. In our work, Studer Group has identified a core of three critical elements that must be in place for great organizational performance once a commitment is made to the pillar approach to goal setting and the Nine Principles^{SM} of Behavior.

Executive Development Coaching Line

A Senior Leadership Module and a Board Development Module are available to train and revitalize leaders and board members to enable them to work in tandem to take their organization to the next level. Tools and tactics taught will serve as accelerants to the Evidence-Based Leadership model already in place. These modules offer a customized one-to-one or team-oriented approach for senior leaders to navigate personal, strategic, or team issues that may block organizational effectiveness.

Emergency Department Coaching Line

A comprehensive approach to improving service and operational efficiency in the Emergency Department. Our team of ED coach experts will partner with you to implement best practices, proven tools, and tactics using our Evidence-Based Leadership approach to improve results in all five pillars: People, Service, Quality, Finance, and Growth. Key deliverables include decreasing staff turnover, improving employee, physician, and patient satisfaction, decreasing door-to-doctor times, reducing left without being seen rates, increasing upfront cash collections, and increasing patient volumes and revenue.

To learn more about Studer Group coaching, visit www.studergroup.com.

ABOUT STUDER GROUP:

Studer Group's mission is to change the face of healthcare by creating a better place for employees to work, physicians to practice medicine, and patients to receive care. Studer Group is an outcomes-based healthcare performance improvement firm that coaches hundreds of hospitals, health systems, medical practices, and end-of life organizations to achieve and sustain clinical results. To learn more about Studer Group, visit www.studergroup.com.

Visit www.studergroup.com/hardwiringflow to access and download many of the resources, examples, and tools mentioned in *Hardwiring Flow.*

ABOUT THE AUTHORS

Thom A. Mayer, MD, FACEP, FAAP

Dr. Thom Mayer is the chairman of the board of BestPractices, Inc., and a medical director for Studer Group. He has been widely recognized as one of the nation's foremost experts in leadership, management, customer service, and flow in healthcare. He is also recognized as an expert in emergency medicine, pediatric emergency medicine, trauma, and sports medicine.

Emergency Departments under his guidance have won prestigious awards from virtually every organization recognizing excellence in healthcare, including Press Ganey, PRC, Gallup, the Institute for Healthcare Improvement, the American College of Healthcare Executives, the Healthcare Advisory Board, and the Robert Wood Johnson Foundation. Dr. Mayer also serves as the medical director of the NFL Players Association.

Dr. Mayer has published over 60 articles and 60 book chapters, and has edited fifteen textbooks. Most recently, Dr. Mayer has written *Leadership for Great Customer Service: Satisfied Patients, Satisfied Employees*, as well as *Leadership for Smooth Patient Flow*, both published by the American College of Healthcare Executives. The latter book was given the 2007 James A. Hamilton Award from the ACHE for the best book on healthcare leadership.

On September 11, 2001, Dr. Mayer served as one of the command physicians at the Pentagon Rescue Operation, coordinating medical assets at the site. The BestPractices physicians at Inova Fairfax Hospital were the first to successfully diagnose and treat inhalational anthrax victims during the fall 2001 anthrax crises, and Dr. Mayer has served the Department of Defense on Defense Science Board Task Forces on Bioterrorism, Homeland Security, and Consequences of Weapons of Mass Destruction.

Dr. Mayer's skill as a speaker is attested to by the fact that he has been the keynote speaker at numerous conferences, including the Press Ganey National Client Conference (twice), the PRC National Conference, and the Robert Wood Johnson Foundation Urgent Matters Conference, among others. He was named the American College of Emergency Physicians Speaker of the Year in the second year that award was given and has twice won the American College of Emergency Physicians Over-the-Top-Award for the highest scores among its speakers. Dr. Mayer was selected to present the most prestigious named lectureships for the American College of Emergency Physicians, the James Mills and Colin Rorric lectures. Dr. Mayer has also spoken at Studer Group national conferences and regional conferences as well.

Dr. Mayer's academic appointments are as clinical professor of emergency medicine at the George Washington and University of Virginia Schools of Medicine and senior lecturing fellow, Duke University School of Medicine.

Dr. Mayer's passion and energy in speaking about cutting-edge healthcare topics have resulted in valuable lessons for leaders and managers in healthcare, and he has received uniformly excellent reviews for his speeches.

Kirk B. Jensen, MD, MBA, FACEP

Dr. Kirk Jensen has spent over 20 years in emergency medicine management and clinical care. Board-certified in emergency medicine, he has been medical director for several Emergency Departments and is chief medical officer for BestPractices and a medical director for Studer Group.

Dr. Jensen is a faculty member for the Institute for Healthcare Improvement (IHI), focusing on quality improvement, patient satisfaction, and patient flow both within the ED and throughout the hospital. He chaired two IHI Communities: *Improving Flow through Acute Care Settings* and *Operational and Clinical Improvement in the Emergency Department*. He currently leads the innovative seminar *Cracking the Code to Hospital-Wide Patient Flow*.

Dr. Jensen is a popular speaker and coach for EDs across the country. He is coauthor of the 2007 ACHE Hamilton Award-winning book, *Leadership for Smooth Patient Flow*. He is the recipient of the 2007-08 ACEP Honorable Mention Speaker of the Year Award. Dr Jensen presents on patient safety, patient flow, operations management, and change management at the ACEP *Emergency Department Directors Academy*.

In addition, Dr. Jensen served on the expert panel and site examination team of Urgent Matters, a Robert Wood Johnson Foundation Initiative focusing on helping hospitals eliminate ED crowding and congestion as well as preserving the healthcare safety net.

Dr. Jensen holds a bachelor's degree in biology from the University of Illinois (Champaign) and a medical degree from the University of Illinois (Chicago). He completed a residency in emergency medicine at the University of Chicago and an MBA at the University of Tennessee.

INDEX

surgical, 211
tracking, 173-174
trauma. *See* trauma.
velocity, 111-118, 139, 233
vertical vs. horizontal, 163-164
volume, 32, 222, 224, 235-236, 269
vs. customer, 66-68
waiting. *See* waiting.
Patient CustoMeter, 65-66
patient-service representative, 158
PATRAK system, 30
Patton, George S., 21
pay-for-performance, 91
peace, 145
pediatric intensivist, 87
pediatrician, 66, 86, 128
The Pediatric Risk-Free ED, 139
Pentagon Rescue Operation, 275
People pillar, 138-139
performance gap, 64-65, 71
perioperative facilitator, 213, 217
Peters, Tom, 8
pharmacy requirements, 181
philanthropy, 139
phone call, 132, 193
physical examination, 7
physician, 8, 25, 80, 111
 behavioral standards, 141-143
 champions, 135-136, 145-147
 confidence, 133-134
 engagement in flow, 121-147
 leadership, 134-136
 love for data, 131
 loyalty, 267
 measurement, 138-141
 orders, 122, 229

preference cards, 127
recognition of, 145-147
relationship with nurse, 134
satisfaction, 43, 184
training, 123-124, 136-137
trust, 133-134
physician assistant, 158, 160, 169, 226, 232, 234
pig-in-the-python effect, 196
pillar management, 99-100, 138-140, 273
plan-do-study-act, 191
play well with others, 123
Poisson distribution, 35, 177, 212
Poisson, Siméon, 35
positivity, 267
postanesthesia care unit, 43, 46, 114, 208, 211, 219
Potomac Hospital, 55
power grid dispatching centers, 77
praise, 145
predictability, 6-8, 28-29, 39, 155-158, 177-179, 212, 218-220, 231
 See also forecasting of service demand.
preoccupation with failure, 78, 80
preoperative area, 226.
 See also surgery.
prescription, 188
Press Ganey, 275-276
prevention, 143
price incentives, 27
primary-care physicians, 128
privacy. *See* patient, privacy.
Problem of the Apostrophe, 126
process variation. *See* variation.
professional competence, 51

S

Index

World War II, 21, 102

X

Xerox, 6

X-ray. *See* radiology.

Y

Yeats, William Butler, 59-60, 86

HOW TO ORDER ADDITIONAL COPIES OF

Hardwiring Flow
Systems and Processes for Seamless Patient Care

Orders may be placed:

Online at:
www.firestarterpublishing.com
www.studergroup.com

By phone at: 866-354-3473

By mail at: Fire Starter Publishing
913 Gulf Breeze Parkway, Suite 6
Gulf Breeze, FL 32561

(Bulk discounts are available.)

Hardwiring Flow
is also available online at www.amazon.com.